"The decision to kill Notarangeli was also made to make a statement to Gerry Angiulo that Winter Hill had a *capable* crew and that they were willing to help Angiulo when he had a problem."

—Taken from John Martorano debriefing, circa 1998

MASCOT BOOKS

www.mascotbooks.com

Capable

©2023 Joe Saccardo. All Rights Reserved. No part of this publication may be reproduced, stored in a retrieval system or transmitted in any form by any means electronic, mechanical, or photocopying, recording or otherwise without the permission of the author.

For more information, please contact
Mascot Books, an imprint of Amplify Publishing Group
620 Herndon Parkway, Suite 320
Herndon, VA 20170
info@mascotbooks.com

The author has tried to recreate events, locales, and conversations from his memories of them. The publisher and the author assume no responsibility for errors, inaccuracies, omissions, or any other inconsistencies herein. All such instances are unintentional and the author's own.

Library of Congress Control Number: 2022906952

CPSIA Code: PRV1022A
ISBN-13: 978-1-63755-192-9

Printed in the United States

To Mary Ann, Mark, and Michael

Denise,
I hope you will enjoy this book. You have been a great neighbor all these years.
Best,
Joe Saccorto

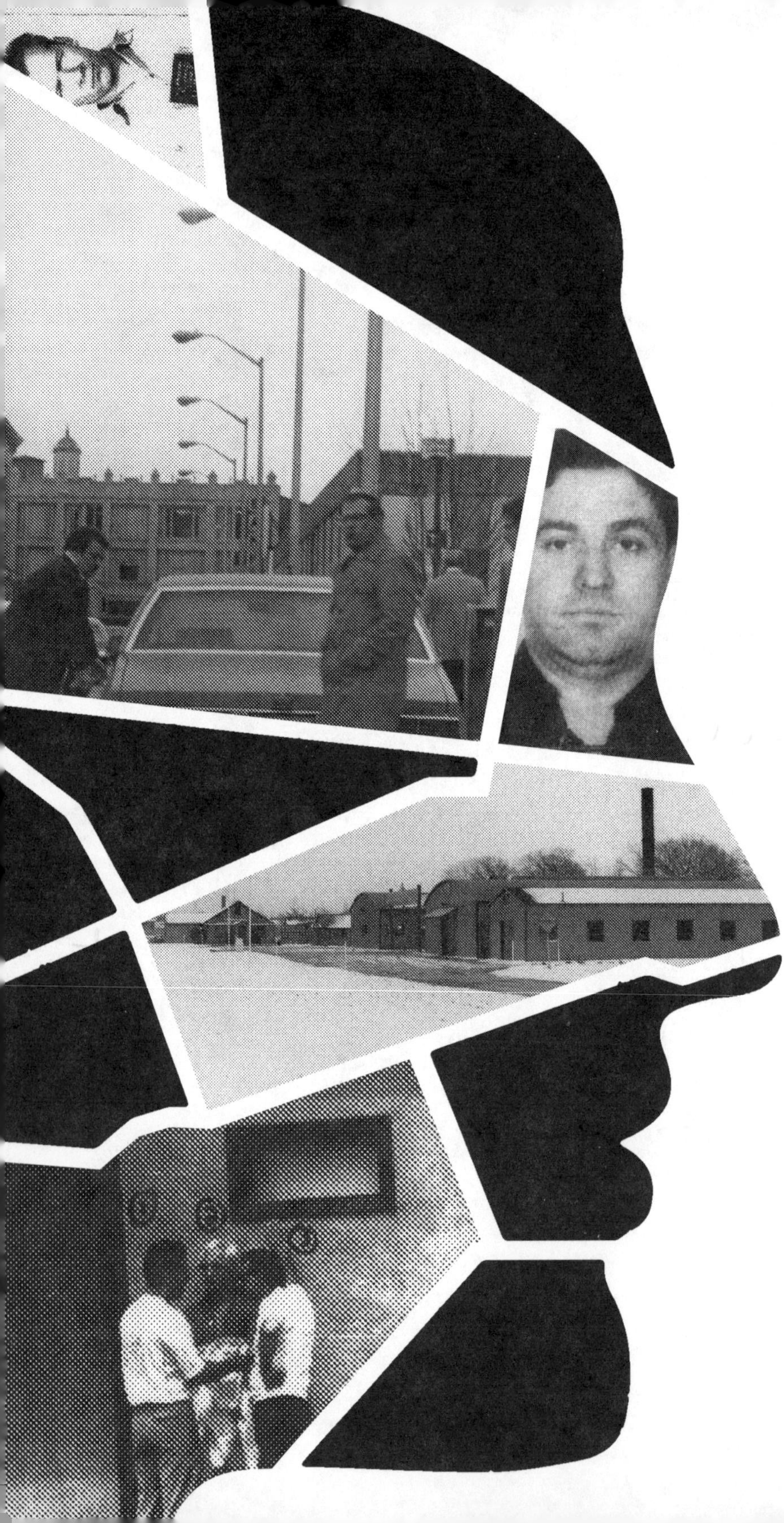

CAPABLE

The Factual History of Innocent Men and Women Murdered by Boston Irish and Italian Mobsters James "Whitey" Bulger, Steve "Rifleman" Flemmi, and John "B'wana Johnny" Martorano, and the Massachusetts State Police Troopers Who Helped Pursue the Gangsters

Joe Saccardo

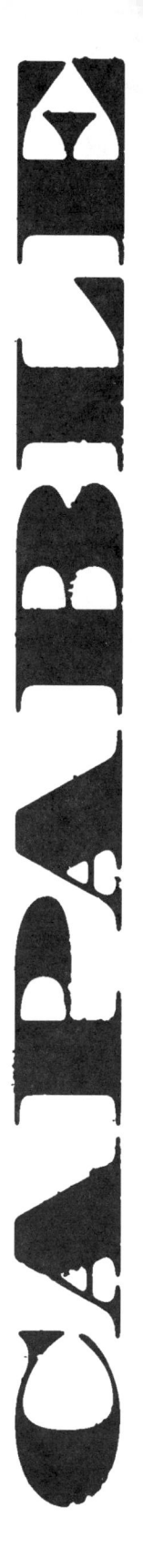

Introduction | 1

Part 1 How It All Began

Chapter 1	My Early Years	6
Chapter 2	John Martorano's Early Years	11
Chapter 3	Only John Martorano and His Brother, James, Know	15
Chapter 4	Johnny Gets His Gun: The Murders	23
Chapter 5	"Oh No, Oh No"	35

Part 2 Mob Wars: The Shooting Sixties and Seventies

Chapter 6	Joe Barboza	46
Chapter 7	La Famiglia Flemmi	53
Chapter 8	Degrees of Separation among Hoods and Cops	57

Part 3 Chasing Bookies

Chapter 9	Operation Grandslam	64
Chapter 10	Pursuing "Legs" Lewis and "Pokerman"	71
Chapter 11	Banker to the Bookies: Heller's Café	83
Chapter 12	The Checkman Cashes Out	99

Part 4 Bugs, Beans, Bookies, and Bad Guys

Chapter 13	The Lancaster Street Garage Surveillance	112
Chapter 14	"Whitey" Bulger and Flemmi: Fish to Beans	119
Chapter 15	The *Valhalla* and the Murder of John McIntyre	130
Chapter 16	The Bad Apples: Corrupt Cops	150

Part 5 Everything Gets Worse

    Chapter 17   Olga's "Mother" | 170

    Chapter 18   Guns, Roses, and the Hussey Family | 177

    Chapter 19   The Drug Trade and Its Impact | 184

    Chapter 20   The Murder of Frances Mansfield | 191

    Chapter 21   Linskey's Lottery or How "Whitey" Became a Millionaire | 199

    Chapter 22   The Tragedy of Debbie Hussey | 207

    Chapter 23   The Criminal and Fugitive Investigation of Bulger (It Is a Bit Confusing) | 216

Part 6 Indictments and Immunity

    Chapter 24   Guns for Immunity/Money for Marion | 232

    Chapter 25   Ivan | 240

    Chapter 26   My Informant, Your Informant | 256

    Chapter 27   Mac and Ivan Go on Trial | 265

    Chapter 28   De Facto Immunity | 277

    Chapter 29   Happy St. Whitey's Day Lasted Sixteen Years | 285

Conclusion | 296
Acknowledgments | 301
About the Author | 303

INTRODUCTION

Why I Am Writing This Book

Let me address the question some people seem to ask: "Why are you writing this book?"

After all, the mobsters who used to brazenly operate in Boston are mostly gone, dead, or in prison. James "Whitey" Bulger, Boston's most notorious mobster, is dead, bludgeoned to death in prison. His colleagues—most of them—are also in prison or dead. For today's Bostonians, the notions of placing bets with the neighborhood bookie seem quaint when you can buy a lottery ticket at every corner store. Why go to a loan shark when you have credit cards, which can saddle you with greater and greater debt legally?

After spending my final four years in internal affairs and twenty-seven years in service to the state police, in 1995, I was appointed to the transit police with the rank of major / deputy chief of special investigations. For three decades, which ran parallel with my law enforcement career, the city witnessed violence from Boston's organized crime.

Some years ago, I decided I would write a book—a kind of memoir—about my thirty years in law enforcement and to further investigate some dangling threads that I can't forget.

I am still amazed that one of the criminals I pursued, a murderer—no, make that a serial killer—is walking free today, free because of a devilish deal made for his testimony against other criminals and an FBI agent.

I want to give an inside scoop on investigative work with tales (some amusing, some tragic) of my years pursuing bookies, professional gamblers, money launderers, drug dealers, and loan sharks.

You will get a taste of my work and that of others in these pages with actual transcripts from the hours and hours of tapes gathered on some of Boston's most diligent organized criminals.

I want to set the story straight on a fellow trooper who was falsely accused of cooperating with mobsters and who saw his career and his life callously ruined. At the same time, I want to contrast this with some members of the FBI who were leaking like a sieve to criminals or who would stop at nothing to protect their assets—even if an innocent man went to jail. I will chronicle the unbelievable and tragic trial of that state trooper who was framed by the FBI.

You will see how the line between the good guys and the bad guys can be blurred and how my own social circle included Stephen "the Rifleman" Flemmi, James "Whitey" Bulger's partner in crime. I have known Steve Flemmi for over fifty years, ever since I met him at a wake. We quickly exchanged pleasantries, which did not give me much time to size him up. I do recall he was smooth. Thank God I never tried to recruit him as an informant, or I could have become another John Connolly, the disgraced FBI agent who became too close to Whitey Bulger. I can tell you he is a manipulative person. He has no problem getting in your face no matter what the issue, but he can also be very charming at the same time. For years, he played the role of family man, despite the blood on his hands. In these pages, we'll talk about one memorable encounter with Flemmi at a wedding. I was close to the family of Marion Hussey, and I want to tell the very sad story of her daughters and sons.

You'll also read about some of the rather colorful characters I encountered through the years of chasing bookies. I often commented that I never met a bookie I didn't like, except maybe one. In these pages, you will meet Eddie "Legs" Lewis, Mike London, Jimmy Katz, Richie O'Brien, Jim Timilty, Burton "Chico" Krantz, and others.

Many innocent men and women were needlessly killed during the Bulger-Flemmi reign. I profile six of those women, three of whom coincidentally were murdered in South Boston, two of whom were indirectly connected to John Martorano, and one of whom he confessed to killing.

Given all the press, books, and movies about Boston's underworld, you may think you know the whole story. I'm writing this book to fill in the gaps about the guys and the crimes that everybody knows. I spent a portion of my professional life trying to nail James "Whitey" Bulger and Stephen "the Rifleman" Flemmi—as well as a pack of other mobsters—and there are stories that the public doesn't know.

Until now.

Most of all, I want to tell about a man whose murderous rampages have far surpassed the toll of the thirteen women murdered in the Boston Strangler case in the 1960s. Johnny Martorano has admitted to killing twenty people, from teenagers to seniors, males and females, black and white. And this book shows you that there may be more victims out there.

I devote a good section of this book to detailing Martorano's murders, particularly those that are less well known. His victims and the families of those victims demand to be heard.

Today, John Vincent Martorano is a free man. A few years ago, he was profiled by a well-known Boston media personality in a best-selling book. He waxed eloquently about his criminal behavior after previously confessing to federal and state law enforcement about his personal involvement in twenty homicides in three states. In 2008, a Miami-Dade County jury found former FBI Special Agent John Connolly guilty of second-degree murder. John Martorano—the actual killer—testified for the prosecution against the agent, whom he had never met. Short of a polygraph test, the veracity of Martorano is in question in this matter. Connolly stands to spend the rest of his life in a Florida state prison while the man known as "The Butcher of Basin Street" proudly perches like a stool pigeon. Connolly served prison time for the murders that Martorano committed. I am sure the surviving family members of the twenty victims Martorano killed feel justice was not served. The year is 2020, and the eighty-year-old serial killer continues to freely walk the same streets of Boston that he once traversed in his long career as a hit man, pimp, and all-around gun for hire.

It bothers me to this day that I and other well-meaning troopers, who were more than accomplished in chasing bookies and the organized crime element, did not recognize that John Martorano was a serial killer in our midst.

He is one of the few surviving associates of the once notorious Winter Hill gang, named after a neighborhood in the Boston suburb of Somerville. My dealing with Martorano and the years of research I have put into his case history have left me with a vivid memory of the man, starting with first time I laid eyes on him in the mid '70s. From the first glance, I knew this guy was the real deal. He had the aura of a legitimate criminal and a capable killer—which he was.

I feel it is time to set the record straight. It is time to show how federal and state law enforcement made a pact with a serial killer. I want to share what I knew and have since learned about Martorano and his criminal associates Whitey Bulger and Steve Flemmi during my years as an organized crime investigator.

This is why I am writing this book.

PART 1

HOW IT ALL BEGAN

CHAPTER 1

My Early Years

Growing up in Dorchester, Massachusetts, I ran numbers for my father.

Dad was a straight-up guy who had worked hard for years at a foundry beneath the old, elevated Viaduct Road leading to the Commonwealth Pier now known as the South Boston Seaport.

He would come home after work pretty beat and too tired to go to the local bar on Dorchester Avenue and play his daily pool numbers, which had to be in to the bookie before seven o'clock in the evening. At fifteen or sixteen years of age, I would trek up to Coley's Tavern with a couple of dimes clutched in my hand to give to Sandy, the local book. He in turn would hand me a three-by-five-inch white piece of paper with my father's "winning numbers." After many decades of sobriety, my favorite bookie's deathbed wish was a bottle of scotch.

In the Greater Boston area, the illegal number pool play was based on the combined payoffs of the pari-mutuel results of the "money horses" (win, place, and show) in certain races at a particular track, such as Suffolk Downs in East Boston. The evening newspapers would record the winning numbers in the sport pages. A little over a decade later, I was a trooper in the Massachusetts State Police Special Service Unit arresting bookies.

That is not so odd for Boston, a place where boys in the same family would grow up on opposite sides of the law.

My dad died three years before I entered the state police academy in 1967, never realizing his nickels and dimes contributed to the illegal activities of the Boston organized crime scene.

I grew up on the third floor of a three-decker. We called it the penthouse. We literally lived on the other side of the tracks—the rapid-transit Red Line tracks, that is—which separated Dorchester from Southie. From our back porch, we could see Carson Beach in the distance with only a minuscule view of the Atlantic Ocean visible. The bow window in the parlor gave us a panoramic picture of many center-entrance, red-brick, colonial-style buildings known as the Old Harbor Project: the home of James "Whitey" Bulger.

I grew up in Dorchester as a preteen, so Southie was my hometown. During the summer months, I would walk through the Old Harbor Project on my way to the South Boston Boys Club (where I nearly drowned learning how to swim). Many a day, I passed through Logan Way, bypassing the Bulgers' red-brick residence, ignorant to who lived there, not that I cared. Just around the corner from the Boys Club, my grandparents owned one-half of a six-family duplex on West Fifth Street, where my grandmother would beckon me to visit for a glass of milk and homemade biscuits.

Only blocks from my grandparents' home, centrally located in Perkins Square, where East and West Broadway intersected, was Joe's Spa, a local landmark where nearby residents gathered for a Coca-Cola or milkshake. Only a few blocks down West Broadway was the iconic nightclub Blinstrub's, fondly known as Blinney's.

In the early '50s, South Boston sponsored some of the first Little League baseball teams in the city of Boston. Renowned Boston Police Detective

Ed Walsh was one of my coaches for a team sponsored by a South Boston company called NIC. Every game we played was on one of two diamonds at Columbia Park, which was surrounded by the Old Harbor Project on the west and Carson Beach on the east. In the winter, the Boston Fire Department flooded the very same fields for hockey and ice skating.

Living in Dorchester and hanging out in Southie never afforded me the opportunity of crossing paths with a state trooper until my uncle Max introduced me to several uniformed troopers assigned to Logan Airport. As a teenager, I was impressed. I never forgot the respect my uncle showed these men. That experience stayed with me as I traversed high school and then enlisted in the US Marine Corps. I graduated in the top 10 percent of my sixty-five-man platoon and got promoted to private first class. I was hoping to be assigned to the military police, but like every jarhead, I ended up being a grunt carrying a machine gun around for several years. Three years after being honorably discharged in 1964, I was proudly wearing the French- and electric-blue uniform of a Massachusetts State Police trooper.

That Dorchester three-decker on Buttonwood Street produced five police officers. The first-floor Flahertys had four boys and three girls. Three of the boys became Boston cops, one was a Quincy cop, and I became a state trooper.

Weeks before entering the academy, I transported to a Boston hospital Marion Hussey (as a favor for a mutual friend), the very pregnant common-law wife of an up-and-coming mobster, Steve Flemmi. Born and bred in the Neponset area of Dorchester, Marion Hussey was an older sister of my friend. We met in 1967, as a result of my hastily being called into ambulance duty to transport the expectant mother to a Boston hospital. Not that it was a nerve-racking trip or anything, but we landed at the wrong hospital. Upon exiting the correct hospital, affixed to my windshield was a $15 parking ticket. Translated into today's dollars, we are talking approximately $150 to $200. It ended well that early summer day for their second son, Stephen, and his parents, Marion and Steve Flemmi. Marion had William and Stephanie with Steve and a daughter, Debbie, from a previous marriage to Tom Hussey. Word got back to the inexperienced ambulance driver that the proud father wanted to gift my family with a bassinet for the upcoming birth of our child.

Never having met Flemmi but knowing of his early reputation for criminal activity, I respectfully declined, most notably because the ambulance driver was entering the Massachusetts State Police Academy within weeks of the offer.

••••

Three months after graduating from the state police academy and still a probationary trooper assigned to the western Massachusetts Pittsfield barracks, I made an unarmed, off-duty arrest of an arsonist. Because of the probationary status, we were not allowed to carry the issued Smith & Wesson revolver home. Troopers were still living in the barracks then, working eighty-hour weeks while getting paid less than four hundred dollars a month. The arrest got me a transfer to my home barracks in Norwell, which was only a twenty-minute drive as opposed to commuting in my own car for two and a half hours from my home in Dorchester to Pittsfield. (Take-home cruisers did not come into effect until 1971, simultaneous with the discontinuation of troopers living in the barracks and working a normal forty-hour week.)

Driving Marion to the wrong hospital to have Flemmi's child was far more nerve-racking than arresting an arsonist trying to burn down apartment buildings in Boston.

Early in my career, I had four different assignments, which were split among the Pittsfield and Norwell barracks, Logan Airport, and providing security for Attorney General Robert H. Quinn. In 1973, I was transferred to the Special Service Unit, or SSU, whose mission was investigating organized crime with a major focus on illegal gambling.

Here, I learned the craft of physical and electronic surveillance, writing affidavits in support of applying for applications for search warrants, and compiling reports after busting bookies in the Greater Boston area. And, more important, I was learning how to testify in court in defense of the affidavits and subsequent arrests.

From 1976 through 1981, I was promoted from trooper to corporal to sergeant. While assigned at Attorney General Frank Bellotti's office, I took a leave of absence in 1981 after being offered the position of director of Transit Systems Security in Miami-Dade County, Florida. Two years later, I returned to the state police and was reassigned to the SSU with the intent of pursuing Bulger and Flemmi. Without telling any of my coworkers, I also sought to find Debbie Hussey, the missing daughter of Marion Hussey, while surveilling her stepfather, Steve Flemmi. I would only learn years later that Bulger and Flemmi had already strangled Debbie to death in the basement of Flemmi's parents' house in South Boston.

Within a year of returning to the job, I had injected myself into a Drug Enforcement Administration investigation focusing on Bulger and Flemmi. It was the beginning of a decades-long effort to see these men brought to justice.

CHAPTER 2

John Martorano's Early Years

Within a stone's throw from an apartment building in the South End section of Boston stood an ugly steel structure, fondly known as the El. For decades, the elevated structure straddled Washington Street, allowing the ear-piercing rattle of orange line trains to punctuate the air. On a January evening in 1963, those trains drowned out the sound of police officers scurrying up a set of stairs to an apartment on Northampton Street to arrest a pimp and his prostitute du jour.

Warmly ensconced in a tiny third-floor cold-water flat was a twenty-two-year-old married white boy with a neck as thick as his thigh, slumbering next to a woman whom police would describe as a pretty "colored girl." Both were dressed in "outer clothing" when Boston police officers from Division 4 surprised the couple with sledgehammers in hand. The police had a search warrant for prostitution, gaming, and narcotics.

The officers took the measure of the rookie pimp, just several years removed from his teens. He turned out to be the manager of the family-owned Basin Street South nightclub, located nearby on Washington Street. He had previously been arrested for a firearm violation and assault and battery. This time, he would be booked for adultery—a laughable crime looking back at the long, violent, and murderous career of John Vincent Martorano. It is my educated opinion that JVM got a pass.

John Vincent Martorano was born on December 13, 1940, to Angelo "Angie" and Elizabeth (Hunt). John and his younger brother, James, did not grow up in a traditional Italian enclave because the tony Boston suburb Milton did not have one. Instead, the town was nationally recognized for the presence of the elite Milton Academy and as the birthplace of former President George H. W. Bush. The influence of an early parochial school education evidently failed John, who, along with his brother, graduated Milton High. He was an excellent high school football player due to his stocky build being close to the ground. John was in his late teens when his father unofficially inducted him into the Boston organized crime scene.

When he was arrested in 1963, he had been married for three years and was a father of two infant daughters. A year and a half later, his wife, Nancy, filed for divorce, later marrying Ed Duff, an associate of her former husband, who ran a bookie operation out of a Fields Corner bar called Mike Baker's located in the Dorchester section of Boston. Duff was also the brother-in-law of Massachusetts State Police Corporal Richard Schneiderhan.

Four decades later, in 2000, Schneiderhan, Duff, and his daughter, Linda Reardon, would be arrested by state troopers on charges of conspiracy and obstruction of justice for interfering with the efforts to capture the number-one fugitive on the FBI's Most Wanted List at that time, James "Whitey" Bulger.

As the dog days of August 1963 settled in, Division 4 officers renewed their acquaintance with Martorano when he was arrested for assaulting a South End man with a "blackjack" (a black-leathered metal club) in the middle of Washington Street. Then justice took a holiday. A municipal court magistrate discharged Martorano's arrest for adultery followed by a dismissal of the assault and battery charge by the Suffolk Superior Court because of a lack of prosecution.

The Martorano story runs long and deviously. It would finally end thirty-five years later, in 1995 when state troopers and FBI agents arrested him on a federal fugitive arrest warrant in southeastern Florida, where he had been hiding in plain sight for sixteen years. Starting in 1998, cooperating witness John Martorano admitted committing twenty murders during a federal and state task force investigation spearheaded by the Massachusetts State Police and US Drug Enforcement Agency (DEA).

Early in Martorano's criminal career, some state and local police officials queried the FBI about Martorano's arrest records. Whatever institutional history and intelligence the FBI may have gathered through the era of Martorano, they never materialized into arrests, as he continued his journey as a major criminal and killer of innocent men and women.

In March 1978, I first met Martorano from a distance. He had pled guilty for participating in an earlier major illegal sports betting operation. I was there during the follow-up court proceedings in Plymouth County Superior Court in Brockton. Martorano was standing alone outside the courtroom dressed in a sport coat and matching slacks with the typical open-collared shirt and his jet-black coiffured hair in need of a shearing. He looked taller and heavier than his state police arrest reported, five feet ten inches and 180 pounds. He was at once stoic and pensive, his lips firmly clenched, probably reciting to himself, "I kill people, and here I am going to jail for one phone call."

Martorano and several of his subordinates pled guilty before going to trial. The judge penalized them to a minimal sentence, but it was Martorano's first time ever being incarcerated for more than a few hours before being bailed; plus, he was fined thirty thousand dollars.

What I didn't know at the time was that he had already begun his career in murder. It involved a young woman who worked for his father, Angie.

Margaret Sylvester was left to rot by monsters who were self-professed tough guys who thought of women as a mere convenience. Monsters like John Martorano.

CHAPTER 3

Only Johnny Martorano and His Brother, James, Know

My underage friends and I may have crossed paths with John Martorano years earlier in November of 1964 when we entered the Beach Street side-door entrance of a sleazy bar known as Jerome's Lounge. We were then refused a drink, angrily left, and entered the Washington Street front door and were promptly served a beer at the bar without having to produce proper identification. We didn't have as good a view of the band or whatever girls may have been performing, but we were happy just to be where we weren't supposed to be: in an area of Boston called the legendary Combat Zone.

The Zone, as it was known, was located in Boston's downtown area and was a favorite destination for servicemen, wise guys, and sometimes just local boys on a binge because of its many bars and strip clubs. November 10, 1964, happened to be the 189th birthday of the US Marine Corps, traditionally followed by Veterans Day. As Marines celebrated at the Intermission

Lounge below, several floors above lay the decomposing body of Margaret Sylvester, a thirty-three-old-divorced mother of a teenage son wrapped in a canvas sack like a bag of potatoes.

At 7:30 p.m. on November 10, 1964, Boston police officers from then-District 16 executed a search warrant for stolen goods (furs) entering Luigi's Restaurant at 699 Washington Street, located above the Intermission Lounge and diagonally across the street from Jerome's, where we had previously enjoyed our illicit drinks.

What must have been going through the minds of the Boston police officers as they gingerly approached a loft area, inhaling the waft of stench emanating from a decaying body? Even hardened street cops aren't prepared for the sight of a young woman lying dead in a fetal position under a window, her blond hair soaked in caked blood from multiple stab wounds.

Did she try to defend herself against the knife-wielding assassin? Was she murdered here or elsewhere? Her burial in a makeshift grave was as dehumanizing as her death. Sylvester had been missing for a few days when someone alerted the police by inventing a fictitious tale about stolen goods in a bar owned by Angelo "Angie" Martorano, the father of John and James.

Sylvester had been a waitress at Luigi's and knew the Martorano brothers well because they tended bar at Daddy's restaurant with her. Her murder was no random act of violence. It apparently was too risky to immediately move the victim, so she was left to rot until the coast was clear. Two sympathetic witnesses, too terrified and intimidated to personally contact the police, concocted a scenario that allowed the police to discover Sylvester's body.

Years later, those men would pay the ultimate price, gangland style, for their ill-conceived compassion. Otherwise, law enforcement possibly would still be looking for her remains. Within days of the discovery of the corpse, John Martorano was being sought for questioning by the Boston Police Homicide Squad, but he was never charged.

The days leading up to the Marine Corps birthday on November 10 were unseasonably mild for late fall. Business at Luigi's was picking up on a normally slow Monday night. Many of the jarheads were celebrating in a combat zone of a different nature without the obnoxious smell of death they prepare for every day. Prostitutes and their pimps, roaming the nearby darkened alleys, could only smell the sweetness of ill-gotten money. Kids from the adjoining neighborhoods, armed with phony liquor identification, were trying in vain to get a beer from the pretty blond waitress. Vice cops making the nightly rounds surveilled the pimps and hookers, who surveilled the birthday-celebrating Marines, who in turn surveilled the strippers.

But nobody saw or heard the angel of death. A stiff kick here, a stiffer kick there. Her pelvis is cracked, and her ovaries are bleeding. She has no defense against the busy knife. It's so blurry. This filthy room is getting darker and darker. Blood and guts are spurting everywhere, landing on the walls and flowing onto the carpeting. Death had come to a building where life was supposed to be enjoyable. Mrs. Sylvester was wrapped in a makeshift casket of cheap cloth and abandoned.

The badly beaten and brutally stabbed body of Sylvester was found two days before the twenty-fourth birthday of Luigi's manager, James Martorano, Johnny's brother. The married father of three children would be arrested and charged with being an accessory after the fact of assault with intent to murder in the death of Sylvester. Despite the fact that a longtime employee of the Martorano family had been murdered in their establishment and the body left for several days to rot while the guilty scrubbed the murder scene, not one member of *la famiglia Martorano* was charged relative to the actual murder of Margaret Sylvester.

A Boston police chemist testified in court proceedings he found blood spattered on the walls and the base of a floor lamp at the scene, but no blood was found on a rug. An investigation would later show that James Martorano had replaced the blood-splattered rug with a new seventy-five-dollar rug on November 9, leading police to believe Sylvester was slain on November 8.

The prosecution's official version of the offense stated in part that James Martorano had knowledge of the murder and assisted an unknown assailant(s) with replacing the evidence-laden rug in order to conceal the crime. Police characters clean up the scene most of the time.

Patricia Cowell was a waitress at Luigi's and a drinking buddy of the Martorano brothers. The twenty-four-year-old mother of a young son appeared in a report by the Boston police on March 29, 1965:

> [Cowell] was present when Marjorie [sic] Sylvester was beaten by James Martorano prior to her death. It is further reported that Patricia Cowell was keeping company with James "Jimmy" Martorano at the time of Majorie [sic] Sylvester's death and that she was with "Jimmy" Martorano at Luigi's Restaurant, Washington Street, Boston.

On the following day, Cowell was interviewed by the Boston Police Homicide Unit, "as a result of information forwarded to that unit by the Intelligence Division."

In her April 1965 grand jury testimony, the Everett native testified that two nights before the murder, she (Cowell), Sylvester, and James Martorano were in Luigi's when Sylvester became loud and argumentative and fell off a bar stool. Cowell also declared James brutally struck and codefendant Andrew Pappas kicked Sylvester.

Cowell would recant her grand jury testimony during James Martorano's trial, resulting in the then twenty-six-year-old prosecution witness being arrested on December 14, 1966, relating to a charge of "responsible presumption of perjury," which "conflicted with the testimony she gave in court." As a result, codefendant Pappas walked out of court with a directed verdict of acquittal on an assault charge. Cowell was sentenced to Women's Reformatory in Framingham, but her conviction was subsequently detoured, and she received a suspended indefinite term and three years of probation. Her attorney was quoted as saying she was a "victim of circumstances, who was in the wrong place at the wrong time."

Thereafter, Cowell virtually fell off the face of the earth, ensuring she would never be wrongly placed as an ill-timed witness to a homicide. She moved out of state, married, and died an early death in 1984 at the age of forty-four in Plainfield, New Jersey.

As Christmas 1966 approached, James Martorano was convicted in Suffolk Superior Court of accessory after the fact of assault with intent to murder in the death of Sylvester. He received four to six years at the Walpole State Prison currently known as Cedar Junction.

The tangled web has taken years to unravel, as Sylvester's death remains unsolved.

Four decades later, in 1998, while trying to save his sorry ass from the death penalty in two states, John Martorano admitted killing two men who had witnessed Sylvester's homicide. Fast-forward to February 2002 at the federal racketeering trial in Boston of former FBI Special Agent John Connolly, who was the handler for his informant, the savvy gangster from South Boston, James "Whitey" Bulger.

Performing his duties as a stand-up citizen, prosecution witness John Martorano, as a result of an earlier plea bargain with the Feds, publicly admitted killing Robert Palladino on November 15, 1965, and John Jackson on September 28, 1966. Martorano rationalized killing the two men because they would have been witnesses against his brother in the unsolved murder of Margaret Sylvester.

Palladino was the first and Jackson the third admitted Martorano murder.

My recent discovery of John Martorano's 1998 debriefing by members of the Massachusetts State Police revealed that Vinny Flemmi, brother of Steve Flemmi (both violent men in their own right), told Jimmy Martorano to leave the restaurant after Jimmy had an argument with Sylvester. According to John Martorano, their father was having a relationship with the murder victim. The next day, Mrs. Martorano called her son Jimmy, asking what had happened to the rug that used to be at the restaurant, but she evidently missed the badly beaten body of Sylvester, which was found that same day. Jimmy told his brother, John, that Vinny Flemmi, Palladino, Jackson, and Jack Azuley, a former Boston cop turned loan shark, were the last ones to be seen with Sylvester. According to John Martorano, a very concerned Steve Flemmi approached him, worrying that Palladino and Jackson would finger his brother, Vinny, for Sylvester's death. It was pure conjecture on Martorano's part. As a favor to the Flemmi brothers for their assistance in helping with the Sylvester murder, Johnny went looking for the witnesses. Martorano states Palladino, while sitting in his car, was defending his position, denying he talked to the police. According to Martorano, the men argued about the denial. Palladino supposedly went for his own gun, but Martorano got the draw and fired first. Palladino's bullet-riddled body was discovered under the old Southeast Expressway, adjacent to the North Station commuter rail terminal. Palladino's car was driven from the scene and disposed of by John Martorano's criminal associate, Frank Oreto Sr. Almost a year to the day after the death of Sylvester and days before the arrest of John's brother James for accessory after the fact of her murder, Palladino met the same fate as Sylvester. Steve Flemmi, the Martorano brothers' partner in criminal activities, has a different version of the events leading up to Sylvester's death.

Less than a year later in September 1966 and several months before James Martorano was convicted as charged, John Jackson, a witness to the Sylvester murder, was ambushed as he approached his apartment in the Fenway section of Boston, according to Johnny. Hiding behind a fence in an area where Jackson usually parked his car was John, accompanied by his shotgun and three accomplices, including two hoods tightly aligned with another Boston assassin, Joe Barboza, namely Tom DePrisco and Arthur "Tash" Bratsos, and a person Martorano refused to identify. DePrisco jumped the fence while simultaneously shooting his forty-five-caliber handgun. From his position behind the fence, Martorano cut down the victim with his shotgun and then threw his weapon down a nearby sewer. Martorano has never identified the fourth assailant.

The following month, DePrisco and Bratsos were in a North End bar called the Nite Life when the two hoods were ambushed ostensibly for attempting to collect bail money for their imprisoned henchman, Joe Barboza. Their bullet-riddled bodies were soon found in Bratsos's car on a South Boston street.

James Vincenzo Flemmi died of a drug overdose in a Massachusetts state prison in 1979.

A year later, Jack Azuley was stabbed to death in his South Boston apartment by a female friend.

Flemmi was arrested in 1995 for various federal criminal charges and had been imprisoned while feverishly claiming he had immunity from prosecution because he was an informant for the FBI. Flemmi stated in his 2003 DEA and State Police debriefing that

> Margaret SILVESTER [sic] was dating Andy MARTORANO at the time of her murder…FLEMMI recalled that either "Wimpy" Bennett of John MARTORANO advised him (FLEMMI) to the details regarding SILVESTER'S [sic] murder. FLEMMI added that his brother "the Bear" never indicated that he (Jimmy Flemmi) had a role in her death.

Flemmi implicates Jimmy Martorano, further stating "that he was told that James MARTORANO had badly beaten Margaret SILVESTER [sic]… because of the romantic relationship she had with the MARTORANO'S father."

According to Flemmi, Sylvester survived the vicious beating "but that at some point someone later killed her when it was noticed that she was in fact still alive."

Flemmi admits that "his brother James 'the Bear' FLEMMI was on scene, at the club the night of the murder." And "it was possible that he told John Martorano" that he and James Flemmi were suspects in the Sylvester murder because of information he received from "Boston Police sources."

Only the brothers Martorano know who killed Margaret Sylvester.*

---

* A Massachusetts Department of Corrections Summary of the Institutional History of James Martorano noted that bartender Joseph Lanzi, who worked at the Nite Life in the North End section of Boston, was murdered on or about April 17, 1967. He made frequent visits to James while he was in Norfolk Prison. The story goes Lanzi was a police informant and was killed by Boston Mafia enforcers, according to mobster-turned-author Vincent Teresa in his best seller *My Life in the Mafia* (1973). He also may have witnessed the dual murder of Bratsos and DePrisco six months earlier.

CHAPTER 4

Johnny Gets His Gun: The Murders

Between the murder of Sylvester and the conviction of James Martorano, on August 21, 1965, John Martorano reported to the police in Weymouth, a blue-collar town south of Boston, that someone had attempted to steal a 1965 tan-topped Cadillac convertible that was owned by a woman from the Boston suburb of Brookline. He also reported that his twelve-gauge, Savage-Fox, double-barrel, Model B shotgun had been stolen from the Cadillac—or should I say, *re*stolen.

His brazen behavior can only be matched by his stupidity, you may be thinking. But let me frame the way a seasoned criminal thinks. Reporting the theft of the shotgun clears him of any future suspicious use of the weapon, especially if his fingerprints are found on it. Martorano said the shotgun was for his protection, evidently supported by a bullet hole in his car.

According to the report, "This shotgun has been recovered and three colored boys [police description] have been apprehended by the Weymouth

Police for this theft." Written in long hand at the bottom of the report was a note that the shotgun was stolen from Savage Firearms in Westfield, Massachusetts.

In the late 1960s, the South End stomping grounds of the Martorano brothers was becoming an extended killing field with the shooting death of a fifty-five-year-old, low-level hood named Wady David, who was found in an alley off Plympton Street on the same day that Johnny had reported his shotgun had been stolen.

The next day, a Dorchester lad named John Cutliffe, an associate of James Martorano's, was wounded in a botched hit that took place uptown from the South End and a block from the Combat Zone. The sphere of criminality where the Martoranos practiced in the '60s and '70s had its apex within the South End, which was bordered on the north by Dover Street (later renamed East Berkeley Street), on the east by Albany Street, on the south by Massachusetts Avenue, and on the west by Huntington Avenue. Basin Street South and the Sahara nightclubs, affiliated with the Martorano family, were situated in the South End. Early in his murderous career, for some unknown reason, John was known around town as "the Cook."

A few months after Johnny reported his stolen shotgun restolen on November 26, the woman who owned the car from which that gun was last observed reported her car stolen again, this time in a bustling ocean-side community, a thirty-minute drive north from her Brookline residence and equidistant from John's home in Milton.

The following January, the Boston police learned from an "anonymous source" the woman with the Cadillac from which the shotgun was stolen came from Kentucky and was a prostitute working for John Martorano, who turned over a portion of her earnings to him.

On October 15, 1968, a female with the same name as the Kentucky woman was arrested with five other "white females" in the middle of the notorious Combat Zone on charges of "being an idle and disorderly person."

The typed report referenced a woman named Barbara, who was one of the six arrested, and notes that she was said to live with John in Weymouth, further stating, "it is alleged that this girl gives him $800 to $900 per week." The anonymous informant alleges that John shook down three or four girls each week for $100 or more, "but the first two girls referred to (the Kentucky girl and Barbara) are his steady income girls."

It is never a résumé-enhancer to beat up the only brother of Johnny Martorano, even though you were a real tough kid from Dorchester, a neighborhood that in the second half of the twentieth century personified toughness. More kids from Dot (except maybe Southie) entered the US Marine Corps during the Vietnam War era than from any other part of the city. Anthony "Tony" Veranis wasn't a jarhead, but he had a reputation as one tough kid.

A welterweight boxer with a heavy fist and a light mind as a result of many years in the ring, winning twenty-five fights, Veranis answered his last bell in a Dudley Street, Roxbury, after-hours bar located over Walsh's TV store in the early morning of April 26, 1966. What was his sin? It was said he had beaten the crap out of James Martorano because of a difference of opinion in a loan-sharking debt (usurious rates on steroids) that Veranis had owed. Veranis confronted Johnny with his mouth instead of his fists, and Martorano ended the dialogue with a quick gunshot to Veranis's head in front of numerous witnesses. The body of the ex-boxer was found within a day of his death in a heavily wooded area known as the Blue Hills in Quincy.

Veranis was Martorano's second admitted murder, occurring eighteen months after Margaret Sylvester's. His first victim was Robert Palladino, one of two witnesses to her murder. Several weeks after Johnny killed Veranis, a memo authored by the intelligence division of the Boston police reported they had received information Veranis owed money to South Boston bookmakers and shylocks. A portion of the memo was conflicted, stating Veranis was in an unknown café in South Boston, where he bestowed a beating upon Johnny, not James, after being threatened by him.

Outlining information from a "reliable source" concerning the Veranis murder, Boston police officials exchanged a memo in May 1967, regarding two female witnesses. Prominently noted, Detective William Stuart had attended a meeting with a Suffolk County assistant district attorney investigating the homicide. He forwarded the names of Denise Maxwell of Dorchester and Revere resident Mary Lou Lawrence, who accompanied Martorano and his buddy Arthur "Tash" Bratsos to the Roxbury nightclub where Veranis was shot. The unsigned memo stated, "Both girls brought to the District Attorney by members of his staff for interrogation."

Denise Maxwell was a patron and waitress at the club. She was born in Detroit, twice divorced, and died in 2013 while married to her third husband. The whereabouts of Lawrence are unknown. Whatever information the women shared with law enforcement officials about the Veranis homicide never materialized. No provenance was attributed to the identity of the police officer who classified the informant as a "reliable source."

Four decades later, John Martorano confessed to the murder of Veranis but did not disclose any witnesses except the deceased Arthur "Tash" Bratsos.

At the age of twenty-eight, while not having achieved a decade of adulthood until 1968, John Martorano was an unfaithful husband, a disinterested father, a purveyor of women, and a murderer. He roamed the streets of Boston with many women (black and white) who sold their bodies in order to provide John with money to satisfy his appetite for perversion. Besides his hooker companions, John rubbed elbows with the essence and personification of sophisticated Boston gangsterism. Boston police detectives would describe the hoods as being more than fashionably dressed in their expensive camel-hair overcoats and leather jackets with open-necked shirts slit to the navel rocking on their heels. Completing the ensemble was John's stolen shotgun.

In a bizarre series of events, Martorano and Boston hoods Tommy DePrisco and Joe "Chico" Amico went on a nocturnal manhunt north of Boston in the city of Medford. In the wee hours of a Sunday morning in February 1966, the trio invaded the residence of a female on Exchange Avenue, not once but on three different occasions, apparently looking for a friend of hers. Two Medford patrolmen reported that the divorced subject of the manhunt was a weekend guest of the female and had been in the Combat Zone, where he got into a "beef with a man over a parking space on LaGrange St." They fought, and he was getting the best of the man when police intervened. Either the trio followed the man, or else they knew him. Finally, the Medford police had had enough of the fools on an errand and arrested them for "being abroad in the night and not giving a good account of themselves."

When police secured a 1963 Cadillac sedan they presumed was Martorano's, a search revealed a fully loaded thirty-eight-caliber Smith & Wesson snub-nose revolver partly hidden under a Massachusetts license plate. The report further stated, "The barrel and trigger guard were wrapped in a white infants [sic] bonnet." Massachusetts State Police firearms forensics reported the firearm neither stolen nor wanted. The missing guest was a lucky man. Early the next month, the midnight riders were found not guilty of illegal possession of a firearm in Malden District Court, with Martorano paying fines for motor vehicle violations.

Shortly after Thanksgiving 1966, two more criminal associates of John Martorano, Joe "Chico" Amico and Jimmy Kearns, were leaving a notorious Revere strip club when they were run off the road a mile from the club after succumbing to a volley of gunfire. Kearns survived, but Amico didn't.

It appears Martorano was employing bully tactics on the local pimp and prostitute population, as evidenced by a November 1968 Boston police memo indicating he and three other hoods, including James Kearns (who was a suspect in the 1966 Kathryn Murphy murder) were "shaking down colored pimps in the vicinity of #411 Columbus Ave., Boston." The report stated one of the men "approached a known prostitute and assaulted her" over monies that "should have turned over to this group."

Later in 1968, Ronald Hicks survived an attempt on his life while witnessing a triple homicide at the Roxbury headquarters of what was known as N.E.G.R.O.—an acronym for New England Grass Roots Organization—a nonprofit community group. In November, Alvin and Arnold Campbell, who were big-deal drug dealers and bank robbers in the black neighborhoods, were arrested for partaking in the slaying of three "community activists" connected with the organization. According to Martorano, he unsuccessfully tried to talk Hicks out of testifying in the murder case. Several weeks later, Martorano met Hicks, jumped into his car while Hicks was snorting cocaine, and shot him in the head. Hicks, a pimp, never got the chance to be a witness against the brothers. He was found shot to death in his Caddy Coupe in the Fenway area of Boston.

Within days, an informant relayed to the Boston police "that Ronald Hicks was murdered by John Martorano," which "did not have anything to do with the Roxbury incident" but "involved drugs." Hicks, a star witness against the Campbell brothers, became the seventh recorded homicide confessed to by the not-yet-classified serial killer Martorano several months before the Campbell brothers were acquitted in June 1969.

Like the Palladino and Jackson murders committed by John Martorano in 1965 and 1966, respectively, the Hicks murder is similar in so far as a crucial witness who could endanger Martorano and his gangster friends was eliminated.

Two of Boston's best intelligence detectives, Robert Chenette and Gerry Bulman, were on the prowl for a nice-looking white female in her twenties with sharp features, about 115 pounds, and maybe five feet five inches. The detectives, renowned for their perseverance, wished to have a conversation to confirm if she was the young lady who was seated on a bar stool next to John Martorano in a joint frequented by black clientele known as the Sahara Club the night he slayed fellow pimp, John "Touch" Banno. Martorano ended the decade of the '60s with homicidal fury, stabbing Banno twenty times in the heart. The good-looking, dark-haired woman was never identified as a possible witness, allowing the demented Martorano to slide again for his eighth murder in four years.

Sometime during the '60s, John Martorano and Massachusetts State Trooper Richard Schneiderhan became acquainted. Schneiderhan's brother-in-law, a small-time bookie named Ed Duff had married Nancy O'Neill, the divorced wife of Martorano. It would be speculative to say the cop and the robber met at the wedding reception, but the bar Duff owned in the Fields Corner section of Dorchester, called Mike Baker's, where Nancy was a waitress, may be a possibility. In any event, both agreed in separate statements that a Combat Zone bar on LaGrange Street named Enrico's was the likely place where the trooper impressed the killer as a result of readily handling himself in a barroom fight.

John Martorano, in 1973, shot at least ten, maybe eleven, individuals, killing five men and wounding five other people, including one woman—three murders and five wounded, all of which occurred in March alone. Michael Milano, an innocent victim of mistaken identity, was felled and his male and female passengers wounded in the Brighton area of Boston.

Martorano was gunning for Al "the Indian" Notarangeli, a bookmaker and owner of a Boston bar known as Mother's Café but instead killed one of the bartenders after he and his companions left the bar. It was alleged on the street that "Indian Al" killed a Gerry Angiulo bookie named Paul Folino. Martorano decided to kill "Indian Al," ostensibly to impress Angiulo, showing him that he and Winter Hill had a *capable* crew and Angiulo could rely on them if he had a problem. Eleven days later, three men were caught in the crossfire of an Uzi-machine-gun-wielding Martorano while driving in the North End section of Boston. Al Plummer, the driver and owner of the 1973 Buick Century, was sprayed with machine-gun fire. Miraculously, the intended target, Al Notarangeli, and two passengers survived. One of them was Hugh Shields, who two years earlier had a photo-finish beating a death sentence in the murder of William Bennett. His bloodstream coursing with who knows what, Martorano's veins must still have been hot and curdling because less than a week later, the rage continued with the murder of South Boston native and "Indian Al" associate George O'Brien and the wounding of his passenger, Ralph DeMasi, on Morrissey Boulevard, Dorchester. If you were a target of Martorano, driving your car became an occupational hazard.

Jake Leary was an ex-boxer who met his demise taking five shots in the head in Fort Lauderdale two days after April Fool's Day. Martorano was a suspect in the shooting of another "Indian Al" crew member but feigned innocence when he testified in Connolly's racketeering trial in 2002, saying he was "not directly, indirectly though" involved.

Martorano chose a new venue for his next hit—inside the Pewter Pot restaurant in Medford—the same town Leary hailed from. The victim and brother of "Indian Al," thirty-five-year-old Joe Notarangeli, was talking in the phone booth on a prearranged setup call when he was shot dead weeks after his good friend Leary.

A suspect in the attempted murder of Vinnie Flemmi in 1965 was next. Trying to use a street mailbox as protection, "Spike" O'Toole could not avoid the machine-gun bullets Martorano was firing in front of the Avenue Laundry at the corner of Dorchester and Savin Hill Avenue, Dorchester. The December killing was the last one for 1973, and his thirteenth homicide was logged in the annals of *My Life as a Cowardly Killer* by John Martorano.

It was said in those days that Martorano was pinned with the moniker "B'wana Johnny" for having killed more black men than sickle-cell anemia. *Bwana* is an East African word for master or boss. He was also dubbed "The Butcher of Basin Street." In January 1968, a black man, a black teenager, and a black woman were discovered shot to death in a 1967 Mercury station wagon parked at the intersection of Normandy and Brunswick Streets in Roxbury at approximately 3:00 a.m. on a snowy morning. Dead was forty-nine-year-old Herbert "Smitty" Smith. Next to him in the front passenger seat was the recent high school graduate nineteen-year-old Elizabeth Dixon, who was shot behind the left ear. Douglas Barrett, age seventeen, was found in the back seat shot at close range above the left ear with the bullet going right through his head and exiting out the closed window, shattering the glass, and causing a hole three inches in diameter. Smith was sitting erect behind the steering wheel with Dixon's bleeding head resting on his knee, a cigarette case still in her hand.

"Uncle Smitty," as he was affectionately known, worked as a bouncer at the Martorano-owned Basin Street bar located at lower Washington Street. Hours before his death, two Boston police detectives spotted Smith at work between 1:15 and 1:30 a.m. having a cocktail. They then passed John Martorano as he was coming out of the club nattily dressed in a black coat, white shirt, and tie. He drove away in a '67 or '68 black two-door Pontiac. The cops also reported seeing Jackie Cincotti (an Angiulo associate) earlier at the club with his "colored girlfriend."

According to Martorano, Cincotti and another Angiulo associate named Rocco LaMattina gave a beating to Steve Flemmi for trying to collect a three-hundred-dollar loan shark payment. Smith held Flemmi, preventing him from landing any blows of his own. Martorano spoke to Smith about the beating the next night, and after their conversation, he set up a clandestine meeting with Smith because he had already decided to kill him. Martorano then retrieved a gun, found Smith in Roxbury sitting in his car, and proceeded to kill all three of the occupants. Martorano didn't have the stones to kill Flemmi's actual attackers because of their connection to the Boston Mafia,* led by Jerry Angiulo and capo Ilario Zannino.

"B'wana Johnny" had no momentary misgivings about what he had just done when he grabbed the keys out of the ignition and, smeared with his victims' blood, crawled away from the scene into the nearby woods like the brutal animal he was. He stated he grabbed a taxi and went to Steve Flemmi's house, where Flemmi gave him a coat. On a cold and snow-driven early Saturday morning, the streets of Boston must have been teeming with cabs just waiting to pick up an overweight white man in a minority neighborhood

---

* The word *Mafia* was introduced in the 1891 New Orleans trial of nineteen Sicilian immigrants who were indicted for allegedly killing the police chief. Authors Joseph Maselli and Dominic Candeloro wrote in their 2004 book *Italians in New Orleans*: "The prosecution raised the specter—perhaps for the first time in American history—of a mafia conspiracy." A day after the trial, nine of the suspects were acquitted, and a mob stormed the jail, removed eleven Italian Americans, and murdered them in the largest mass lynching in American history.

covered in blood as he carried the stench of the deaths of three innocent people into the night.

The parents of Elizabeth, Ruby, and Charles Dixon spent a harrowing afternoon on January 6 being interviewed by homicide detectives at Boston Police Headquarters. They stated Elizabeth attended Boston Latin but was a 1967 graduate of St. Joseph's High School in Dorchester. Her parents had no idea who their unemployed daughter was with the night of her death; they only remembered Elizabeth said she would be out late.

Martorano made sure that her mom and dad never had to worry about her whereabouts again.

Nineteen-seventy-four started with the February slaying of Al "Indian Al" Notarangeli, who was the original target of Martorano's misidentified bartender. He tried to make peace at a meeting with Martorano but in the process received an ill-fated death sentence while clutching a Bible. Martorano's shooting victim was found in the trunk of a stolen car in Charlestown the next day.

While John Martorano was running from the law, a late Sunday night phone call made by the lawyer for Steve Flemmi was answered by detectives in the intelligence division of the Boston police. John Nee and Joe Cunningham were contacted by Attorney Robert Dinsmore on May 5, 1974, to arrange the surrender of five-year fugitive Flemmi, who was indicted in 1967 for the murder of William Bennett. The initial meet was to take place the next morning at the Squire Lounge, a strip club located north of Boston in Revere. Within a half hour of the original time for the meet, Dinsmore telephonically changed the location to his Park Square office in Boston, where Flemmi was arrested and later released on bail. Also, a warrant was lodged by the state police against Flemmi for assault and battery with intent to murder and assault and battery by means of a dangerous weapon for bombing the car of Barboza's lawyer. An FBI agent was notified, but as the *Congressional Report* noted, "As Rico promised, Flemmi was released on bail and the attempted murder charges against him were dropped." Seven months later, charges were dismissed against Flemmi and Salemme for the murder of William Bennett.

Flemmi was introduced to Bulger the same year he returned, wasting no time getting back to business logging his first homicide. He and Martorano killed James Sousa in December 1974 and buried the still missing corpse in a town north of Boston.

The daily activities and observations of Boston Police Organized Crime Detectives Vernerin and O'Reilly became interesting while they were on their regular rounds of the city in April 1975 when they paid a social call to a hangout known as Chandler's in the South End. The Martorano brothers and a few other hoods had an economic interest in the establishment. As reported by the detectives, sitting at the bar was a half-assed wise guy who was "sporting a black eye and appears to have lost some teeth." Previous to their visit, the detectives heard about a story of the owner of several bars in the Boston area "having some trouble" because "someone connected in the North End entered one of his places and apparently was sent there either about loan-sharking or bookmaking—it's not known." The bar owner told the interloper to go to hell and then proceeded to "kick the hell out of the guy causing two black eyes and the loss of many of the man's teeth" because this loser "made some nasty remarks about Eddie's mother," according to the story the detectives heard.

Eddie himself was then visited by Whitey Bulger and refused his demand that he pay for the damages along with some sort of compensation. Bulger didn't want any trouble, only an agreement. Several days had passed when Eddie was summoned to Chandler's, where the ante was driven up by a meeting with the man who had just killed James Sousa four months earlier. After spending considerable time trying not to bend to Flemmi, he agreed to pay for "the replacement of any and all teeth by the messenger," who was an employee of Flemmi's, as related by the unknown storyteller. The Bulger and Flemmi coalition was in full bloom, with Special Agent John Connolly waiting in the wings to nurture the budding relationship. Eddie Connors, who owned a bar in Dorchester, was killed two months later by Bulger,

Flemmi, and Martorano. My educated guess is Eddie, an ex-boxer, beat the crap out of Flemmi's flunky.

John Martorano killed Eddie Connors and Tommy King in June and November, respectively, establishing his sixteenth and seventeenth homicides. His accomplices, Bulger and Steve Flemmi, shot Connors in a Morrissey Boulevard phone booth in Dorchester. They shot King in the back of the head at Carson Beach in Southie and buried his body along the banks of the Neponset River in Dorchester. Along with Martorano, Flemmi confessed, and Bulger was found guilty of both murders in 2013.

CHAPTER 5

"Oh No, Oh No"

The lower-end South Boston neighborhood, after World War II and the Korean conflict, was a bit gritty, maintaining its character well into the 1950s and '60s. Triple-deckers and public housing dominated the landscape. There were no manicured public parks like those at City Point. Asphalt playgrounds substituted for the sandy beaches of Pleasure Bay. No yacht clubs lined West Broadway as the South Boston Yacht Club did on Columbia Road. Soda jerks served up milkshakes in Joe's Spa located at Perkins Square, where East and West Broadway met. A dime fare or hanging onto the rear of a streetcar for a free ride took you to the Point, but your return trip always led you back to the tenements and projects.

A small parochial girls' high school, named after a venerable South Boston native, Richard Cardinal Cushing, anchored the lower end of West Broadway. At 4:30 a.m. on Sunday, June 26, 1966, a year after her graduation from Cushing, Kathryn Louise Murphy was found shot to death in front of

220 Westview Street Extension, a stone's throw from her Ames Street, Franklin Field, home in Dorchester.

The nightmare for a family enduring the of loss of a daughter to a ruthless killer was shocking enough, but when it was reported that Murphy socialized with some of Boston's gangster element, it was difficult for many of its citizens to fathom.

Bookies, loan sharks, drug dealers, hijackers, and professional car thieves were interviewed by the Boston Police Homicide Unit; some of them would be reported missing and presumed dead or found themselves at the business end of a semiautomatic pistol. Although he didn't make the police interview cut, John Martorano was possibly one of the last to be seen with Kathryn Murphy.

Murphy's bullet-riddled body was left in the gutter to bleed to death as a result of four close-range shots to the rear of her head and one in the back; while clutching her purse in one hand and a lighted cigarette in the other, she uttered her last words: "Oh no! Oh no!" after apparently being pushed out of a car, according to the medical examiner. The *Boston Globe* reported several days later, confirming she was shot in "the back of the head as she lay on the street." Lieutenant Edward Sherry of the Homicide Squad stated she was shot from a thirty-two caliber automatic. Neighbors described two men sitting in a car nearby the scene where she was found dead in an outfit of forest-green slack suit with brass buttons. The site was but a hundred yards from the apartment she had shared with a younger sister, brother, and her mother's soon-to-be broken heart.

This pretty nineteen-year-old girl, a typist for the old Boston Mutual Insurance Company, frequented bars where you would never find insurance executives pulling up a stool and tossing a cold one. She had a boyfriend in the army and many girlfriends. Her dad died in 1960, six years before Kathryn. Several weeks before her death, Kathy had borrowed $250 from well-known Boston hood, Steve Flemmi.

Flemmi, Bulger, and the Martorano brothers were leaders of what was identified in law enforcement circles in the '70s and '80s as the Winter Hill/South Boston organized crime group.

Flemmi was an informant for the FBI as early as 1965. He helped to recruit Bulger during the '70s. The Martorano brothers were then able to take a default position in the organization with the protection of Bulger, Flemmi, and the FBI.

The weekend of June 26, 1966, was going to be like any other early-summer stretch for Kathy Murphy. She had arranged to be picked up by her girlfriend Ann and then meet Joan and go out for a ride. She wore the green slack suit; it was perfect for a warm June night. Safely tucked away in her wallet was an identification indicating she was two years older than nineteen. She had enough money for a few drinks but not enough to pay off the remainder of the money Steve Flemmi had lent her. Kathy was just a year out of high school with an entry-level job that paid her a meager wage. She lived in public housing and didn't own a car. What was so important in her life that she had to borrow money from a gangster?

Like any loving mother, Mrs. Murphy had good reason to be concerned for her daughter. Kathy's sister Ellen was eleven at the time of her death. Recalling the time forty-eight years later, Ellen knew something was wrong but was too young to understand what was happening. She stated several weeks before her death, Kathy had hemorrhaged vaginally, which had resulted in a trip to the emergency ward at the Carney Hospital in Dorchester. She speculated her sister may have had a miscarriage.

Kathy's evening started at Walter's Bar, a Dudley Street establishment owned by the Bennett brothers. They were criminal associates of Steve and his brother, Vinnie. The bar was located in the Uphams Corner section of Dorchester straddling the Roxbury line. During the day, the area was fairly safe, but the night could be a bit sketchy. Diagonally across the street from Walter's and above an appliance store was an after-hours club that was cooperated by Steve Flemmi and Walter Bennett. (Two months earlier, Johnny Martorano had slaughtered Tony Veranis at the same club.)

Steve and Walter remember seeing Kathy having a drink with her girlfriends before they left sometime after midnight. Every movement Kathy made after the witching hour is pure speculation. I believe she made the innocent mistake of trusting a cold-blooded killer for a ride home to her death.

In a confidential summary debriefing report, circa 2001, authored by DEA Special Agent Dan Doherty, cooperating prosecution witness Kevin J. Weeks, former bodyguard and confidant of James "Whitey" Bulger, divulged a conversation concerning the Murphy homicide he had with Bulger's partner in crime, Steve Flemmi. Weeks's interviews spanned the year 2000, and his memory of criminal events covered over two decades.

Paragraph 77 of the Weeks report said the following:

> Shortly after JOHN MARTORANO was removed from the Plymouth House of Corrections and began cooperating with the DEA/MSP that he (Weeks) had a conversation with FLEMMI at the Institution regarding MARTORANO. FLEMMI claimed that MARTORANO was involved in 50 murders. FLEMMI further stated that in the 1970's MARTORANO was involved in 5 contract murders in Laval, Canada. [More on that later.] FLEMMI further advised WEEKS of a story involving James KEARNS and MARTORANO back in the 1960's or early 1970's. FLEMMI stated that KEARNS and MARTORANO were at a club one night and KEARNS picked up a girl, Kathleen [sic] Murphy. According to FLEMMI, KEARNS' steady girlfriend showed up at the same club and KEARNS asked MARTORANO to take Kathleen [sic] MURPHY home. While driving her home, MARTORANO requested sexual favors from MURPHY. FLEMMI told WEEKS that MURPHY subsequently "freaked out" and upon exiting the vehicle started yelling that she was going tell her father.

> FLEMMI stated to WEEKS that MARTORANO shot her five times as she exited the vehicle. FLEMMI also told WEEKS that KEARNS was either charged with the homicide or a suspect in the homicide.*

Murphy's father had died in 1960, and her being shot five times was reported in the Boston newspapers. Kevin Weeks with Phyllis Karas wrote a book *Brutal* in 2007, which was based on his more than twenty years of criminal life as part of the Bulger-Flemmi relationship. The book was more than informative, but Weeks neglected to mention his 1998 conversation with Flemmi about Murphy. Flemmi's 2003 debriefing was made public as a result of a two-week window of opportunity before it was sealed by a federal judge in 2009.

John Martorano, who engineered an immunity plea by testifying as a prosecution witness in the racketeering trial of FBI Special Agent John J. Connolly in 2002, was questioned by his defense attorney Tracy Miner, who cross-examined Martorano about murdering women.

> Miner: It's not your testimony that if you saw it was a woman, you would have stopped, is it?
> Martorano: If I knew it was a woman, I wouldn't have done it. But I couldn't stop and leave people behind. [The no witness rule]
> Miner: Because it is your testimony that you don't kill women?
> Martorano: *Positively, if I don't have to.* [My emphasis]
> Miner: But sometimes you have to, right?
> Martorano: I never run across that situation.
> Miner: How about Kathleen [sic] Murphy; do you recall her?

---

* Editor's note—the names in capital letters are as the report was written.

Martorano: Don't know her.

Miner: Do you recall a girlfriend of Billy Kearns?

Martorano: Billy who?

Miner: Kearns.

Martorano: Billy Kearns, yeah.

Miner misidentified Billy Kearns for James Kearns. She further delved into Martorano going out with Kearns and taking Kearns's girlfriend home. She asked if he was testifying he did not kill Murphy, and he responded, "I don't even know the name."

Steve Flemmi was debriefed as a premier cooperating witness by the Massachusetts State Police and DEA in 2003, and he reiterated his claim that James Kearns drove Murphy to another Boston after-hours joint, then called the Sahara Club, on Shawmut Avenue, which was owned by John Martorano, but was "unsure who was responsible for Kathleen [sic] Murphy's murder." Allegedly waiting was the misogynistic owner of the club, Johnny Martorano. Flemmi further related he didn't recall lending Murphy money but indicated it was possible. Boston police speculated a sexual component may have been a motive in both deaths. Kathy must have initially felt comfortable with her ride home but then refused the sexual advances or was forced into submission upon arriving in her neighborhood. She was slain in proximity to her home, for possibly threatening to expose a sexual deviant who became angry enough to kill.

Two questions came to the fore: was there any available physical evidence (i.e., sperm) recovered from Kathy's body, and should John Martorano come under suspicion?

Within forty-eight hours of the murder, the homicide squad questioned and released twenty-seven-year-old James R. Kearns of the South End after he stood "on his constitutional rights and declined to answer questions," as reported by the *Boston Globe*. His girlfriend conveniently provided an alibi, stating he was bedded down with her at the time of the murder. From 1956 through 1966, Kearns accumulated twenty-two criminal violations, including rape, forgery, receiving stolen property, larceny, and auto theft. He was able to beat several of his arrests. Whether his girlfriend conveniently supplied alibis beneficial to his defense in those ten years is unknown. Kearns died in a federal prison in Arizona in 2005.

Conflicting stories abound surrounding the events leading up to the brutal slaying of Kathryn Murphy. One such tale involves a Boston native sitting out the rest of his life as a death-row inmate in Raiford, Florida. "Big" Billy Kelley, who made his living stealing cars, loaning money at high interest rates, and doing drug deals, was convicted for the October 3, 1966, murder-for-hire shooting and stabbing death of Sebring citrus farmer Charles Von Maxcy. The former drug dealer and loan shark has proclaimed his innocence since 1984.

Criminals from Boston allegedly partook in assisting Von Maxcy's wife, Irene, by orchestrating the murder with her con-man lover and sometime pimp, Boston native John Sweet. He reached out to Walter Bennett, the Dudley Street bar owner and operator of the after-hours joint where Tony Veranis was killed and where Kathryn Murphy may have had her last drink. Bennett facilitated the hit for twenty-five thousand dollars. Steve Flemmi passed on the opportunity, but Kelley and fellow thief Andrew Von Etter had registered their names, or unknown parties did, in a nearby Daytona Beach motel around the time of Maxcy's murder. In a series of gangland hits, Von Etter was eliminated in February 1967 for fear he would bring law enforcement heat to the disappearance and possible slaying of his associate's brother, Edward "Wimpy" Bennett. In 1981, Sweet implicated Kelley in the murder of Von Maxcy.

I wrote Kelley in 2014, hoping to jog his memory surrounding events leading up to the murder of Kathryn Murphy because he was one of the last people to see her alive. In response to my first letter, he answered with an eight-page handwritten explanation. Overall, he wrote he has a tremendous amount of remorse for her death and how she died, to the point he would have "tossed your letter in the trash, but you picked the person who has haunted my thoughts for almost fifty years, which I will explain as I write this letter." Further into his missive, he wrote, "I can't give you the name you'd like to hear, but I will tell you this, the guy who killed Kathy has been dead for quite a few years." On page 4, he referenced the Howie Carr book *Rifleman*. "Did you see Kathy's photo on page 48? Even more interesting is the one on, page 49." Without looking, I knew a 1965 mug shot of James Kearns would be staring right back at me.

In his last paragraph before signing off, Kelley had one lament: "In case you wonder why I answered your letter, I guess it's out of respect for Kathy, and maybe she wants you to know exactly what happened to her."

At one point, I was getting too close to the truth of the matter because after a chain of nine letters spanning seven months, he wrote, "I've told you the truth, there is nothing more, so Joe do me a favor, don't write anymore. We are just wasting each other's time. Good luck. Billy."

I didn't let go that easily. In February 2015 in a letter to Kelley's appeals lawyer, I requested and received an audience in Tampa, Florida, later that winter. Because of my personal interest and extensive research into the Murphy homicide and into Kelley's case, during a three-hour conference with four lawyers, I maintained Kelley's innocence in the Von Maxcy murder but cited his selective veracity in the Murphy homicide. As of this writing, he is living out the rest of his life in bad health on death row.

James Kearns was certainly a person of interest in Kathryn Murphy's demise. Within days of the homicide, the *Boston Herald* noted a report of a car being abandoned on the Southeast Expressway in Boston, in close proximity to the scene of the Murphy murder approximately at the time of the shooting, which was 4:30 a.m. on a Sunday. The car was discovered by former Metropolitan District Commission police officers at 5:15 a.m. At that hour and day, an early-morning drive at normal speed from the murder scene to where the car was abandoned would take less than fifteen minutes. I believe the Mets just missed a possible murder suspect because James Kearns was a professional car thief. Even the most ardent car thief doesn't heist a car that has just been returned home by its owner between 4:00 a.m. and 4:30 a.m., unless he needs a ride fast from a crime scene after splitting up with the ride that brought him there in the first place. Neighbors who heard gunshots and heard Murphy cry out, "Oh no!" saw two men leaving the scene in an unknown car.

A 2016 interview with Kathy Murphy's boyfriend, who had been serving in the US Army at Fort Carson, Colorado, at the time of her murder, indicated he was "devastated" upon being notified of her death. He had not seen her for at least six months but had been writing her on a regular basis. The army allowed him death leave to attend her funeral, and during that time, he was interviewed by the Boston Police Homicide Squad. "I gave them everything I had," he said to me, adding, "She used to go to Walter's Lounge in Dorchester. I may have been there with her or my brother. I forget." He couldn't fathom a motive other than speculating rather sorrowfully, "Maybe she heard something or overheard something she wasn't supposed to hear."

From 1960 through 1978, there were approximately seventy-five gangland-related homicides in Boston and environs of which Martorano accounted for at least eighteen or an estimated 20 percent. His fugitive status in Florida did not impair his ability to perform out-of-state hits in 1981 and 1982 in Oklahoma and Florida, respectively.

PART 2

MOB WARS: THE SHOOTING SIXTIES AND SEVENTIES

CHAPTER 6

Joe Barboza

Think of your mother, sister, daughter, wife, or girlfriend being suddenly taken off this earth, her very existence eliminated by men of no moral bearing. While the number of women murdered during the gangland wars and beyond did not reach near the number of men killed, one was too many. Mobsters killed each other at a record pace but did not want to be accused of killing innocent women. Average women, who didn't possess weapons, were murdered for no other reason than killers chose to protect themselves and fellow killers from what ironically turned out to be a loosely knit array of corrupt federal, state, and local law enforcement officials.

From the early 1960s until the early '70s, the wise guys depleted their own ranks, making the funeral and flower business a ton of dough. The *smart* wise guys were those who chose not to participate in the firing range that defined the streets of Boston, where approximately fifty victims of all ages, races, sexes, and reputations met death or near death or went missing.

The so-called gangland war of the '60s produced a landmark year in 1965, which resulted in over twenty-five shootings, a majority of which were homicides and missing persons believed dead. Ironic that the Vietnam conflict was escalating parallel to the Boston killing fields.

In 1961, George McLaughlin, a gangster from Charlestown, in a state of drunkenness, reportedly hit on another mobster's woman at a beach party in the North Shore of Boston. Because of the affront, the abused victim's husband and a friend, all longshoremen from Somerville and Charlestown, beat McLaughlin to a pulp. The two Townies were confederates of Winter Hill gang leader James "Buddy" McLean. Georgie wanted Buddy to give them up to be murdered by the McLaughlin brothers, but Buddy respectfully declined. This was the trigger that set up a tit-for-tat warfare among Boston's Irish hoods in Somerville and Charlestown in the 1960s that would eventually leave more than fifty people dead.

A twenty-one-year-old bank teller from Boston wasn't on any gang war hit menu, but William J. Sheridan was fatally shot for no apparent reason on the evening of March 14, 1964. A small gathering of friends was breaking up a party after midnight in the Roxbury section of Boston in the apartment of Maureen Dellamano, George McLaughlin's girlfriend. McLaughlin murdered Sheridan in cold blood with a gunshot wound in his head during an altercation between the two men in the doorway of the apartment. Two days later, a district court complaint and federal fugitive warrant was issued for the arrest of Charlestown's finest, George McLaughlin.

Canton was a growing suburban town south of Boston. A reliable source reported to the Canton police in October 1964 that he had observed George McLaughlin driving his red and white Oldsmobile accompanied by two local thugs, Ed Gabree and Lenny Bickford, who were well acquainted with the Boston police. McLaughlin and Gabree, thieves and tailgaters, had drawn the attention of law enforcement before George became a fugitive from justice, hiding out in the hometown of his brother "Punchy."

Canton police had the Magnolia Street home of George's brother Edward

"Punchy" McLaughlin under surveillance at the request of the Boston police months before Punchy survived a second attempt on his life just before Thanksgiving 1964. Rival Somerville hood and tough streetfighter, James "Buddy" McLean was gunning for Punchy. Buddy shot his brother Bernie McLaughlin to death in 1961, just outside the Morning Glory Café in the City Square area of Charlestown.

FBI agents arrested George McLaughlin on February 24, 1965, in a Boston apartment bedroom within reach of three revolvers in a top dresser drawer. Up until the age of ninety-three, as 2021 approached, he would remain a prisoner at the Bay State Correction Center in Norfolk for life.

Punchy went down without a fight in October 1965 while sitting at a bus stop in West Roxbury as a result of a fusillade of bullets shot from a thirty-eight-caliber "long barrel." Buddy McLean was subsequently shot to death a week later while sitting in his car in front of a Somerville lounge.

The carnage continued well into the '70s along with a proliferation of hijackings—Punchy's buddy Eddie Gabree being one of the most proficient at it. Gabree was arrested at midnight on May 23, 1973, in the rear parking lot of Eddie Connors's Savin Hill bar known as Bulldog's, as he and five other thieves surrounded three cases of stolen tuna.

Two years later, Eddie Connors was assassinated by Bulger, Flemmi, and John Martorano, a little over a mile from where Connors viewed his stolen loot. The prospect of selling hot tuna also fizzled for "Big" Billy Kelley, who is spending his adult life on death row in Florida. The owner of the tuna stolen from a warehouse on Dorchester Avenue in South Boston was unable to identify the property as his, after being visited by two private investigators of unknown affiliation. The defendants were found not guilty.

Whether he knew it or not, Gabree was on the radar screen of the Boston office of the FBI in 1977 as a well-known tailgater due to his years-long criminal behavior, which began when he was a juvenile. He stole everything in sight beginning at nine years of age in 1943, eventually becoming a Boston alumnus of the infamous Lyman Boys School for Delinquents.

A real-life Oliver Twist character known as a fence was supplanting the likes of Gabree along with a local crew of forty to fifty hijackers facilitated by N. Giarro Enterprises. From March 1977 to June 1978, there were sixty-seven hijackings and thefts of tractor trailer loads in New England from which three million dollars in stolen property was exchanged and funneled through a nondescript ten-thousand-square foot warehouse located in the Boston neighborhood of Hyde Park at 1616 Hyde Park Avenue, which was an FBI sting being operated by a kid from Chelsea.

Special Agent Nick Gianturco, operating under his undercover pseudonym, Nick Giarro, played the central role in a joint FBI and Massachusetts State Police venture. The investigation was given an unusual moniker, "Lobster." For two years, in daily hand-to-hand buys of millions of dollars' worth of stolen merchandise, Agent Gianturco put his life on the line dealing with brazen thieves who were capable of stealing Christ off the cross. The major operation produced arrest warrants for forty-six suspects in the nation's biggest crackdown of truck hijackers, as reported by the FBI. Not surprising, a majority of the arrested were native Townies (Charlestown) or hailed from Southie.

Police characters of minimal means and mindless ambitions spread like Boston baked beans as the so-called gangland war gripped the city of Boston and convulsed the survivors.

By the time the dust settled in the mob war, more than fifty Boston hoods were dead or missing.

Some of the missing may have disappeared into the US Marshals' Witness Security Program,* like the initial inductee, Joe "the Animal" Barboza.

Joe Barboza deserves his own category of criminality.

---

* The US Marshals Service Witness Security Program has protected, relocated, and given new identities to more than 8,600 witnesses and 9,900 of their family members since the program began in 1971. No participant following program guidelines has been harmed or killed while under the active protection of the service, according to its website. At the time of Barboza's assassination, he had exposed himself publicly in violation of Witness Security Program guidelines.

It is alleged that Barboza was solely responsible for at least 20 percent of the carnage in the '60s. Murder your neighbor, and you get life in a state prison if convicted. Murder everyone in a group as large as the starting lineup for the New England Patriot football team, and the federal government hands you a makeover and a reset button for the rest of your life, courtesy of Uncle Sam.

Barboza lied for a morally corrupt FBI Agent, H. Paul Rico, about the brutal slaying of a local Irish boxer known as Teddy Deegan. Barboza asserted at a Suffolk County Superior Court trial in Boston that six members of organized crime killed Deegan. His perjured, uncorroborated testimony led to the erroneous convictions of innocent men all of whose surnames ended in a vowel. In the process, an Irishman was murdered, resulting in the Italians taking a big hit from the Portuguese Barboza and the Hispanic Rico. A July 1968 teletype item to the director of the FBI from the special agent in charge of the Boston office recommended letters of commendation for Special Agent Rico and others who "were responsible for the development of government witnesses Barboza and Glavin."

In 1975, H. Paul Rico retired from the bureau, taking a position as director of security for World Jai Alai in Miami, which was owned by Tulsa businessman Roger Wheeler. That same year, Bulger was reopened as an FBI informant with Agent Condon as his handler. Twenty-five years later, during congressional hearings, Rico testified without displaying any remorse about sending the innocent men who were convicted in the murder of Eddie Deegan in 1965 to jail for life when he sneeringly pronounced, "What do you want, tears?" In 2004, Rico died in a Tulsa hospital while under police guard, awaiting trial for conspiracy to commit murder in the case of World Jai Alai owner Roger Wheeler in 1981. Steve Flemmi, Bulger, and John Martorano were named as his coconspirators.

While Steve was earning his reputation as a marksman in 1951, H. Paul Rico joined the FBI, and Barboza, at age twenty, led a prison riot and escaped from Concord State Prison in 1953. Ten months later, he was headed back to prison to serve ten to twelve years for serious criminal charges. Former FBI informant Vinnie Flemmi had been responsible for at least a half dozen murders as recognized by the bureau bugs, but within months of his incarceration, the narrow streets of Boston continued to flow with the blood of a dozen gangland slayings, mostly by the hand of Joe Barboza. Near the end of May 1967, the special agent in charge of the Boston FBI office received a letter from Director Hoover stating, "a review of the Bureau reveals that no investigation of Barron (Barboza) has ever been conducted by your office." Barboza is recorded on the Patriarca bug seeking permission to kill people, yet not one agent, as reflected in the Hoover letter, opened a case file or at least a threshold investigation when in fact the local and state police had near certain knowledge of his various criminal movements without the benefit of the intelligence accrued by the bureau.

Theoretically, Agents Rico and Condon were protecting Barboza and, more important, the Patriarca bug. They knew he and Vinnie Flemmi had committed the murder of Teddy Deegan but were willing to sacrifice him at the altar of bureau awards, incentives, and prominence. Contrasting the Hoover letter, the Boston special agent in charge of Rico and Condon recommended them for incentive awards for persuading Steve Flemmi to convince Deegan's killer, Barboza, to testify against Patriarca.

While Martorano was on a killing spree in 1968, Agents Rico and Condon made numerous visits courting the semi-imprisoned Barboza while he was being held in protective custody by the US Marshals Service, at a seaside safe house in the north of Boston fishing community of Gloucester. The professed reason for checking his well-being was to keep "the Animal" caged and in check, in order for him to testify at several gangland murder trials and, more important, the upcoming and very confusing Deegan trial. Barboza committed perjury on an astonishing level at the Deegan trial, resulting in four innocent men, Limone et alia, being found guilty of a murder they did not commit. Postconvictions would produce FBI commendations, which were thrown around like confetti for FBI agents who suborned perjury.

Joe Barboza was truly an animal. He was a brutal, vicious hitman, and Rico allowed himself to believe a psychotic liar in the murder of Eddie Deegan when illegal FBI electronic surveillance, along with street-level intelligence, proved otherwise. He wasn't alone in his malfeasance. Suffolk County prosecutors and individual Boston police investigators deserved to be taken to task as well. As the cliché goes, they were sold a bill of goods by Barboza. Needless to say, hindsight is always a false prescription for insight. Rico also induced another informant to lie under oath in a Rhode Island murder case. That case and the criminal convictions of Limone et alia were all later overturned. The only living legacy Rico left was the estate of the men Barboza wrongfully accused of killing Deegan, who sued the US government and won an award in excess of a hundred million dollars in 2007.

As written in the last page of the last paragraph of the 1975 book Barboza wrote with Hank Messick, titled *Barboza*, he (Barboza) came to terms with himself when he was quoted as saying, "The Mafia laughs at me being in prison, but I laugh even louder because I'm still way ahead and they can never get even. Never." "Never" lasted less than a year after the publication of this book about the miscreant life of Joseph "the Animal" Barboza (alias Joe Donati, Denati, Bentley, and Barron). He was murdered in the streets of San Francisco, where his heartless body was found on February 11, 1976. The suspected assassin, Boston Mafiosa Joseph Anthony Russo, didn't leave his heart in San Francisco: he left a monster.

CHAPTER 7

La Famiglia Flemmi

Paralleling the murderous career of Barboza were those of his close associates, the Flemmi brothers. John and Mary (Misserville) Flemmi had three sons: Stephen Joseph born on June 9, 1934; Vincenzo James born on September 5, 1935; and Michael born on July 9, 1937. Michael entered the Boston Police Department in 1968. Steve enlisted in the army and became a paratrooper, serving two tours in the Korean War, where he was known by his alias, Michael Stephen Fucielo. After he was honorably discharged from the army, he was known as "the Rifleman."

Vincenzo did not serve in the military but earned the moniker "the Bear"—maybe because he was so cuddly.

Armed with a resume that would have made Prohibition-era Chicago hood Al Capone blush and proud at the same time was Vincenzo Flemmi. In May 1965, two assassins with shotguns went big-game hunting and attempted to kill "the Bear" as he exited his Dorchester home at 699 Adams Street. First on the scene was District 11 Boston Police Officer William Devereaux, who recalled a priest arriving to administer last rites as Flemmi was lying in the street bleeding profusely as a result of stomach wounds. The officer was aghast when Flemmi looked at the priest and said, "Get the fuck away from me. I don't need your fucking prayers."

And yet, this was a hood recruited by Paul Rico as an FBI informant.

That same month, Vincenzo Flemmi, who went by either Vinny or Jimmy, was the subject of a conversation overheard on the Patriarca bug, where it was recorded that "Barboza was with Flemmi (Vinnie) when they killed Deegan." The next month, Vinnie has a meeting with Rico confirming "he is willing to aid the Bureau, as he can help put away the individuals who attempted to kill him." The following day, June 9, the Boston FBI special agent in charge sent a memo to Hoover reporting,

> from information obtained from other informants and sources, that BS-919-PC (Vincent "Jimmy" Flemmi) has murdered Frank Benjamin, John Murray, George Ashe, Joseph Francione, Edward "Teddy" Deegan, and "Iggy" Lowry…and from all indications, he is going to continue to commit murder.

The upside of the illegal bug was it generated intelligence that Vinny was a hitman on a par with his buddy Barboza.

Vincenzo Flemmi was closed as an informant three months after Agent Rico was advised of the six murders mentioned in the June 9 memo. Resulting intelligence recorded through the Patriarca bug and relevant transcripts contributed to Rico et al having foreknowledge of the homicidal tendencies and criminal transgressions of Vinnie Flemmi. In a memo to Director Hoover, Rico suggested that Flemmi might embarrass the bureau because he was being charged with assault with a dangerous weapon with intent to murder, upon which he exercised his criminal constitutional prerogative to flee. La famiglia, as practiced by the Mafia, was its greatest strength.

The Commonwealth of Massachusetts exercised its constitutional duty sending Rico's top informant to prison for four to six years for armed assault with intent to murder twenty-two-year-old Dorchester resident John Cutliffe. The Massachusetts Board of Probation arrest record for Vinnie Flemmi listed seventy to eighty entries from 1949 up to his incarceration in March 1966, ranging from speeding to attempted murder. A seventeen-year criminal history of brutality by "the Bear" did not seem to jolt Rico's conscience.

The same month Vinnie Flemmi departed for state prison, a brief excerpt from the personnel file of Rico rated him as excellent and stated he had been assigned exclusively "to the development of Top Echelon informants and had worked primarily on this important program and had exceptional talent in his ability to develop informants and his participation was outstanding."

The FBI took a page out of the Mafia's playbook, and lo and behold, three months after throwing Vinnie to the curb, they found Steve Flemmi waiting.

On February 2, 1967, brother Steve joined the FBI team and was classified as a "Top Echelon" informant. For administrative and clandestine purposes, he would be identified as BS 955 C-TE.

An ex-con and cooperating police witness spent the afternoon of September 5, 1969, being recorded by the Boston police and FBI rendering a four-page statement based on conversations and meetings he had with Steve Flemmi and his close criminal associate Frank Salemme in conjunction with setting up the December 1967 hit of William "Billy" Bennett. (Earlier that year, his brothers Walter and Edward "Wimpy" went missing and are presumed to be dead.) Ex-con Robert Daddieco and Salemme were close friends, and now he was giving up the man known as "Cadillac Frank." Daddieco had a lot to say after the murder.

> Frankie and Steve went off to make a phone call. About fifteen or twenty minutes later Daddieco was in the car and observed Bill Stewart [sic] talking to Steve and Frankie about two car lengths in front…Steve and Stewart [sic] left and they were

gone about ten minutes or less when Steve came back and said that Billy was dead and he was going back to move the car that Grasso was using that night.

Daddieco also fingered "the other guy they used to get Billy" but didn't remember the man's name. Whether Agent Rico had knowledge of the interview, he called Flemmi and informed him he and Salemme were going to be indicted for the Bennett murder and the attempted murder of Barboza's attorney and stated, "I suggest that you and your friend leave town." Salemme was later convicted of bombing the attorney's car and spent in excess of fifteen years in prison. Flemmi fled to the Las Vegas area with Peter Poulos, an accessory to the Bennett murder, but Poulos never survived the month with his travelling companion and was slain in the desert outside of Las Vegas.

The Clark County Sheriff's office investigated the murder but felt at the time it was "hampered, and after a few months the FBI took control of the case." "While a fugitive, Flemmi stays in touch with Rico. Yet, Rico does not share this information with the fellow agents responsible for finding Flemmi," as chronicled in the US Congress Committee on Government Reform report in 2004. Even though the local court issued murder warrants for the pair, Homicide Detective Chuck Lee said, "everything came to a sudden stop." The Poulos homicide is still active and is carried as an open case by the sheriff's office in Las Vegas. Flemmi admitted murdering Poulos when he testified at "Whitey" Bulger's federal trial in 2013, but like John Martorano, he has never appeared before a judge of competent jurisdiction to plead guilty.

CHAPTER 8

Degrees of Separation among Hoods and Cops

A 1990 play written by John Guare titled *Six Degrees of Separation* popularized the theory that everyone is six or fewer steps away, by way of introduction, from any other person in the world. According to Wikipedia, the commonly known theory of six degrees of separation was originally explained by Frigyes Karinthy in 1929. If your world was the neighborhoods of Boston, however, there was only one degree of separation. If you accept this theory, no less than a dozen neighborhoods connected a chain of a friend of a friend in a minimum of one step instead of six, which is in conflict with Karinthy.

But, of course, he didn't come from the neighborhoods of Boston known as Dorchester or South Boston.

Natives of Dot were affectionately referred to as Dot Rats—not because they finked out on others, but there were so many from the hood who knew a friend of a friend (if that makes sense). If you came from Jamaica Plain (JP), Charlestown (Townies), and maybe even East Boston (Eastie), you would better understand the proposition.

In the last half of the twentieth century, Boston was a homogeneously populated urban city. Along with attending the local neighborhood public or parochial school, one could walk to a nearby park in Southie and play Little League baseball in the summer or hockey in the winter on the same flooded baseball fields. Catholic Youth Organizations (CYO) sponsored baseball, softball, and basketball for all. Or maybe you belonged to the parish Scout troop or joined the Boys and Girls Clubs that were starting to flourish in the city. As a result of everyone attending one of the many fine parochial or public high schools, homogeneity was allowed to flourish. You took public transportation known as the "T" everywhere. Lifelong friendships and relationships were established and endured as a result of one degree of separation, which brings us to the wise guys and their degree of separation.

James "Whitey" Bulger and his gang, the Mullins, came from Southie. The Flemmi siblings grew up in Roxbury and lived in Hyde Park and Dorchester. Frank Salemme, who was nearly assassinated gangland style in 1989, spent his youth in Jamaica Plain. Although they grew up in the Boston suburb of Milton, the Martorano brothers spent most of their adult life conducting criminal business in Roxbury and the South End. The five Angiulo brothers who headed up the Boston branch of the New England Mafia were born, raised, and lived most of their lives in the heavily Italian North End conclave of Boston.

The degrees of separation among FBI Agent H. Paul Rico, State Trooper Richard Schneiderhan, and Boston Police Officer William Wallace Stuart are a little blurry but nonetheless significant.

For a period in the '50s, Schneiderhan resided in the same Roxbury neighborhood as the Flemmis and before that the South End. Stuart's parents also lived in the South End, where he was born in 1928. When he was accepted into the Boston Police Academy in 1954, Stuart lived in Dorchester. Rico spent most of his life where he was born, in the affluent suburban town of Belmont, just miles away and only a few degrees of separation from

Schneiderhan and Stuart.

The law enforcement careers of these men concurrently spanned over three decades from the '50s through the '70s, which mirrored one of the most horrendous eras of crime and corruption perpetrated by neighborhood gangsters, and were allowed to metastasize with the assistance of a few bad neighborhood cops.

I don't think those of us who lived through the '60s will soon forget that tumultuous decade, but you have to admit the music was memorable as a backdrop to a raging and uncontrolled gang war in Boston that engrossed family and friends of a different nature, where nobody gave a damn about your politics or the war raging in Vietnam.

But undisturbed and less conflicted sixty miles south, in the city of Providence, Rhode Island, was FBI informant BS 837-C hard at work.

A long, rambling nine-page letter from FBI Director Hoover, dated June 21, 1961, and titled "CRIMINAL INFORMANTS—CRIMINAL INTELLIGENCE PROGRAM," introduced the Top Echelon Informant Program. The second-to-last paragraph states, "This program has, as its purpose, the employment of quality criminal intelligence informants. The two most important components of this program are the selection of individuals for development as informants and the designation of the Special Agents who will participate."

John F. Kehoe Jr., a special agent in the Boston FBI office and a Dorchester native hardly ever had to take the hour-long drive to Providence to meet his snitch because the informant's intelligence was mailed to him in the form of transcribed tapes and logs. Nor did he have to select "individuals for development" because the FBI had installed three illegal electronic surveillance bugs—commonly known in police jargon as black-bag jobs—as its inaugural item in the Top Echelon Informant Program. Ultimately, Kehoe's choice of Paul Rico as a designated agent for the program proved to be disastrous. Kehoe was the antithesis of Rico. He later became the head of the Massachusetts State Police as commissioner of public safety in 1971 after a twenty-nine-year career with the FBI following his 1941 graduation from Boston College.

The target of the first secret bug was the leader of the Mafia in New England, Raymond L. S. Patriarca. Beginning in 1962, his office at the Coin-O-Matic Distributing Company at 168 Atwells Avenue in Providence and that of his business associate Louis Taglianetti were bugged. A second bug was surreptitiously installed in January 1963 in the Combat Zone at Jay's Lounge, which was run by Jerry Angiulo, the underboss for Raymond Patriarca. A third unauthorized bug was installed in May 1964 within the Boston State Street office of the Piranha Finance Company.

From January 1962 until December 1968, the FBI maintained bugs in Providence and Boston, administratively being characterized as informants. Executive privilege was later claimed over a federal prosecution memorandum related to conversations overheard in what essentially was a warrantless invasion of privacy, which in layman's terms pertains to the unambiguous lack of any court order signed by a federal judge in the performance of an illegal trespass onto the property of the subject target. It wasn't until 1968 that Congress passed Title III of the Omnibus Crime Control and Safe Streets Act (Wiretap Act). The bill passed in large part "in response to congressional investigations and published studies that found extensive wiretapping had been conducted by government and private individuals without the consent of parties or legal sanction."

In the middle of the federal bugs, Stuart was promoted to first grade detective in 1964, along with a $2.00 per week raise, bringing his gross salary to $122 a week. During a six-year period in the '60s, he was involved in a least a half dozen cruiser accidents. He was never faulted but received serious injury in at least one accident. During those years, he would also be commended by the special agent in charge of the Boston FBI office for successfully being involved in a variety of federal criminal investigations.

While performing his duties as an intelligence officer, Stuart submitted many reports referring to unknown sources and reliable informants, citing local gangsters and organized crime figures, a majority of whom would be killed in the escalating gang wars. Stuart's sphere of intelligence and surveillance work encompassed the geographical boundary of Roxbury, particularly the Dearborn Square area of Dudley Street, where he crossed paths many times with Agent Rico; his partner, Agent Dennis Condon; and the Flemmi, Martorano, and Bennett brothers.

Within days of the third bug operating out of Piranha Finance, Agent Condon wrote a memo citing that an informant (name redacted) told him Vinnie Flemmi "feels he can now be the top hit man in this area and intends to be." Several months later, his partner, Agent Rico, authored a memo wherein an unnamed informant "indicates that he thinks Vincent 'Jimmy' Flemmi has committed several murders." The agent's admonition about informant information characterizing Flemmi as a prospective hit man rings hollow. Not the information but the messenger. Conceivably, one or two confidants with whom Flemmi would vocally share his ambition about being a "top hit man" would be Joe Barboza and/or Flemmi's brother, Steve. Barboza had a man crush on Vinnie, thereby ensuring his loyalty. In retrospect, it is implausible Steve would ever consider giving up his brother to the bureau, months before he was targeted as an FBI informant in November 1964 or thereafter. With three active unauthorized bugs humming and Rico as the designated agent for the program, redacted and unnamed sources would suffice for hard intelligence garnered from conversations illegally obtained.

The "other informants and sources," as relied upon by the FBI, would have to become more reliable because in 1968, a seven-year electronic surveillance operation in Providence and Boston targeting Patriarca was terminated. Hundreds of hours of illegal recordings and transcribed logs were discontinued and secreted away by the bureau, only years later to be named "the Patriarca transcripts" by legendary *Boston Globe* columnist, Richard Connolly.

The Massachusetts State Police Organized Crime Gaming Unit, or Special Service Unit, had been hitting bookies at a constant pace in Suffolk County since the early '80s. Besides Boston, three communities—Winthrop, Revere, and Chelsea—encompassed the county. When a new trooper came into the unit, he or she was immediately dispatched to Chelsea to learn their craft. At the time, there were probably more bookies in Chelsea than books in the local library. Winthrop had its share of resident betters and bookies while Revere bar owners loved illegal video poker machines. Our gaming unit also had the mission of pursuing organized crime figures throughout the state, which became part of our daily assignment.

PART 3

CHASING BOOKIES

CHAPTER 9

Operation Grandslam

One of the most aggressive joint Massachusetts State Police and FBI organized crime investigations conducted in eastern Massachusetts occurred in 1975. Troopers assigned to the Special Service Unit partnered with FBI agents from the organized crime section of the Boston office. Agents Pete Kennedy and Tom Daly spearheaded the operation known as Grandslam.

The central focus was to attack the grip Boston Mafia had on illegal gambling, especially sports. Day in and day out for six months, from June to November, troopers and agents monitored the conversations and conducted physical surveillance of the leading figures and bookies associated with Mafia capo Jerry Angiulo and his lieutenant, Ilario Zannino, alias Larry Baione.

Hundreds of hours were expended surveilling the bookies by troopers travelling from one bookie office to another, which encompassed almost every Boston neighborhood and several of its suburbs. The physical surveillance stretched from a Dorchester bowling alley to the oceanfront home of Baione in the swanky North Shore town of Swampscott. Low-level bookies, practicing the trade from various apartments and extending their reach to bosses keeping track of the action in fancy homes in affluent towns were all being heard and watched on a daily basis for months without their knowledge.

Weeks into the operation, a coming-home party was going to be sponsored by longtime bookie and target of illegal sports betting, Abe Sarkis, for newly released federal prison inmate and Mafia leader Larry Baione. Boraschi's Restaurant in Dedham, owned by Sarkis, was the venue for the Baione party. The pair grew up as close friends in the diverse South End neighborhood of Boston, the same neighborhood where Trooper Schneiderhan spent part of his youth.

Trooper Charlie Henderson and I got the assignment to put the peek on Baione and his invited guests. It was like a bar mitzvah for bookies and a Mafia convention, all rolled into one party with Mafia goons providing security. Jerry Angiulo's brother Donato and Mafia associate Angelo "Sonny" Mercurio made a cameo appearance. Bookies and gangsters we had been following for weeks were fawning all over Baione with several applying the immortal Mafia kiss of respect on each of his ruddy cheeks. We could hardly finish our drinks and dinner, provided by the Feds, while watching the theater of the benign from our dining room table.

While the party continued late into the night, Charlie and I sat in our surveillance van in the restaurant parking lot, awaiting the departure of Baione. Sometime after midnight, he came out of the restaurant with a group of hoods, and they drove off, with him comfortably seated in the rear seat. For the next hour or so, the group took a sightseeing tour of Baione's old haunts in the neighborhood streets of Jamaica Plain and South End, finally pulling up in front of the Hanover Street Café Pompeii in the North End at three in the morning. While we tried to fit into a sparse crowd of late-night expresso sippers, to our surprise, Baione met Jerry Angiulo in the café. No visible pecks on the cheeks were exchanged.

Our subsequent report of the welcome-home party and early-morning meeting Baione and Angiulo shared not only surprised Charlie and me but the Feds as well. We were informed by longtime bureau agents that our observation of the two Boston Mafia leaders together in public was the first made by the state police, as well as the FBI.

In the middle of the operation, Johnny Martorano killed Eddie Connors and Tommy King in June and November, respectively, establishing his sixteenth and seventeenth homicides. His accomplices, Bulger and Steve Flemmi, shot Connors while he was standing in a Morrissey Boulevard phone booth in Dorchester. They shot King in the back of the head near the shores of Carson Beach in Southie and buried his corpse along the Dorchester banks of the Neponset River. Along with Martorano, Flemmi confessed, and Bulger was found guilty of both murders in 2013.

After months of electronic and physical surveillance conducted against the largest sports bookmaking consortium in Boston environs, preparations were made to execute search warrants for over thirty bookie offices. As part of the logistics, FBI agents and troopers who had *not* participated in the investigation were going to be utilized to assist in the raids. Several days beforehand, many of these individuals were designated point men (team leaders) and were then shown the location they were to raid. However, the day before D-Day, FBI informants advised the word was out on the street that the raids were imminent. We had a leak. Then Corporal Richard Schneiderhan—the already corrupted and self-admitted confidant of John Martorano and Steve Flemmi—in all probability was a point man or had knowledge from troopers under his command who shared information about the operation.

A week later, on Sunday, November 16, 1975, federal search warrants for five of the major players were to be executed at 1300 hours. As point man, my responsibility was to keep Abe Sarkis in-pocket (under surveillance in bureau lingo). He had been under my view since the early morning, leaving his home in Milton and going directly to his restaurant in Dedham.

At one point during my surveillance, I observed Sarkis taking sports book on his restaurant pay phone and placing the evidence in his jacket pocket. At approximately 12:45 p.m., Sarkis came out of his restaurant, got into a waiting Jeep with two males inside, sat in the parking lot for about ten minutes, and then proceeded to leave for Route 1. Out of fear Sarkis would join a funeral procession for a low-level wise guy passing by on Route 1, our team jumped the gun, stopped the car, and detained and searched Sarkis for incriminating gambling apparatus.

To my surprise, without hesitation, an agent I had never met before jumped into action. Special Agent John Connolly immediately took over the scene, placating the astonished bookie-at-heart. Sarkis had thousands of dollars on his person, along with gambling materials, and Connolly wanted to know why he carried that much money. What I didn't know then was two months preceding the raids, Connolly had officially recruited "Whitey" Bulger as his confidential informant.

A new word appeared in the lexicon of illegal gaming in the early '70s. Some called it extortion and others the cost of doing business, but most bookies called it rent. Pay to play, retire, or incur the wrath of extortionists. Confidential state police informants confided that certain bookies were being threatened to pay a percentage of the gross to the likes of whom? Those independent bookies (of which there were many) not affiliated with Jerry Angiulo were well aware of the brutality of John Martorano, Flemmi, and Bulger, and knew the odds were unfavorable, so of course they smartly paid the piper. Through the years of chasing bookies, I often commented, I never met a bookie I didn't like, except maybe one.

Case in point...

The FBI handed off a tip to SSU regarding a bookie operating out of an apartment building located on the Revere Beach Parkway in Revere. (A trooper could spend his or her entire career bagging bookies in Revere.) In any event, sport bookies and agents are like clockwork, always coming and going at precisely the same time depending on what time the games are being played. The Feds provided a name, phone number, motor vehicle registration, and address for a prospective bookie living in a five-story apartment building but no physical description. The best I could do was walk into the building with unsuspecting tenants with a key. After spending a couple of weeks clocking this bird, calling him for the sport lines, which he graciously shared, I had enough probable cause to draw up an affidavit, which was signed by a Chelsea District Court clerk magistrate. On a quiet Sunday afternoon in early January 1976, three FBI agents and two troopers gained unimpeded entrance carrying a sledgehammer into the apartment building without being noticed. The bookie's metal door was locked, so with my no-knock search warrant in hand, I knocked on the door. Normal procedure called for the sledgehammer. He declined to come to the door, yelling out something like, "Who is it?" or "What do you want?"

I yelled back that I lived in the building and was having car trouble. I asked if I could use his phone because my old lady locked me out. Within seconds, he opened the door and then turned his back on me as we were storming the apartment shouting, "Police!" He then suddenly realized what was going down and reacted by bolting from our grasp while trying to unsuccessfully pull out two telephone lines and reaching for a loaded .25-caliber Titan automatic weapon on the coffee table. A search of the premises revealed a .357 Magnum, a silver-plated .38-caliber Special Smith & Wesson snub nose, and several boxes of ammunition. Surprisingly, the muff possessed a valid firearm identification permit. I'm sure when his boss got word of the raid, the twenty-two-year-old novice bookie got a little street justice. Bookies make their money with a pen not a gun.

Plymouth County Assistant District Attorney William O'Malley (who was eventually elected district attorney) submitted an application applying for authorization to wiretap a bookmaker in the South Shore town of Weymouth. Concurrent with the wiretap, Trooper John Naimovich went undercover and worked as a bookie in the seaside town of Scituate, not far from Weymouth. This was my first exposure to the often intractable

Naimovich, who was sometimes called Ivan. He was assigned to Plymouth County, and I was with the Special Service Unit. The late Quincy police detective Peter Gallagher turned out to be a great balance during the wire and very knowledge, but the senior Naimovich was in charge.

Before sunrise, ten days from Christmas 1976, seventy-five state and local police fanned out over Boston and the South Shore, arresting nineteen individuals for alleged illegal gambling violations. Naimovich had a warrant for Martorano and arrested him on the sixteenth. The ink wasn't dry on Martorano's bail papers when FBI informant Richie Castucci was shot to death by Martorano, Bulger, and Flemmi. The body was found in his Cadillac, which was parked in the Northgate shopping mall in Revere, on December 30, 1976. He became the eighteenth homicide and third or so police informant Martorano quieted.

A five-minute incriminating phone call made by John Martorano to a Weymouth bookie was recorded during our interception. Like Naimovich, Martorano was the boss and demonstrated his capacity as a supervisor, as witnessed by the call. A court-ordered voice analysis was requested for Martorano and performed by troopers assigned to the attorney general office. It was revealed in 2013 at the racketeering trial of Bulger that Corporal Schneiderhan, who administered the exam, assisted Martorano in passing the voice analysis. He instructed Martorano to place some sort of a device in his mouth, which threw off the machine.

To the surprise of prosecutors and police, four of the main players, including Martorano, pled out in 1978. The move ensured no disclosures at trial by the defense nor any prosecutorial penetration into the organized crime group. Martorano appeared in court, where he and his cohorts pleaded guilty and received four to six months in the house of corrections at Plymouth. He was an intimidating person in the courtroom.

As an example, while investigating several prisoners at the Plymouth House of Corrections sometime later, I bumped into James Timilty and Richie O'Brien, who had paid rent to Martorano and Bulger. O'Brien would later testify to exactly those circumstances in the 2013 Bulger trial. I queried them about how Martorano was handling prison life—this being his first incarceration—and they responded, "He has never said a word to us." The boys got the nonverbal message and gave him a wide berth the entire term. The misguided instituting of rent by members of the newly minted Winter Hill organized crime crew, who set up headquarters in the Boston suburb of Somerville, would not end with Operation Lighting.

Except for Gloria Gill (a woman claiming to be his wife) and his lawyer, Martorano had no visitors and even turned away a friend from Quincy. He made a few phone calls to his attorney, Marty Weinberg, and fewer to Gloria. She had an unfortunate accident in 1969, falling under an oncoming MBTA rapid transit train at South Station. The train operator told the Boston police he observed the woman "take a swan dive." She was treated for a "laceration of the lower right leg" and released from the Massachusetts General Hospital.

As part of a then prerelease stipulation, Martorano needed a sponsor for employment upon release. In May 1978, he was working the jail pay phones, making calls to the Berenson Properties of 66 Long Wharf, Boston, owned by real estate developer Theodore S. Berenson. The next month, Berenson was scammed for $60,000 by Bulger, Flemmi, and Martorano. Using photos of a multimurder crime scene supplied by FBI Agent Connolly, the trio somehow convinced the gullible Berenson he was involved, and they would not reveal the photos if he paid.

Whether Martorano landed a job is questionable, but in 1980, Berenson had his picture taken with Bulger and Mafia associate Phil Waggenheim by the Massachusetts State Police when they were conducting electronic and physical surveillance at a Lancaster Street garage, located at the edge of the west end of Boston.

Martorano missed the photo opportunity due to the fact he was working on his tan as a federal fugitive in sunny southeast Florida.

CHAPTER 10

Pursuing "Legs" Lewis and "Pokerman"

After testifying in Chelsea District Court concerning illegal gambling, Trooper Joe Sinkovich was driving his unmarked cruiser through a couple of side streets leading to the Tobin Bridge, which connects the city of Chelsea to Boston due south. He was sharp enough that midmorning fall day in 1983 to recognize several cars and license plates parked in the area.

That previous summer, troopers from the Special Service Unit, led by Sinkovich, arrested several bookies in the Hyde Park section of Boston. Thankfully, he took time to make a call to our Framingham office, located in a western suburb of Boston, notifying me of his observations. He knew I would be very interested in why a couple of high-level bookies, whom we had previously tracked for weeks, had parked their expensive cars within blocks of a sleazy bar in the area of Chestnut Street.

I immediately raced to the area and recorded every license plate within two blocks of the bar. Sinkovich could not have ever imagined that the embryonic stages of an epic twelve-year odyssey was about to begin, turning the mass killer John Martorano into a jail-free snitch; eventually incarcerating cooperating witness Steve Flemmi for life; and causing James "Whitey" Bulger to flee and then be captured after sixteen years and stand trial where "Himself" was found guilty of ten murders and sentenced to life in federal prison. Many of the bookies arrested by SSU during those years had been extorted by Bulger et alia to pay protection money in order to stay in business, according to state police informants. More difficult to imagine was yet another monumental travesty of injustice perpetuated against the citizens of the Commonwealth of Massachusetts by the Department of Justice.

But it all started with our pursuit of a well-known bookie named Eddie Lewis, some months before I raced to Chelsea.

Informants are crucial to gaming investigations. State police detectives would identify informants as "It-1" or "CI-1" and if not, then "Smith" or "Jones" was as good as any moniker you could apply. I used Smith and Jones in my affidavit to secure search warrants for the premises used by several bookies within the greater Boston Jewish faction of an organized crime illegal gambling syndicate.

In June of 1983, our informant provided us with information that would have long-standing consequences. Let "Jones" tell you in his or her own words: "I am receiving the wagering lines and placing wagers on sporting events over telephone (617)787------, and that this is part of the Edward Lewis operation, and that color codes are used to identify the agents and bettors." He or she further stated "that at the end of each night's wagering, the person at telephone number (617)787----- copies on paper a record of all the wagers which were registered during this period, and then personally delivers these records of wagering activity to Lewis at his residence at Broadlawn Park in Chestnut Hill."

The telephone number provided by "Jones" led me to the Brighton area of Boston and a person who was convicted in 1975 for violating state gambling laws. In August of 1983, while conducting physical surveillance, I had the good fortune to overhear the male occupant of the address at which the preceding phone was listed, conversing on the phone using common language familiar to bookmakers, while I was legally standing outside his apartment door. Corporal Bob Haley and I continued surveillance of the Brighton man, who subsequently led us to Chestnut Hill and the condo building of Edward Lewis, longtime bookie personified.

Born in 1920 to Asher and Rose Lewis, Edward Lewis grew into a handsome, tall two-hundred-pounder with a ruddy complexion and hazel eyes. His nickname "Legs" was not lost on his family and friends. Neither was his bookmaker expertise. Lewis maintained a crew of agents all over the Boston area. He supplemented his illegal income with involvement in the travel business, including junkets to Las Vegas.

I don't know what the bookie's definition of luck is, but Lady Luck was with Haley and me when our Brighton boy and another familiar convicted bookie were both observed entering the condo building where Mr. Lewis resided.

Football betting season was approaching as we were getting closer and closer to Lewis. We got so close that one evening after observing our Hyde Park bookie enter the Lewis condo building, I secured myself inside the common hallways and observed him enter the front foyer door with a key and proceed directly to number seventeen and place slips of paper under the door, whereupon I was able to take notes of handwritten notations indicative of wagers being made on baseball games for that evening, which, in proverbial affidavit phraseology, "were in plain view." On diverse occasions, I was able to repeat the surveillance a half dozen times. The mailbox listings revealed an E. Lewis occupying condo number sixteen.

Several days later, in midafternoon, who arrives in the Broadlawn Park parking lot in a brand-new 1982 dark-blue Lincoln Continental, driven by Jimmy Katz? None other than our guy, Eddie Lewis. Both Katz and Lewis had been partners in the very lucrative sports betting business for years, so much so, that Lewis sent agents to Miami for the winter in order that they be available for his snowbird bettors. In gambling circles, Lewis was known as "Legs" and Katz as "the Sniff" (something about cocaine).

Both men had previously been arrested in 1980 by the state police gaming unit and convicted for serious conspiracy gambling charges in Norfolk Superior Court, where each pled guilty and narrowly missed jail time, instead receiving six months in jail, suspended for one year, two years' probation, and a ten-thousand-dollar fine.

After entering 55 Broadlawn Park for the seventh time within several weeks, the Brighton bookie, Marcus Goldenberg, performed his usual delivery, placing betting paraphernalia under the door of number seventeen. Within a half hour, a middle-aged woman wearing a house dress exited number seventeen, walking through the common hallway toward number sixteen, where she was observed handing off the betting slips that had been left under her door to number sixteen. We exchanged friendly greetings in the hallway as she was returning to her apartment and Lewis to his, marked number sixteen. After several moments, I stood in the hallway outside number sixteen and covertly overheard two male voices inside conversing in the lingo of bookies.

After a few minutes, I left the hall area and took a up a physical surveillance in the parking lot outside. Within minutes of my exiting the building, so did Jimmy Katz. He drove away in his new sport-bettor-financed Lincoln. Our informant information provided by "Jones" had proved to be reliable.

With football season underway, Jones said the Brighton bookie had relocated his office to West Roxbury, a quarter of a mile from the Lewis residence in Chestnut Hill, using two newly subscribed phone numbers. Jones and I met one evening, and Jones placed a wager at my direction on a football game with a man utilizing a color code for the purpose of identifying the bettor on one of the new phones. Several mobile surveillances of the Brighton and Hyde Park bookies confirmed the usual practice of delivering receipts or betting slips to the Lewis condo for the sports games wagered that day.

I sat down to write up what I had observed. Twenty-one pages later, my affidavit was presented to a Suffolk County Superior Court judge respectfully requesting he issue a warrant and order of seizure authorizing the search of three persons, three apartments, and two motor vehicles.

In early September 1983, members of SSU and Boston police detectives made a forcible entry executing search warrants for the Brighton bookie, his apartment, and his car, finding numerous illegal gambling apparatus. Our Hyde Park bookie temporarily slipped our grasp.

Several days later, troopers from SSU made a peaceful entry into the Broadlawn Park condo number sixteen, where Edward Lewis and his wife and daughter were completely caught off guard. So was Katz, who was sitting at a desk with Lewis comparing notes on the recent wagers bet with their syndicate.

That evening, troopers from SSU not only surprised Lewis but his partner in crime, James Katz. Gaming paraphernalia and $10,450 along with other items were confiscated from Lewis. Although we did not have a search warrant for Katz, the search was justified based on the language of the warrant, subsequently $1,100 dollars was seized from his person. No arrests were made, but a million-dollar letter was seized from Lewis's briefcase.

Sale of the Boston Celtics

According to a July 29, 1983, story by United Press International, "In 1983, Jewish mogul business man Steve Belkin backed out of a deal to buy the Boston Celtics basketball team, citing too much negative media publicity and his 'guilt by association' with close business associates." Belkin owned a travel company called Trans-National. His vice president, Henry Lewis, had been "convicted, of kidnapping charges in 1969, and again on bookmaking charge in 1977. He resigned from Trans-National in July 1983; he was allegedly under investigation for gambling charges," according to UPI. Lewis's brother, Alan, was president of Trans-National. Their father, Eddie "Legs" Lewis was on the payroll for Trans-National as a sales consultant.

While employed at the travel agency, he had been an active bookie working for Boston Mafia capo Larry Baione. He had been convicted in 1980 for illegal sports gambling. And then in September 1983, Edward Lewis's condo was raided by the state police gaming unit.

Steve Belkin, a 1971 Harvard Business School graduate and travel industry entrepreneur, should have had more smarts than to employ the father and brother of his partner, Alan Lewis. His brother Henry was vice president before resigning his position in July 1983 and father Ed was an active bookie with a 1980 conviction for illegal gambling while on the payroll for Trans-National as a sales consultant.

In a July 25 press conference, several days before the UPI story broke, Belkin said Hank (Henry) was fired after six months of formal negotiations regarding his employment. What he did not state was that company employees knew that Henry Lewis was intending to leave or quit.

At the same news media performance, Belkin insisted he was unaware that Eddie Lewis had been convicted of bookmaking, although other reports indicate Alan Lewis had made his 25 percent partner aware. In fact, Belkin and Alan Lewis had purchased Regency Travel from Ed and Henry Lewis, earning a million dollars for the father and son bookmakers.

Alan Lewis resigned as president and chief executive officer of Trans-National, Inc., in August 1983 in protest of the withdrawal of one million dollars of corporate funds used to negotiate the purchase of the Boston Celtics. Belkin apparently never advised Alan Lewis, his director and president, possibly violating his fiduciary duties and skirting applicable law.

Shortly after Ed Lewis had his illegal sports betting emporium heavily disrupted, Steve Belkin agreed to speak to me regarding employment of the Lewis family in his travel business. When he was confronted with certain aspects of my inquiry relating to his business dealings with the Lewis family, I distinctly recall Belkin saying he was friendly with the then sitting Massachusetts governor and soon to be failed presidential candidate Michael Stanley Dukakis. I surmised Mr. Belkin wanted to make me aware he had political clout, so I interpreted his comment was that of a veiled threat.

Our informant "Jones" continued to provide reliable information. He told us "every Wednesday morning several high-level bookmakers connected with the Lewis faction as well as other bookmaking groups meet at a Dunkin' Donuts in the North End of Boston for the purpose of settling their sports betting accounts." Jones further stated, "Within sports bookmaking circles, Wednesday is a common day to settle wagers." On Monday, bettors and agents would settle up with the bookmakers within each respective group. On Tuesday, the bookmakers would settle up with a main person who was representative of the activities. On Wednesday, representatives of each separate group or faction would meet and exchange or collect wagers that were laid off between various groups. Jones's information reinforced what was common knowledge within the SSU.

Jones said people in these meetings included Jimmy Katz, and he also named a person in attendance who was connected "to the North End faction of bookmakers." At that time, the North End was not only heavily populated with law-abiding Italian immigrants, but it was also the power base of the scurrilous Boston Mafiosa and its leaders.

Following a month of physical surveillance and coffee at Dunkin's, the SSU and Boston police detectives served two of three search warrants on Wednesday, October 19, 1983. The suspected bookies had more than enough incriminating illegal gambling evidence in their possession to justify the search. Area spectators watching the police officers included several convicted bookmakers for whom we did not have warrants. One guy readily admitted to having two small envelopes, each with $5,000. No arrests were made at this time, but we had the collective pleasure of disrupting a $150,000-a-day illegal gaming operation run by Lewis and Katz.

SSU Senior Trooper John Naimovich, the indefatigable state police expert on illegal gambling, presented the accumulated evidence gathered to a Suffolk County grand jury. Indictments were then returned against Ed Lewis and five of his cohorts followed by their arrests in October 1984.

It would be over two years later, preceded by a handful of motions and court chicanery, before Lewis would be found guilty of conspiracy, organizing and managing gaming facilities, and other charges resulting in fines of $15,000 and a suspended three- to five-year state prison sentence with three years' probation. Dispositions for Lewis's Brighton bookie delivery boy, after he pleaded guilty, were not as harsh as those for Lewis but nonetheless punishing with a small fine.

Katz pled not guilty to all the same charges imposed upon Lewis and was found not guilty of all but one charge. He was fined $3,000. And three years hence, in 1989, the elusive Hyde Park bookie pled guilty to minor gaming charges with minimal penalties. At the time, it was estimated by SSU troopers via intelligence, informants, and good old-fashioned street work that nearly half of the Lewis operation had been dismantled without the benefit of a wiretap. Or so we thought.

You recall the FBI and SSU joint operation named Grandslam back in 1975 that was leaked? A few days lapsed after the initial raid on the Lewis condo and before his seized phone book was scrutinized. The phone book was a gold mine for investigators. The Lewis personal phone book listed not only the FBI's main target—Larry Baione—but his three nonpublished phone numbers along with the numbers of other targets or suspected gamblers/bookies, such as Abe Sarkis and Mel Berger.

Over two dozen well known Mafia-connected bookies of all ethnic backgrounds were noted along with Burton "Chico" Krantz, who supplied the handicapping process for sports betting, also known as the line. Seven phone numbers were listed for Jimmy Katz, along with John Martorano and his former associate and convicted bookmaker Richie O'Brien. A Boston police officer whose father was a prominent Mafia figure and a state trooper who went on to prominence made the phone book. We had enough phone numbers and probable cause to tap the phones of every top-notch bookmaker of the illegal gaming syndicate operating in the greater Boston area for years to come.

It may be conceivable in today's description of having legs that the nickname "Legs" was appropriate for Lewis and his sustainability in the very competitive and illegal sports-betting environment in which he took his lumps (arrests), yet he maintained the ability to manage his business but apparently not without the help of a small bank located within a neighborhood bar in Chelsea.

When Trooper Joe Sinkovich told me about the bookie cars he saw in Chelsea, what I didn't know was why Lewis, Katz, Chico Krantz, and other assorted convicted bookies and agents had been hanging around a Chelsea bar in a heavily populated Hispanic neighborhood. That was not the usual territory for these bookies and their agents.

It took a little over three months to make a cursory connection.

In January 1984, I was a corporal still assigned to SSU when I received informant information that local bookmakers were meeting in a Chelsea bar called Heller's Café for the purpose of cashing checks with Heller's owner Michael London. He would exact a percentage of a minimum one point or more per-check. Up until this moment, all we had was a bunch of bookies who had been surveilled on diverse dates and times by troopers from SSU cashing checks with Mike London, but we did not discern any illegal gambling in our presence. In April, following a fire, the Chelsea bar closed for repairs. Our case was also closed pending any further activity warranting its reopening.

While we were trying to figure out a way to strategically attack Heller's, an anonymous male called the then state police headquarters, complaining about video poker machines located in various bars and clubs in Revere, a city just north of Boston. He also stated the owner of one of the clubs was a bookie who took action (shocking). That correlation is akin to proclaiming the Boston Red Sox play baseball in Fenway Park. The caller further stated on Thursday and Saturday night, "high stakes" card games were being played at a men's club (unbelievable), and he had recently seen video poker machines stored at a business for distribution. File case #85-47 was born. SSU was all over it.

As the summer of 1984 was approaching, we had the unsavory assignment of having to go into bars and restaurants in a seaside community, trying to locate these video poker machines. It was brutal. Imagine sitting in a bar drinking beer and playing video poker games and getting paid to do so. I wanted to meet the anonymous caller who was putting us through these unsavory working conditions.

A typical surveillance would encompass a trooper sidling up to the bar, ordering a beer, and then heading to the video poker machines, if available. In one bar called Bill Ash's, the bartender was observed serving up has many rolls of quarters as beers and exchanging quarters for a hundred dollars within a forty-five-minute span. One patron hit a game for twenty dollars more, likely spending double that amount for his troubles. And it appears the bartender was doing double duty as a bookie. The trooper's expenses amounted to five dollars for three beers with tip and five dollars for wagers placed on the video poker machine.

With a show of force for our summer of discontent, troopers from SSU, armed with multiple search warrants, literally stormed the shores of Revere Beach, invading establishments whose owners had the audacity to publicly display the games. Names like the Caravan, Shipwreck, Speakeasy, Bill Ash's, and five other legitimate bars had their machines confiscated on the spot, necessitating a rental truck to transport the evidence to our supply depot in Framingham. (Geez, if we win the case, do we have to return the machines to their rightful owner?) "Pokerman" was on life support.

At the turn of the 1990s and 133 indictments later (all based on illegal video poker machines), *Commonwealth v. Club Caravan* and eighteen companion cases wound their way to the Appeals Court of Massachusetts in Suffolk County. The wife of a cop who fronted ownership for her husband and a firefighter who was the proprietor of one of the bars would get entangled in our summer sojourn. Doug Perry, Suffolk County assistant district attorney, did a masterful job of successfully maneuvering many appeals through the court system. What had my affidavit and our splendid investigation seven years in the past wrought besides a beer belly?

In the back rooms of at least nine or so Revere drinking joints stood two or three video poker machines, inconspicuously draining the hard-earned money of the addicted players. Some innocent family may have gone without enough food for the week because daddy (or mommy) thought more about beer and games.

Depending on the location, the typical take for one machine would be in the vicinity of $800 gross per week and a profit of $250 after an even split with Revere Amusements, the owner of the machine, which left a measly $300 payout for the suckers bearing quarters.

After superior court guilty findings and subsequent appeals, three state appeal judges would view a video of Trooper John Naimovich reciting his opinion concerning his thoughts on skill versus chance at winning in a digitized poker game. Under the state gambling laws, chance was illegal, although the lower court "disregarded as an expert opinion" that of the trooper when he asserted that the machines employed "absolutely no skill," thus leading to a dozen indictments being dismissed, which were not based on actual use of the machines. Conspiracy and various gambling charges prevailed, as did the reputation and expertise of Naimovich.

Ten years would pass since the summer of '85 concluded with the near extinction of illegal video poker machines sucking the money from the citizens of Revere and environs. But the defendant and appellant owner of Revere Amusements, Arthur Marder, was desperately trying to prevail, this time in the US Court of Appeals for the First District of Massachusetts as a result of Internal Revenue Service criminal investigative agents and the US Attorney's office picking up where SSU and the Suffolk DA's Office left off. Marder owned all the machines seized by SSU in 1984. It was edifying to know that the Feds thought enough of the state police gaming unit investigation in Revere to prevail and get the convictions. The state and the Feds were then able to recover thousands and thousands of dollars in the form of fines from what turned out to be a low-budget investigation as evidenced by one trooper's expenses and minimal overtime.

The same year SSU drove poker machines out of Revere Beach, Marder migrated to Palm Springs, California, to better enjoy the Pacific sunsets as opposed to the Atlantic sunrise. His son Steven then ran the company for his father. The father and son duo weren't bookies in the contextual sense of the word, but Marder's company was bagging quarters somewhere in the vicinity of half a million a year from 1981 to 1989, supplied from an artificial dealer who possessed an infinite amount of playing cards, where customers were gambling on chance against enormous house odds. Without the protection of organized criminals, local politicians, and possibly several closed-mouthed indictable Revere cops, Marder could not have proliferated for so long a period.

Arthur and Steven Marder were unsuccessful in appealing their federal jury convictions on twelve counts of illegal gambling, including RICO (Racketeering Influenced and Corrupt Organizations) charges, using interstate facilities in aid of racketeering, operating an illegal gambling business, and money laundering. At the age of sixty-three, the former video poker king, who provided me and my fellow troopers a lot of fun and free beers on the state police, was finally sentenced to federal prison in January 1993 for at least thirteen years. His son Steven received a six-year sentence. It is unverified if the Marders had ocean-side cells.

CHAPTER 11

Banker to the Bookies: Heller's Café

Sitting in my unmarked cruiser attempting to look inconspicuous in a predominately Latino neighborhood, I was trying to figure out how the hell we were going to surveil this place known as Heller's Café. Under the shadow of the Tobin Bridge, the nondescript bar contained a bank teller's cage with bulletproof glass adjacent to racks of whiskey and coolers full of beer. From April to August 1985, we had done enough physical surveillance to realize renting an apartment within view of the target was not an option. Parking in the area of 110 Chestnut Street in Chelsea was at a premium, but that didn't make a difference because parking would be obvious to owner Mike London, who had a habit of stepping outside his bar to observe the street. The parking lot adjacent to the gas station across the street was nixed because the attendants spent more time in Heller's Café than at the gas pump. However, as the winter of 1985–86 slowly subsided into April showers, "Sammy" provided an early hope for May flowers for investigators.

Since 1983, Sammy had been a productive informant for SSU and particularly Trooper John "Ivan" Naimovich, who had turned Sammy after arresting him for bookmaking. I had spoken with Sammy on several occasions over the SSU private telephone line, mostly to convey messages to Naimovich. Those messages and resulting meetings between Sammy and Naimovich informed us that London charged a commission of 1 to 2 percent or more to cash checks for bookies from illegal gambling proceeds as long as the bookies had two references.

Sammy's firsthand knowledge of potential money-laundering activities and illegal gambling along with preliminary physical surveillance of Heller's provided a strategy for getting us probable cause for a wiretap.

But we were still without a suitable vantage point to peek on London, his bar, and the criminal element patronizing the teller's cage. I wondered how many times I would have to drive around the area looking for the best possible location. As it turned out, I didn't have to drive any more. Staring at me less than fifty yards away, within distance of Heller's, was a nice big white construction trailer. Something like this would not arouse suspicion. But there was only one place we could possibly site a construction trailer close enough for our purposes, and that was underneath the Tobin Bridge, in a lot diagonally across the street from Mikey and his bandits. Now we had the ways but not the means. We set the stage. Now we needed the actors, the supporting actors, resources, and funds.

In early in 1984, we had proposed a joint state police investigation targeting London to the Suffolk District Attorney. An important part of the investigation was Assistant District Attorney Mike Gaffney. We met in his office, where I prepped him on Heller's. Even though he was dubious about our ambitions, he fronted us seed money from the county's law enforcement funds. I was so thankful to him I wanted to name our forthcoming investigation "The Gaff." The joint endeavor did not materialize but six thousand dollars in seed money was used a couple years later to fertilize another growing investigation.

Mike Foley, a rather serious yet gregarious Irishman in the fashion of John Wayne's character Sean Thornton in the 1952 movie *The Quiet Man*, was a friend and a lieutenant on the state police in charge of the detail patrolling the Tobin Bridge. We wanted to place the trailer on property under the bridge, which was owned by the Port Authority, a semiautonomous branch of the state bureaucracy, and we needed the port's permission. Foley and I met with the operations manager of the bridge where a bit of cajoling persuaded a rather skeptical fellow to agree to let the state police place the construction trailer under the Tobin Bridge.

Things were moving at a fast pace as the winter snowbanks of 1986 that had piled up began melting, leaving the streets of Chelsea rather messy. By the end of March, we had preliminary funding, allowing the trailer to be placed in such a position where we could utilize a video camera provided by the Boston office of the FBI, who were now our partners along with the Criminal Division of the Internal Revenue Service. We were more than fortunate to be partnered with FBI Special Agent Matt Cronin, born and brought up in Hartford, Connecticut, and IRS Special Agent Bob Rooks, originally from Detroit, Michigan, a US Marine Corps Vietnam vet who described himself as an accountant with a gun. As a result of funding from OCDETF (Organized Crime Drug Enforcement Task Force), the money and resources followed.

Standing outside his bar one day, dressed in a white bartender's apron and Birkenstock sandals, Mike London played sidewalk superintendent, laughing and pointing at utility company workers hooking up electricity that would provide power to our trailer. The video camera was placed in the trailer bathroom window. London would be cast as the leading man in Operation Hades, which was now in the movie business, filming check cashers, drug dealers, bookmakers, loan sharks, and some of Boston's most notorious wise guys entering and exiting the front and side door of Heller's Café.

Several miles north, in the adjacent city of Revere, was a two-bedroom rented apartment on the second floor of a typical red-brick building tucked behind a major Revere shopping mall. Who was renting the unit, a far more comfortable location than the trailer, wasn't so typical for Revere. A team of FBI agents from the drug squad were transplanted form their Boston office to a new office that would become the plant where they would strap on earphones for weeks, secretly listening and recording conversation from "the Checkman."

Michael Barry London, a native of Chelsea, was living in the affluent suburb of Marblehead, north of Boston, when he was arrested at the age of thirty by the Chelsea police for setting up and promoting bets. The charges were subsequently dismissed in 1970. He would be convicted in 1975, this time in Boston federal court, for gambling offenses and was sentenced to two years suspended, two years' probation, and a five-thousand-dollar fine He listed his occupation on an arrest report as owner of Heller's Café.

London's check-cashing business evolved soon after, in a café with limited food service, as M&L Associates. It was a brilliant idea according to records from one of his banks. M&L cashed checks totaling approximately $10.2 million during the last three quarters of 1985. This allowed his family to move into a million-dollar mansion, located in Weston, one of the most expensive metro Boston suburbs, where the per capita income is perpetually the highest in the state. On the weekends, London would drive his new Mercedes-Benz 500 SEL sedan to Hyannisport, the Cape Cod summer home of President Kennedy's family, where he and his family spent leisure time in a beach house more spectacular than his McMansion in Weston.

Massachusetts General Law chapter 272, section 99, provides for the interception of wire and oral communications but no provision for the use of something called a pen register. By contrast, federal law allows pen registers to be utilized as a court-ordered pretext to a federal wiretap or electronic bug.

The purpose of a pen register is only to record the telephone numbers of incoming and outgoing calls. Because we were a federal operation now (due to the participation of the FBI and IRS), for four months commencing in April 1986, court-authorized pen registers were installed on two telephones located within Heller's: one for a coin-operated pay phone and the other in what became known as the cage or teller area. We were not able to use a trap-and-trace device on the phones, which would have identified incoming calls because of switching station equipment problems.

However, pen register analysis disclosed heavy outgoing telephone traffic directed to known drug dealers, bookmakers, and others recorded by the phones under electronic surveillance, which were being monitored by federal agents and troopers at the operational site known as the office or plant, secretly located in the belly of the beast, the city of Revere, where several among the hierarchy of Boston organized crime resided.

FBI Special Agent Matthew Cronin authored an impressive affidavit outlining in detail the many drug dealers, bookmakers, and other assorted police characters fraternizing Heller's on a daily basis. Mixed in with video and physical surveillance of pedestrian traffic in and out of Heller's, hand-to-hand drug deals made by undercover DEA agents and state troopers, pen register analysis, and informant intelligence provided by both the Feds and state police resulted in the affidavit being approved by a federal judge for an application to apply for a wiretap on two phones and two bugs in the cage area for Heller's Café.

On October 28, 1986, a federal judge issued orders authorizing the interception of wire and oral conversations at Heller's. By 6:48 that evening, we had our first incriminating money-laundering call taken by London with a convicted bookie ("S.D.") on a pay phone with an extension behind the bar. What follows is a condensed version of the conversation, which reads like a script from a Martin Scorsese movie:

> Mike London: My old friend that fucking yells at me all the time. Go ahead, what is it?
> SD: The fucking hours you work are unbelievable.
> ML: Yeah, so, and you come in here fucking wired [bounced checks] up to your ears and you yell at me for not giving you money on time.
> SD: 'Cause everyone gets paid, and I don't get paid.
> ML: Not everybody comes in and gets me wired checks for

twenty-five at a clip, 'member that.

SD: Yeah, but let me ask you this question. All the years I been doin' business with ya.

ML: Yeah.

SD: How many bounced checks have I given ya?

ML: Excellent. Triple A.

SD: Huh?

ML: Triple A. I could never say a bad word about ya.

SD: That's correct.

ML: But if I do somethin' with you, it's not out of any disrespect to you.

SD: Yeah.

ML: It's the way I look at the paper [checks] that I'm lookin' at.

SD: Right.

ML: You give me, you give me last week a check for 985 [nine thousand eighty-five hundred dollars] or 89 or somethin'.

SD: Right.

ML: Everything was wired. All those checks looked bad to me. I put one check in one bank, one check in another bank, one check in another bank. [The intent was to separate good and bad checks in order to flout money-laundering statutes, also known as structuring.]

SD: Right.

ML: That takes time. Takes two days, three days.

SD: What if you hit a brick, ah, what if you hit a brick wall? What happens to me?

ML: If I hit a brick wall?

SD: Yeah.

ML: You're fucked for all your money.

SD: Huh?

ML: You're fucked for all your money.

SD: That's right.

ML: What happens if you give me a check, if you give me a check, and I give you, ah, twenty-five at a clip, and you go outside and get killed and all the checks bounce. What happens then?

SD: Yeah, but you got a shot to get your money, though.

ML: For who?

SD: 'Cause you g…

ML: For who? Where am I gonna get it from, you, Frank Jordan, Frank Jordan, Sam Jones, Bill Russell? Who am I gonna get it from? [Losing bettors would sign checks in the names of sports celebrities, such as Boston Celtics greats Jones and Russell.]

SD: Hold on. But 99 percent of my checks are good though.

ML: Not necessarily, don't say that.

SD: Yes, yes, because (unintelligible).

ML: You had some big ones come back.

SD: …I make sure the check is good before I bring 'em to ya.

ML: Well, it makes no difference anyways. I, I like you, and, hey, you're honorable, and, and that's all that matters ta me.

SD: You know.

ML: Whatever you say ta me makes no difference, Steve.

SD: Yeah.

ML: And never forget that.

SD: Yeah.

ML: I think you're an honorable guy, and you're a solid guy, so it makes nuthin' to me.

SD: Yeah.

Our first intercepted phone call showed that London was immediately in violation of several money-laundering violations, such as knowingly structuring checks under ten thousand dollars with the intent to bypass currency transaction reports, which had been in existence since the '70s.

Because of some technical problems, the oral (bug) interceptions didn't go online until November 6. But then we caught a two-way conversation in the teller's cage involving London and Mafia capo Vinnie Ferrara. London tells Ferrara about a couple of bookies they are trying to extort (i.e., pay rent).

> ML: You shouldn't even think that because I'm the guy that told ya they were two fucking assholes. Am I right or wrong? That ain't, that ain't your concern. Your concern is to get a dime [one thousand dollars] a month rent.
>
> VF: All I can say is, one more time, I'm gonna give them a slap in the mouth. I will just do that. Just, just talk to this guy, the other guy, I just wanted to, I felt like doin'. I'm just too tired…

Later that same day, London made a call from the bar phone to an executive at the then-named Essex Bank in the neighboring city of Lynn, which was a primary supply of cash for his illegal check-cashing scheme. This call is condensed and very telling.

> JS: Essex Bank.
> ML: REDACTED
> JS: Yeah, twenty thousand [dollars]
> ML: Twenty!
> JS: Uh hm.
> ML: Ah, you're murdering me, you're murdering me. Murder, tell that bank to order somethin' during the middle of the week. Tell 'em I'll give 'em, I'll up my balances close to a hundred if they do.
> JS: What (unintelligible) didn't have anything.
> ML: No. It's for three days, two days. Only Monday or

> Tuesday is the only day I get money, and I only order fifty in large [$50,000] for me on a Saturday.
>
> JS: Hm, all right, I got twenty that's (unintelligible).
>
> ML: No, twenty's not gonna help me.
>
> JS: It's not?
>
> ML: What? No. I got, I got money here. I, I, I can get by for tonight, but ah you know uh I put tremendous pressure on the other banks tomorrow. I must have a hundred thousand in checks here now. You know what I mean? I like to turn over once at night.

In spite of rumors on the street the Feds and staties were on the prowl, London had no compulsion about conversing freely on the phone or in the cage area. Several days after the previous phone call, London was talking to a bookie in the cage, whom London and Ferarra were trying to seduce into becoming a prospective client for their extortion racket. London said, "There's nothing wrong with paying rent. You get protection out of it. What, what, what's wrong with it? I mean if they're [Mafia] gonna, if they're still here and they can straighten out for you, it certainly pays for itself in one year, doesn't it? Providing they charge a nickel [$500], and I, believe me, Sonny, I don't know. I don't ask it. You know I run my own business. I don't even want some of them in here."

This was not true. London was setting up as many unsuspecting bookies as he could gather for Ferrara.

Later that same afternoon, London is pontificating on how it all works to an unknown male, while both were in the cage.

> ML: That isn't the rule of thumb, though. The rule of thumb is that if you're not laying nothing on your own and you're giving your business to a connected guy, [Mafia] then you don't pay rent. There's Sonny here they went after. I, I, I'm gonna warn

Sonny. If Sonny comes up with a lie, he's gonna get a slap.

UM: How do you know?

ML: This is Sonny that comes in here. One of Joey Y's agents now. [Joey Yerardi's criminal record includes a federal gambling conviction in 1976.] He was throwing away 10 percent of his business, and there's ninety. They got nine, they got five guys' names that bet with him. You don't understand me. And, and they can call in business. They went after Joey Smith (unintelligible) start paying a dime [$1,000] a month. They know what they are doing (unintelligible).

UM: If anybody's out (unintelligible).

ML: Well it's worse because he [Ferrara] wants to kill people.

UM: The guy's crazy. (unintelligible)

ML: That money don't go to them, believe it or not. It goes in a kitty, but it's not their money. They turn all that in. That goes into the…

UM: Where did Vinny get all his money? (unintelligible)

ML: Vinny must have corralled twenty guys already. Between five hundred [dollars] and a thousand [dollars] I know of seven or eight.

UM: Well you, you said he don't get none of that.

ML: It goes, it goes to a kitty.

UM: Where did he get his money for his houses and all (unintelligible)?

ML: He's a shrewd kid, Vinny. Where did he get, where did he make that score?

UM: Yeah.

ML: He was bettin' those computer games last year; he made the money…He's a gambler, who the f…can rely on gamblers? Where's he make his money now? Shylocking [loan-sharking]. Ah, ah, ah, collecting money, ah deals you know. I see

him. I see him picked out one guy for seventy thousand [dollars] in the last month. They borrowed money from a guy and told the guy to go f…himself.
UM: The guy wasn't connected?
ML: The guy wasn't connected.
UM: They can do that.
ML: Well they do a hundred things. They're doing something all the time.

Further into what turns out to be a twenty-minute conversation between London and this unknown male, London blurts out, "Yeah, Stevie [Flemmi] don't collect no money, for ya. You know that, don't you?" Near the end of London's rent tutorial, he proffers, "Stevie likes Vinny. Stevie and Vinny are friendly."

Although Stevie (Flemmi) and Vinnie (Ferrara) were both competing for business in the extortion of independent bookies, they maintained a mutual respect while keeping a collegial distance.

On Veteran's Day, November 1986, London made a call to Vanessa's Restaurant, located in the Prudential Center on Boylston Street in Boston. He asked for Sonny, stating, "This is your friend over in Chelsea." London wanted Angelo "Sonny" Mercurio to come to his bar to straighten out a rent problem, but Sonny blew him off because he had his own problem to attend to. Mercurio was not the Sonny who was being set up by Ferrara to be extorted; he was one of the extortioners. He was also a Mafia soldier in cahoots with Ferrara and what remained of the new breed of organized criminals based in the North End, within walking distance of Vanessa's.

On that same day, London took a call from Burton "Chico" Krantz. Krantz wanted to settle a betting figure with London, asking, "What's that for, phone?"

London responded with one word, "Rent." London had a complimentary pet name for Krantz, "the President," presumably as a result of his expertise in handicapping sports events for other bookies nationwide.

This kid Sonny, as referred to by London, was an independent bookie now in the grasp of London and Ferrara. Our wire picked up London telling him, "The other guys are gonna get your name. Stevie [Flemmi] and Whitey [Bulger]." Several days later, Sonny was literally boxed in the cage talking with London and Ferrara, where Ferrara told him, "Here's what I want to do with you. I want him [London] to do the numbers. Just go on with being my friend. Any way I can help you I will."

I can't help but repeat the old cliché: with friends like Ferrara, who needs enemies?

The greedy, callous hands of bullies were putting a choke hold on bookmakers who were making a ton of money but were fairly harmless.

London had an insatiable appetite for his work—money laundering, illegal gambling, and loan-sharking. On the day before Thanksgiving, we caught him on the phone talking to Ronnie in a long, protracted conversation about his business and stress. The following has been condensed.

> London: Where you going?
> Ronnie: I'm going to Myrtle Beach.
> London: Oh, you know something, Ronnie?
> Ronnie: What?
> London: When I grow up, I want to be just like you.
> Ronnie: Why?
> London: Well, you take time off, you're a golfer, look at poor me. I have to sit here every fucking day, work day in, day out for a lousy fifty thousand a week.

Further into the recorded telephone conversation, London wishes he was in Myrtle Beach, working off some stress.

> London: My hunch is that this winter's gonna get me. This winter will be my last winter.

Ronnie: Well, I'll tell ya, Mike. When ya do crash, it's gonna be a fucking heavy hit for ya

London: Why?

Ronnie: Because it's fucking debilitating.

London: Oh, I'll get myself a job as a bartender somewhere or something.

London had incredibly prophesized his own demise.

It was now November, and our electronic surveillance monitors in the plant were made up of a contingent of FBI, IRS, DEA, and Customs agents and a US Marshal or two. I was told even Special Agent John Connolly took a shift. The state police handled physical surveillance from what was now two construction trailers beneath the Tobin Bridge. I'm not sure if we told the bridge operations manager about the second. We had plenty of help and a variety of indictable conversations, but further interceptions would be necessary and appropriate, compelling Agent Cronin to don his affidavit hat and pen.

About this time, I met with Trooper Naimovich to confirm and consult on informant updates. While seated in a Revere restaurant relaxing and enjoying a cup of coffee, I noticed two badass mobsters, Richie Devlin and "Red" Brady, seated nearby. Both had been filmed going in and out of Heller's, but each was sitting at separate tables with fellows who turned out to be as nefarious as our video stars.

I pointed them out to Naimovich, who surprised me with the fact that he had a federal arrest warrant for one of the diners, Ralph DeMasi, who was seated with Devlin. DeMasi must have smelled us out, causing him to depart the restaurant, leaving his jacket on his chair. The other hoods soon followed. Cute trick but it didn't work.

Naimovich went to his unmarked cruiser as if to get something (his weapon) while keeping an eye on the group, while I phoned the nearest state police barracks in Lynnfield. From my perch at the restaurant kitchen windows, I was able to observe the hoods reassemble in the rear parking lot of the restaurant.

In what seemed like only minutes, three state police cruisers came screaming into the area with Staff Sergeant Jim MacDonald leading the charge. Within minutes, we surrounded the smartasses, ordering all to hit the pavement. I clearly remember the sound made by one of the troopers jacking his shotgun as being very exhilarating.

After searching them and their cars for weapons, only to find pocket knives and being advised of negative warrant checks on the others, Richie Devlin queried me if I knew his state trooper cousins. Troopers with guns and shotguns drawn were to Devlin a mere inconvenience, more on a level of a traffic stop. We transported the arrestee DeMasi back to a nearby motel where he was staying, so Devlin could retrieve DeMasi's belongings so he didn't have to pay for another night because he would be locked up at no cost in the Lynnfield barracks. After getting permission from DeMasi, we conducted an unsuccessful search for weapons in his room. Upon completion, Devlin handed me a pair of sunglasses that I had accidentally dropped in his car during the search. He was a gentleman during the whole process, including returning my sunglasses, which he could have kept as a souvenir.

DeMasi was one lucky SOB. Ten years earlier in 1973, he was shot ten times in Dorchester while a passenger in a car driven by William O'Brien. O'Brien was slain, but DeMasi miraculously survived. The hit was by Bulger and Johnny Martorano. DeMasi would live to testify at the federal trial of Bulger in 2013.

As for Devlin, he would be shot to death outside an East Boston eatery twenty years hence. Richard "the Pig" DeVincent, who was sitting at the same table with Mafia associate and Devlin's partner "Red" Brady was found shot to death, Mafia style, in 1996.

And as of this writing, both DeMasi and Red Brady survive.

On December 1, we reupped the electronic surveillance at Heller's. After I read the affidavit, it came to my attention that a concurrent joint FBI investigation, with the intelligence unit of the state police was being conducted.

Cronin's affidavit required a mandatory stipulation stating any anticipated electronic interceptions of Ferrara required Cronin to report that his conversation was recently intercepted. On October 28, 1986 (two days after we first went online at Heller's), a federal judge authorized a bug to be placed in a storeroom at Vanessa's Italian Food Store, located in the Prudential Center at 800 Boylston Street, Boston. The FBI and state police now had the optimum opportunity to garner additional indictable information from both locations to present to a grand jury.

Vanessa's was a small sandwich shop located across from a Catholic chapel in the middle of a fifty-two-story office tower in the Back Bay known as the Prudential Center. The unimpressive shop was run by Angelo "Sonny" Mercurio, a ranking Mafia member. To access the Prudential Center, underground parking was available, or pedestrians walked in from many surrounding street entrances, which made it difficult to physically tail a surveillance-shy mobster.

My curiosity got the best of me, prompting a recon mission to the shop in early December. I was trying to locate the phone on which London had called Mercurio several weeks earlier. Adjacent to the sandwich counter and to the right was a twenty-foot-long hallway with a door leading into the shop. Upon entering the door, to the left was a black phone sitting atop a stand from which I retrieved the numbers I was looking for. Located to the right of the hallway was an empty glass-enclosed room with brown construction paper covering the windows from floor to ceiling.

Shortly thereafter, I met with the Mitch Dembin, the assistant US attorney in charge of monitoring the ongoing Heller's electronic surveillance. I lobbied hard for an affidavit to jump onto the acquired telephone numbers from Vanessa's, primarily because Mercurio was a legitimate target for an offshoot wire, given reliable information he was part of a small core of the remaining faction of the Angiulo crime family, not to mention his connections with London. He was also recorded talking about extorting bookies via rent. Mercurio would be a potential target for RICO violations.

For reasons that later became apparent to me, Dembin politely demurred.

Reputed Mafia soldier Sonny Mercurio jumped from the junior varsity while under indictment for his involvement in extorting bookies Sagansky and Weinstein and become a made member in good standing as an FBI informant for Agents Ring and Connolly in 1988, which didn't stop him from contributing his talents to "this thing of ours." As late as June 1989, Mercurio continued "his dual status as informant and defendant," according to the Wolf report. He was indicted earlier for racketeering crimes committed in the '80s and fled. Upon his capture, Mercurio tutored a federal judge about going on the lam, stating, "Power of the lam means you get a lesser sentence. I advocate everybody run away."

An empty storeroom next to Vanessa's was used for more extortionist felonies. A week or so after my excursion to Vanessa's, Mercurio and Ferrara were caught on the bug in the storeroom, sorting out their bounty extorted from rent-paying victims. Ferrara was overheard bragging about three bookies who were paying $250, stating, "Now I got their 250, which is Gerry's [Angiulo] end, right?" Steve Flemmi, a trusted associate of Angiulo, provided the bulk of information for the Vanessa investigation known as "Jungle Mist."

Dominic Isabella was overheard meeting with the Vanessa crew and was previously filmed spending many hours at Heller's Café until he contracted throat cancer, and Mike London temporarily took over his gambling and loan-sharking business. Although he was getting along in years, the man was pretty active. He owned a bar in East Boston and was described by his fellow hoods as a "capable guy." One day, Isabella made a call from a phone located in the cage area of Heller's to a man who owned a local printing business. Isabella proclaimed he needed health insurance and wanted the unsuspecting man to put him on his employee health plan. In a deep, raspy voice, Isabella said, and I paraphrase, "You gotta do me a favor, and youse can't refuse." Not quite Marlon Brando's Don Corleone quote in *The Godfather*, but the businessman understood the meaning. Isabella died of throat cancer several years later.

CHAPTER 12

The Checkman Cashes Out

The evening before we were preparing to serve search warrants at Heller's Café, an FBI surveillance team kept the proprietor, Mike London, "in pocket," which was an oft-used bureau term for "we got this bird under heavy surveillance."

My observation post was across the street from the bar in the video trailer. London left the bar at approximately 7:30 p.m., which was normal for him. What was abnormal was he placed a small gym bag in the trunk of his Mercedes-Benz. Cripes! What the hell has he got in the bag?

I'm imagining that London got the word about our upcoming raid the next day from some leaker in our United Nations of law enforcement, and now he was absconding with our potential evidence in a nondescript bag possibly containing banking, bookmaking, and loan-shark records and all the cash he kept in the cage, which no one ever tried to rob him of. Now he was out of my pocket and on his way to sticking it up our keisters

Suddenly, an FBI agent yells on my bureau radio, "He [London] almost hit the guardrail." Geez, he's on the Tobin Bridge, and I thought to myself, *He is jocked and driving under the influence with our evidence safely packed away in his trunk.* I called all the appropriate authorities looking for advice, but they were unreachable.

Hopefully he was just heading home, probably half in the wrapper, to his expensive house in Weston. Maybe he was traveling westbound on the turnpike and in all probability planning to exit onto Route 128.

My next call was made to the State Police Troop E barracks in Weston. The alert troopers stopped London exiting the pike and arrested him for operating under the influence. They transported him to the barracks and towed his car to a garage in Waltham, where the troopers conducted an inventory search of the car (which is proper procedure). They found several thousand dollars in the glove compartment. I arrived just in time to observe the troopers inventory the gym bag in the trunk.

The suspense was killing me, not to mention the fact I might have to draw up an affidavit to reinforce the search. When they opened the bag, the contents smelled a bit nasty, probably because the aroma came from London's dirty barroom laundry. Step back and soak in the irony.

London showed up a little late for work the following day, obviously being delayed because of his early-morning court appearance. His day didn't get any better when a small army of federal agents and state troopers overwhelmed him that same afternoon on December 17, 1986.

We had search warrants for everything: the bar, the teller's cage, the rat-infested cellar, and London himself. We seized all the records I feared the night before might have gone south in the gym bag, plus over $130,000 in cash. The largest one-man money-laundering scheme in the country at that time was being cleansed.

It appeared "the Checkman's" hangover wasn't subsiding because his usual jocularity and sarcasm were missing under the pressure cooker boiling beneath the surface.

The first bookie to reach out to London later that day was Jim Katz. Some years earlier, I had the pleasure of ejecting him from the Marshfield Fair horse track because of his bookie conviction when we caught him red-handed consorting with Eddie Lewis about matters of high-level bookmaking in the Lewis condo. Katz was eventually admitted into the federal Witness Security Program.

Our wiretaps were still operating when we recorded London telling Katz it was "a big problem, big, big problem." (That would prove to be an understatement.)

The conversation further deteriorated between the two bookies.

> ML: Ripped the whole joint apart.
> JK: Did they take everything, Mike?
> ML: Everything, I don't have a fucking thing in this joint.
> JK: Yeah, green [money] and everything.
> ML: Everything.

Katz told London that "the Staties are the guys from the BM [bookmaking] squad, you know." London was confused and thought the cops were from a drug unit. Katz answered, "No, no, no, that guy arrested me three times for bookmaking. Don't tell me who they are."

Katz ended the cryptic conversation with a hint of humor stating, "Well, one point, at least we know one thing, we're even [money wise] so there's no problem."

London laughed.

After the raid on London's bar, the storeroom at Vanessa's was abuzz with conversation among the Angiulo rent collectors, worrying whether or not Heller's was bugged. As we picked up on our wire, Ferrara griped, "If it wasn't, it's bugged now, so I don't go in there no more."

The electronic bug in the Vanessa storeroom lasted from October through April 1987. In mid-January, Vinny Ferrara, a recent graduate of the

Boston College Evening School (now called the Woods College of Advancing Studies) and his coconspirators were overheard extorting two of the oldest surviving illegal numbers bookies in the state.

Harold "Doc" Sagansky (also known as Doc Jasper) and his partner "Moe" Weinstein were well into their eighties when the young Turks led by Ferrara thought it a good idea to force these two octogenarians to pony up a half million dollars, ostensibly for protection from the real bad guys. Sagansky was a trained dentist but could count numbers play better than a mouthful of teeth. Nickels and dimes made him a wealthy man investing in Boston properties, including a motel adjacent to Fenway Park, the home of the Red Sox. At some point, the family surname was anglicized to Sage.

Presumably, Doc and Moe had already been paying a cut of their numbers business to Ferrara's boss, Jerry Angiulo, who was incarcerated. Not only that but the daily state lottery number substantially reduced the illegal numbers racket. During the Angiulo era, the difference between winning with the bookies and the state lottery was if you bet with the bookies, no taxes. (The numbers play was outpaced by the allure of illegal sports wagering and for high rollers was more exciting.) At least that was the reason Doc gave Ferrara for not being able to meet their demands. Ferrara and his band of bullies—Dennis Lepore, Bobby Carrozza, Dominic Isabella, and Mercurio—held Moe against his will until the next day, releasing him after Doc handed over half of the requested ransom. Two-hundred and fifty-thousand dollars was then split between the junior varsity abusers of the elderly.

Exactly six months from the day Heller's was raided, the London and Ferrara consortium of extortion, money laundering, and rent collapsed, just like the soon-to-be October 1987 22 percent drop in the stock market crash known as Black Monday. With a search warrant, troopers and Boston FBI agents marched into the storeroom adjacent to Vanessa's sandwich shop. Little was found, but a search of Ferrara's car produced his phone book filled with names of a who's-who of Boston Mafiosi and beyond. The phone book found on that June day would prove to have far-reaching implications for a trooper and his informant.

Here's what they don't show in the movies: the long, painstaking, and sometimes tedious work that comes after legally recording conversations.

It took many months for FBI Agent Cronin and me to review well over three hundred indictable phone and oral conversations, which had been culled from several thousand hours, to reduce them to one hundred or so transcribed tapes to be used for the Mike London trial. We also had hours and hours of video surveillance footage to go through. Meanwhile, IRS Agent Rooks was preparing a money-laundering case against London, which required scouring through twenty-five thousand checks London had cashed. In addition, nearly two dozen bookmakers and agents were identified, many of whom were subpoenaed to the federal grand jury along with a handful of civilians, of whom several became cooperating witnesses.

The Feds have something called an "overhear notice," which means that if a person is intercepted on an electronic surveillance and you can identify them, by law, that person has to be notified. Well, we had a sports bettor whom I identified, who was playing heavy with London and winning big on the Boston Celtics basketball team. On a slow afternoon, the overhear notice gave us a reason to get out of the office, so we headed to the bettor's attorney to advise him his client had been intercepted. The attorney said he was no longer representing the man. The bettor owned a very successful glass-cutting business in Dorchester and had what turned out to be an expensive house in the adjacent city of Milton. So, Cronin, Rooks, and I pulled up in front of the house where a couple of high-end cars were parked in the circular driveway. No one answered the door, but an attractive young lady responded from the second-floor balcony that our bettor was not at home. I yelled his name several times, and suddenly, he appeared on the same balcony.

After proper identification, he agreed to meet us out back of the house. We explained the overhear, but we wanted a little conversation about his lifestyle only to be thwarted with a shout of "Just give me the notice!" We handed it over the bushes. He had a spectacular, unconventional-style swimming pool in the backyard the shape of which none of us could discern. I contacted a fellow trooper who knew the man and came from the same area of Dorchester the glass company was located, and he told me a remarkable story about the $150,000 pool that was constructed in the shape of a glass cutter.

It was a great break from the tediousness of preparing for trial.

The original assistant US attorney in our case, Mitch Dembin, transferred to the West Coast in the middle of preparing to indict and charge London. He missed out on an art heist the newspapers were headlining as the biggest in our country's history. On March 18, 1990, two individuals dressed in police uniforms gently forced their way into the Gardner Museum and carted off paintings worth millions of dollars while Bostonians settled into their homes after celebrating St. Patrick's Day. I mention this because among the twenty-five thousand checks cashed by London were a half dozen payroll checks from a Boston gas station made out to Steve Flemmi. Like Dominic Isabella, Flemmi was probably enrolled in the proprietor's employee health insurance. Among the Flemmi checks was one from the Gardner Museum made out to a resident living on the same street as Flemmi's hangout, the Marconi Club, adjacent to the nearby gas station. The club and gas station were located in a small Italian neighborhood known as Cherry Valley, the center of illegal gambling activity conducted by Flemmi and his associates and the residence of an original Gardner theft suspect. When the check of the pensioner was discovered, it was revealed that the former security guard at the Gardner Museum had actually died two years before the theft.

Fourteen months after the art theft, Leonard DiMuzio, the former resident of Cherry Valley went missing. It was just before Easter 1991, and it was eleven weeks before his badly decomposed body was discovered in the trunk of his own car in a municipal parking lot across the street from East Boston's favorite neighborhood restaurant, Santarpio's. His tortured body of forty-three years literally drained from the trunk because of the severe decomposition. The shooting death of DiMuzio, a Marine Corps Vietnam veteran, is still under investigation, as is the multimillion-dollar Gardner Museum art theft.

Finally, on May 10, 1990, Michael London was arrested and charged with laundering over two hundred million dollars in a four-year period. His indictment did not garner the same sensational headlines as the Gardner theft; nonetheless, the news reverberated throughout the criminal community beyond the metro Boston area.

The media would characterize London's Heller's Café as the mob bank. Collectively, we would call London the "Banker to the Bookies." The federal grand jury, upon presentation of numerous electronic wire and bug tapes by Assistant US Attorney Marty Healey, handed down fifty-one counts of tax evasion and currency violations plus bookmaking, loan-sharking, illegal drug sales, and other criminal activities. One reporter from the *Boston Globe* had to remind readers that fellow SSU member Trooper Naimovich "was acquitted of a charge of passing information to Ferrara about possible grand jury proceedings to the alleged Mafiosa was observed meeting in Heller's café with a reputed bookie who acted as an alleged go-between for Ferrara." Naimovich was much smarter than that to meet a "reputed bookie" in Heller's for all to see because he had helped lock up many of the bookies we observed going in there.

Six years after London's M&L Associates check-cashing business was raided, ten individuals were charged with money laundering and bookmaking along with indictments charging four metro Boston check-cashing establishments with money laundering in a four-million-dollar plot. Some of the same bookies who sustained London for many years were charged including Chico Krantz and Jim Katz, who both later secured positions of prominence in the federal Witness Security Program.

An old friend showed up as we were preparing for trial. In September 1992, during the preparations for the London money-laundering trial, newly assigned federal prosecutor Michael Kendall met with three-time convicted bookie and prospective government witness Eddie "Legs" Lewis and his attorney Morris Goldings. There was another interested party in the room: Boston Latin School–educated St. John's University School of Law graduate

Assistant US Attorney Fred Wyshak, who had transplanted from Newark, New Jersey, back to Boston to the Organized Crime Strike Force. Wyshak was in the embryonic stages of probing Bulger and Flemmi, and he wanted Lewis to turn on them. Even though Lewis might have been facing jail time for contempt, he verbally flipped Wyshak the finger.

The London trial went on for months. In the midst of the trial, in January 1993, Lewis flew back to Boston from his retirement home in Miami Beach for an interview with Kendall. Subject: rent. Lewis was staying at the Copley Plaza Hotel in Boston's historic Copley Square so I thought it would be a gesture of goodwill if I drove Lewis to the federal courthouse. Kendall agreed. He invited me to share breakfast with him at the hotel. It was going to be casual conversation. Ground rules: no talk about the upcoming London trial. I asked for and got a tutorial on illegal sports betting. I remember him telling me, "Manage the money." He turned out to be a fascinating man and a stand-up guy for a seventy-two-year-old facing up to eighteen months for civil contempt charges in the London money-laundering trial. During the trial, Lewis refused to answer defense attorney Frank DiMento's questions of whether he paid rent to Bulger and Flemmi even though trial Judge Mark Wolf ordered him to answer. Ultimately, Wolf did not make a federal case out the refusal and allowed Lewis to maintain his dignity, thereby diminishing his fear of reprisal by the extortionist heavies, Bulger and Flemmi.

A very informative article appeared in the *Federal Law Enforcement Bulletin* titled "Analyzing Sports Betting Records" written by FBI Special Agent R. Phillip Harker in 1979 wherein he proclaims,

> The success of any bookmaking enterprise is dependent on the bookie's "line" information, his ability to lay off, and the business he receives from his "customers," for without the bettor, the man who pits his "knowledge" of the sport against the organized operation of the bookie, bookmaking would not be the multi-million-dollar business that it is today.

By the time London went to trial in January 1993, our investigation had spanned ten years, and in the interim, I was promoted from corporal to captain, accounting for four different assignments of which my last was internal affairs. I had hoped when I was promoted to staff sergeant in 1988, I would be able to remain in SSU, act on intelligence gained from the London wiretap, and continue to pursue Bulger and Flemmi. The new commissioner had other ideas and made me a Troop A patrol supervisor.

After a seven-week trial ending in February, a jury convicted London of twenty-nine of thirty-one counts of racketeering. His wife and four children were in the courtroom when the verdict was announced and began to cry, releasing their emotions that they had held in check every day during the trial. Assistant US Attorneys Michael Kendall and Dina Chaitowitz had presented a tedious and extremely difficult case to jurors in a fashion they could more easily understand, resulting in an overwhelming and history-making conviction.

In June 1993, London was sentenced to fifteen years and eight months in prison and three years of supervised release. A fine of $5,000 was imposed. In addition to the fines, London was ordered to forfeit $865,000 in cash that was involved in money-laundering offenses of which the state police received nearly a half million dollars. (That buys a lot of cruisers.) In addition to over $1,366,500 in fines and forfeitures, in a separate forfeiture action, the federal government also seized London's bar in Chelsea because of his involvement in drug trafficking. The IRS froze thousands of dollars in assets in order to collect unpaid taxes, interest, and penalties in excess of one million dollars. According to Henry Katz (one of London's two attorneys), his client declined an initial plea bargain deal offered by prosecutors consisting of two and a half years in prison and a $250,000 fine.

In a little-known caveat, subsequent to the London trial, Assistant US Attorney Fred Wyshak asked Cronin, Rooks, and me if we would be interested in coming to work with him at the organized crime strike force, which at the time reported directly to the US Department of Justice in Washington,

DC. We all declined for different reasons, but for me it would have resulted in a political pissing contest with Colonel Henderson, and if Wyshak had persisted, it would have been a difficult pill to swallow for Henderson to transfer a captain who would report exclusively to the US attorney's office rather than the colonel.

London filed an appeal of his federal district court conviction to the US Court of Appeals, First Circuit, Boston, citing numerous questions of law in his case. The judges sitting in the en banc court of appeals ruled on September 18, 1995, that "This was a complex case involving a sophisticated defendant, complicated financial dealings, and links to organized crime." In summation, "The judgment of the district court is affirmed."

Two federal prosecutors assigned to the Boston organized crime strike force were just starting to scratch the surface in exposing the heavily rumored proposition that James Bulger and Steve Flemmi were FBI informants. The Heller Café tapes were an integral investigative tool Assistant US Attorneys Fred Wyshak and Brian Kelly would use to try to penetrate the FBI Top Echelon Informant Program. And for that reason, Wyshak recruited DEA agents and state police troopers instead of FBI agents. Past history revealed, as early as 1988, when *The Boston Globe* exposed what would prove in later years to be the truth, that Bulger was playing on both sides of the fence. But the Michael London prosecution was the beginning of the end.

It would take a dozen years, from the first surveillance at Heller's Café in 1983 to the capture and arrest of Frank Salemme and John Martorano and RICO indictments of Bulger and Flemmi for a myriad of federal, state, and local law enforcement who stumbled, made mistakes, and fought through interagency rivalries, police corruption, and prosecutorial malfeasance to finally succeed in rendering the eventual destruction of the Irish and Italian mob in Boston.

In their critically acclaimed best seller *Black Mass* (2000) and movie of the same title, former *Boston Globe* reporters Gerry O'Neill and Dick Lehr penned a chapter relating to the successful Heller's investigation. At the risk and expense of self-aggrandizement (and I am speaking for former FBI Agent Matt Cronin and IRS Agent Bob Rooks, as well as myself), I will quote the following words:

> Fittingly, it was left to Joe Saccardo of the Massachusetts State Police to target Boston's version of Meyer Lansky. London juggled two accounts in a local bank with about $800,000 in family money and withdrew up to that amount each week as the checks cleared.

Further,

> Saccardo began to lobby for a second wave of prosecutions out of Heller's Café—all the bookies who were paying rent. He didn't know what the crimes should be, but he began to wonder if something in the mix could be used against Bulger.

Slight correction: With all due respect to the authors, I knew *exactly* what crimes to pursue, especially in light of the Heller's investigation, which gave me an indelible footprint to follow. I was just not afforded the opportunity to do so by the state police command staff (because of internal politics) in spite of a federal investigative position offered later in 1993 by Assistant US Attorney Fred Wyshak.

Boston Globe columnist Kevin Cullen, author of several books about Boston gangsters, whose knowledge of local organized crime is profound, wrote the London money-laundering investigation was not only the forerunner but laid out the groundwork for bringing to justice the Bulger and Flemmi organized crime group. He wrote an insightful, complimentary column in 2011 titled, "Here's to Honest Cops Who Made a Difference." Cullen artfully brought to the fore many prominent federal, state, and local law enforcement professionals "who risked their careers, chasing Whitey."

I was honored to be mentioned in the same column with such a fine group of working street cops. Cullen further stated, "When [Joe] Buddy Saccardo, another great state cop, found the bookie's bank in a dive bar in Chelsea, it was a matter of time before [Trooper] Foley would round up the bookies. And when Foley and [Trooper] Greaney got [the President] Chico Krantz, the biggest bookie around, to flip, Whitey's days were numbered."

Amen.

PART 4

BUGS, BEANS, BOOKIES, AND BAD GUYS

CHAPTER 13

The Lancaster Street Garage Surveillance

The most proficient bookmakers, circa '70s and '80s, who were also embroiled in the Mafia illegal gambling syndicate were the so-called Jewish faction, who made their bones in the west and south end sections of Boston. These men set the lines or what the odds would be, calculated the vig (10 percent profit), managed the money, paid rent, and took a beating (figuratively) primarily because of the tenacity of the Special Service Unit. During this era, troopers gathered an enormous amount of raw intelligence and arrested bookies, including Mafia bosses who ran the day-to-day operations. The same cast of characters kept emerging from the sports bookie scene, such as Eddie Lewis, Jimmy Katz, Howie Levinson, Mel Berger, Burton Krantz, and Mike London, known as the "Checkman." SSU learned these names in part through wiretap intelligence.

Logistically, to run wiretaps, the SSU had to acquisition electronic surveillance equipment from the attorney general or district attorney offices.

(below) In the center is John Callahan, a potential investor in the Miami Jai Alai Fronton, formerly owned by the deceased Roger Wheeler. Wheeler was murdered by John Martorano in 1981. Callahan became collateral damage when he was killed by Martorano that same year.

BULGER Record Form No. 35 1428-AZ   ASSOCIATE WARDEN'S RECORD CARD   FPI-LK-5-1-56-55M-8414
         Rev. Oct. 1940

Offense Robbery of FDIC Bank	Race White	Age 9-3-29
Sentence 20 Years Begins 6-21-56	Married no	Deps. none
Date Imp. 6-21-56 At Boston, Mass.	Citizen Yes USA	Relig. Cath
Date Rec'd 11-13-59 fr Atlanta	Physical Cond. Regular Duty	
Par. Elig. 2-20-63	Mental Cond. High Average Intellig	
C.R. 11-24-69 Max. 6-20-76	Education: S.A.T. 10.2	
Comm. Fine None G.T. 2400 days	G.S.	

PREVIOUS RECORD:
Jails 6   Ref.
Pens: Fed.   State
Detainers: Fed.   State
Escapes: Fed.   State
CUSTODY:
Crimes Involved: (Enumerate)

PSYCHOLOGICAL & APTITUDE TESTS:
IQ 113

Occupational Skills:

Avocational Interests:

Aliases:

BULGER, JAMES J., JR.

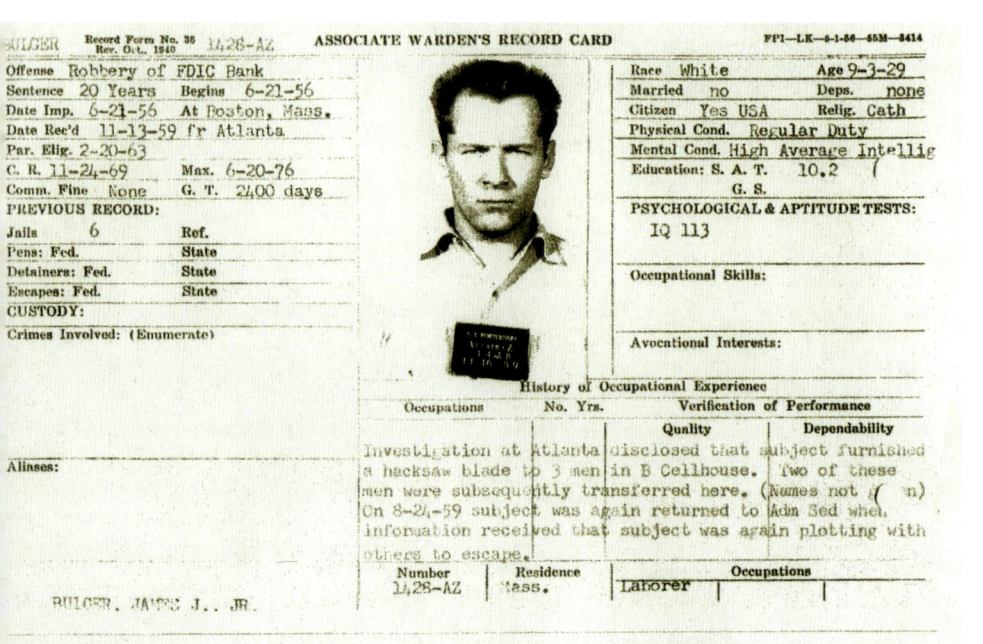

History of Occupational Experience

Occupations	No. Yrs.	Verification of Performance	
		Quality	Dependability

Investigation at Atlanta disclosed that subject furnished a hacksaw blade to 3 men in B Cellhouse. Two of these men were subsequently transferred here. (Names not given) On 8-24-59 subject was again returned to Adm Seg when information received that subject was again plotting with others to escape.

Number	Residence	Occupations		
1428-AZ	Mass.	Laborer		

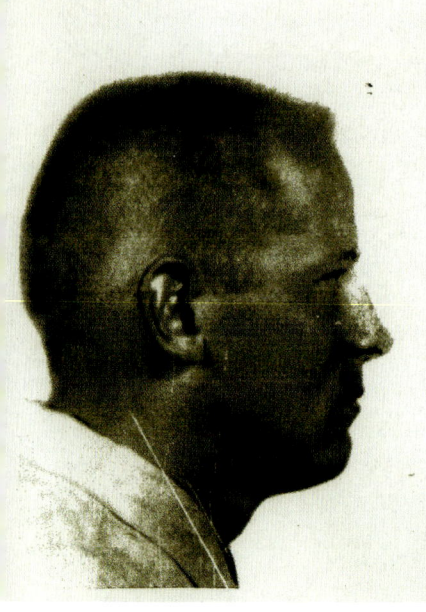

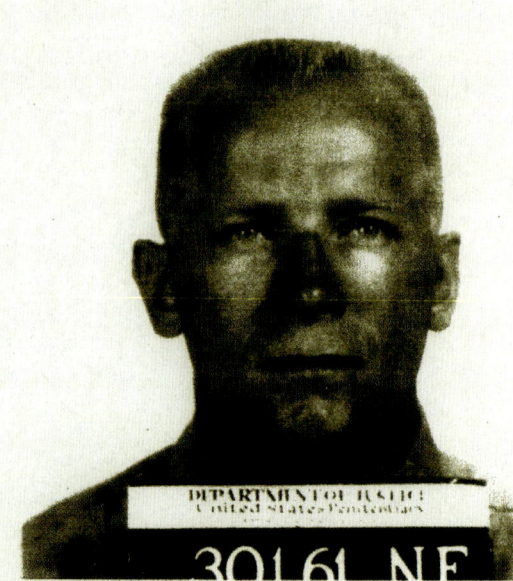

DEPARTMENT OF JUSTICE
United States Penitentiary
30161 NE

(left) Copy of James "Whitey" Bulger's index card with information for his entry into the federal prison system in 1956.

(below) Grounds and Quonset buildings for the Massachusetts State Police Academy, located in Framingham. A year later, the writer passed through those same buildings as a graduate of the state police.

(above) Pictured in the middle is Angelo Martorano, father of John. On his left, James. Unknown date.

(right) A Boston Police mug photo of Steve Flemmi.

BOSTON
129 260

(above) John Martorano exiting the Plymouth Superior Court in Brockton and entering his car in 1976.

(below) An exclusive photo of Vinnie Ferrara, J. R. Russo (center), and Bobby Carozza (right) leaning on a building in Maverick Square in East Boston in the late '80s. At the time, the trio was the second tier of the former Angiulo crime syndicate.

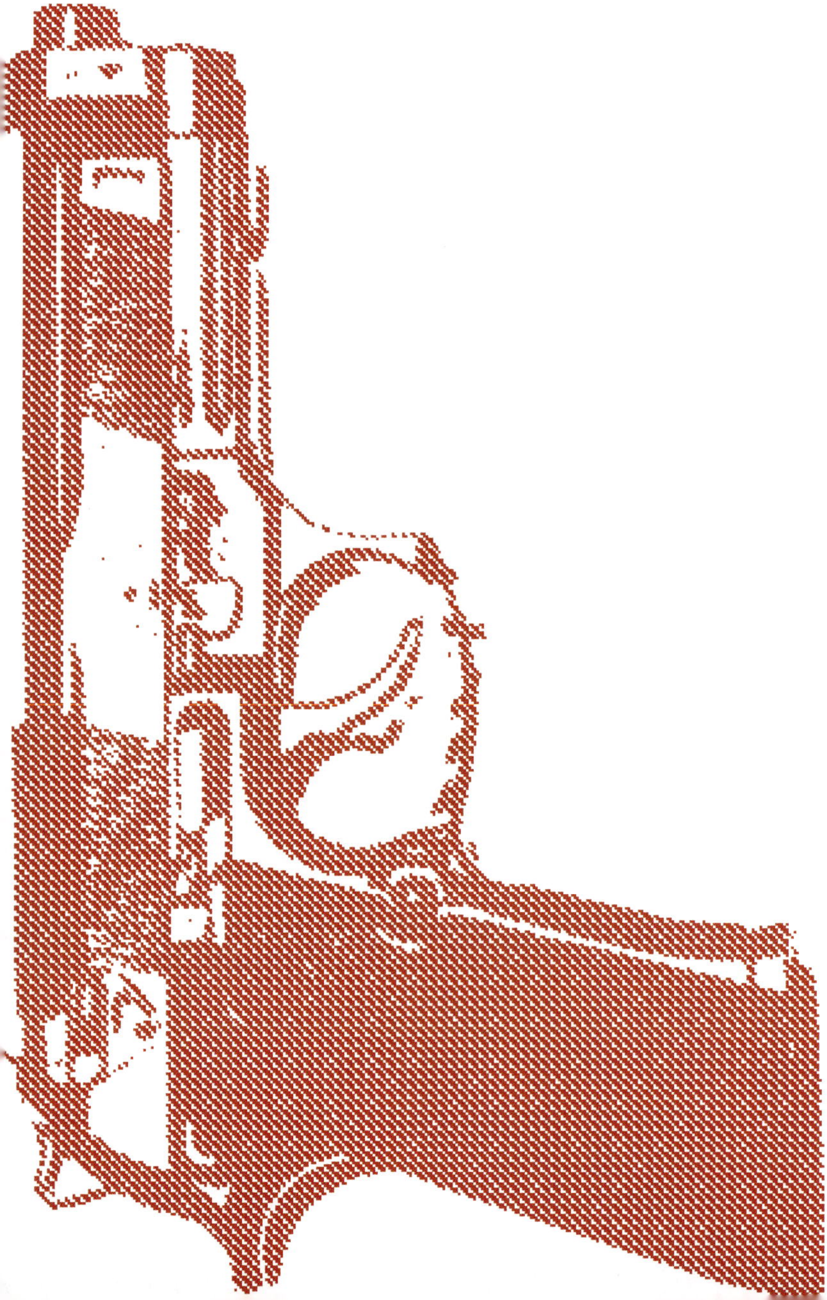

Troopers had to submit affidavits indicating probable cause to apply for a search warrant signed by a state superior court judge.

In the spring of 1980, troopers from the Boston State Police Headquarters Major Crimes Unit, while serving an arrest warrant for a couple of prison escapees, stumbled across a rare scene. A curious look out the escapee's third-floor window from the fleabag rooming house, located a block from the old Boston Garden on the edge of the west end, yielded an interesting sight. Milling about on the sidewalk below in front of the 19 Lancaster Street garage were the partners of the fugitive John Martorano. Strutting about in broad daylight and in open view were the unofficial arbiters of The Gaelic and Garlic Society, James Bulger and Stephen Flemmi, just a five-minute walk from the North End Prince Street headquarters of underboss Jerry Angiulo.

No way in hell would Angiulo have allowed Bulger and Flemmi to openly conduct "secretive" meetings in the garage with major level bookmakers, loan shark enforcers, and close associates without Angiulo's blessing and of course a monetary tribute. Lancaster was an infrequently used, one-way cut through side street that was perfect for observing any oncoming pedestrian or motor vehicle traffic.

A voluminous affidavit was authored by troopers assigned to major crimes, coordinated with SSU troopers who contributed confidential informant intelligence relating to area bookies. Suffolk County Assistant District Attorney Tim Burke took on the monumental task of making application for electronic surveillance of the garage. Previous to the signing of the warrant, convicted felons and bookies were observed making over three dozen calls from the garage pay phone, including Bulger and Flemmi. This was a missed opportunity. Although there was sufficient probable cause to tap the pay phone, state police bypassed state and county prosecutors and produced their own equipment by placing a microphone in various areas of the garage. From July 24 to August 19, troopers made eight surreptitious entries into the garage to fix or alter the technical performance of the malfunctioning equipment. Six months of physical, video, and electronic surveillance of the garage caught every level of organized crime figure and major bookmaker (such as Mel Berger) within the metropolitan area of Boston.

And then suddenly the operation went south. Bulger and Flemmi stopped their routine of four to five visits a week, as did nearly all the other hoods. The two then set up shop at a bank of pay phones located in a Howard Johnson's parking lot off the Southeast Expressway near the Andrew Square section, a few blocks from the South Boston Old Harbor projects where Bulger grew up. Futile attempts were made by the troopers to tap all the pay phones before the pair abandoned the site. No indictable incriminating conversation was produced from the garage microphone or the pay phone taps.

The question begs, why didn't they wiretap the garage pay phone?

The tenor of the times had dictated the decision. There was a power struggle involving the hierarchy of the state police challenging elected state and county prosecutorial autonomy in how troopers assigned to these offices should conduct investigations at the direction of the hierarchal Bureau of Investigative Services commanded by Lieutenant Colonel Jack O'Donovan. The decision was made by O'Donovan to foreclose any logistical participation in the Lancaster Street bug by political attorneys, reinforcing the vision of an independent state police.

One problem. The prosecutors controlled the electronic surveillance equipment, hence a malfunctioning homemade bug and no access to available wiretap equipment for the pay phones at Lancaster Street. Thus, the state of Massachusetts's favorite contact sport—politics—reared its ugly head, preventing what could have been a wholesale beheading of an oligarchy of La Cosa Nostra, or LCN (Italian for "This Thing of Ours"), and Winter Hill organized crime members.

Fallout from the Lancaster Street investigation created bad blood between the state police and the Boston office of the FBI because of a perceived leak. Although a handful of troopers had knowledge of the Lancaster Street fiasco, there was no lack of finger pointing at a particular FBI agent, John J. Connolly, of South Boston. For better or worse, Connolly, nicknamed by his less-than-enthralled fellow agents in the Boston office "Giovanni Cannoli," was the target of widespread rumors and innuendo within the ranks of the state police since the failed Lancaster bug. The word on the street was he was a leak for Bulger and not to be trusted. However, there may have been other sources for the leak. A prosecutor in the Boston office of the US attorney had prior knowledge of the state police request for federal assistance in the probe because "The Massachusetts State Police consulted O'Sullivan [Assistant US Attorney Jerimiah] to discuss obtaining authority for electronic surveillance of the Garage," according to the 1999 Wolf report. The state police also did not want the FBI to be told, as they believed Bulger and Flemmi were bureau informants. Remember this was 1980, long before it was disclosed in 1999 the two hoods were Top Echelon FBI informants for decades, since the 1960s and '70s.

The guru and renowned expert in all things organized crime, affidavits, and wiretaps had been stationed in the AG's office since the '60s. Corporal Richard Schneiderhan was the last word in many electronic surveillance investigations before his fellow troopers initiated the telephone hook up to go online.

The electronic bug inside the garage did not materialize on its own. A trooper assigned to the Norwell barracks who was formally assigned with Schneiderhan in the AG's office was called upon to display his electronic genius. There was a familiarity between the two men due to Schneiderhan graduating from the state police academy in 1959 with a relative of the Norwell trooper. Not to take the heat off, the deceased O'Sullivan and imprisoned Connolly, I would not be surprised if the trooper innocently confided bugging the garage with the corporal who years later was proven to have a corrupt relationship with Flemmi and John Martorano.

Concurrent with the Lancaster Street surveillance, FBI Special Supervisor Agent Ed Quinn, formerly of Dorchester's Saint Margaret's parish choir, a Boston College grad, and a veteran Marine Corps captain, prepared with trepidation with his C-3 (Organized Crime Squad) agents for a Title III wire intercept at the Prince Street headquarters of the Angiulos. Quinn was targeting the chief Mafiosa family in Boston.

However, if the state police investigation at nearby Lancaster Street had been successful, many of the Mafiosi Quinn was targeting would have been indicted or arrested while the bureau scrambled for probable cause.

Did the FBI have knowledge of the state police bug in the garage? Did someone in the FBI leak it? What is factually true and a matter of official FBI files—after Lancaster Street went south and just prior to the Prince Street intercept known as Bostar—is Steve Flemmi was reentered into the Top Echelon Informant Program where Bulger had rested comfortably for almost seven years. Flemmi ultimately provided needed information of the interior structure for the affidavit to secretly place a microphone in the offices of 98 Prince Street in stark contrast to the earlier illegal bugs of Patriarca and the Angiulos in the mid '60s.

Special Agent Quinn, the son of a Boston cop, skillfully displayed leadership and persistence as supervisor of C-3 when he and other squad members, such as Jack Cloherty and Nick Gianturco, to name a couple, dismantled the Boston branch of LCN in 1981, nearly two decades after Special Agent Rico failed in the 1960s.

For many years, law enforcement in the Boston area had the erroneous concept that the Boston FBI Organized Crime Squad revolved around Whitey Bulger. According to my sources, nothing could be further from the truth. In the decade of the '80s, the work done in combatting LCN was difficult, demanding, and very successful with each and every agent contributing. Besides the 1983 indictment of Gennaro Angiulo, resulting from the secret intercept of his North End base of operations, lengthy investigations were conducted involving many Boston LCN members and associates, including the first Mafia induction ceremony in 1989 in a Medford, Massachusetts, home of an LCN associate.

Less than ten years after the Boston office of the FBI performed the most effective intrusion into how the Mafia conducted business, Steve Flemmi was being deposed in a civil suit brought forward by the family of one Flemmi's homicide victims. Flemmi was deposed on many subjects, but the one area of questioning that reverberated for years to come was whether he and James Bulger paid money to any FBI agents besides Agents John Morris and John Connolly. He named four or five agents whom he had paid. Soon thereafter, the Boston media contacted the agents, and all vigorously denied the allegation. Other allegations made by Flemmi were reported by the *Boston Globe* regarding non-FBI issues that appeared to have no credibility as reported in a follow-up *Globe* story. US Attorney Special Prosecutor John Durham interviewed each named agent under oath in addition to an exhaustive and prolonged investigation conducted by the independent Organized Crime Strike Force based out of Washington, DC. Three federal investigative agencies were utilized to determine if there was any credibility to Flemmi's allegations. The IRS did a detailed financial audit on the agents, all of whom cooperated with the investigators. One agent requested former federal prosecutor Attorney Paul Kelly to contact the Strike Force to advise that Agent Nick Gianturco was willing to take a polygraph test. Ostensibly, the Strike Force refused to meet with the agent due to exculpatory evidence that may be created, which would have to be released to defense attorneys in any future trials. All of the preceding information as well as testimony from immunized key witnesses Flemmi, Kevin Weeks, and John Martorano did not produce evidence of the named FBI agents receiving money from the Bulger group except Morris and Connolly.

Addendum

The contact sport of Massachusetts politics got ugly a year after state and county prosecutors rebuffed efforts by state police brass who tried to infringe on their jurisdictional prerogatives. Legislation was proposed to eliminate via forced retirement and budgetary shenanigans, the Bureau of Investigative

Services command staff, including the chief protagonist of Whitey Bulger, Lieutenant Colonel Jack O'Donovan. Senate President William Bulger, a South Boston Democrat, younger brother of Whitey, and boyhood friend of FBI Agent Connolly was placed smack in the middle of the political ring. No amount of pushback by the powerful politician could diminish the coarse dialogue of suspicion. To this day, the autonomous leprechaun author of the damaging and mischievous legislation that had the potential to bring down the State Police Bureau of Investigative Services heavy Irish-American command staff, remains autonomous. So much for the incestuous "boyo" brotherhood of the FBI, or First Born Irish.

CHAPTER 14

"Whitey" Bulger and Flemmi: Fish to Beans

With permission of then unit leader Lieutenant Charlie Henderson, I began a cursory investigation into the criminal activities of Bulger and Flemmi, starting with physical surveillance in July 1983, as they skirted about South Boston. Past experience of being involved in the wiretap that put John Martorano in jail had taught me a little bit about criminal association along with current informant street talk that Bulger and Flemmi were extorting "rent" from independent bookies. I wanted to explore the issues. (Unknown to me was that this was weeks before they killed professional thief Arthur "Bucky" Barrett at the same house where Debra Davis met her gruesome fate several years earlier.)

Several known addresses of Bulger were randomly checked with negative results. Sources revealed if one wanted to contact "Himself" (Bulger), one would be instructed to leave a message at a Southie bar known as Triple O's Lounge, because Bulger allegedly went there several times a week for that purpose.

During the early part of 1984, both Bulger and Flemmi started to frequent a South Boston bar known as Olde Time Tavern. On diverse dates and times, the pair were observed in and out of the tavern, sometimes arriving alone, leaving together, and meeting with known local hoods, including Kevin Weeks. The same month, both Bulger and Flemmi started to show up daily at the South Boston Preble Circle construction site of a building that was being prepared for a liquor store, namely Stippo's. South Boston resident Stephen Rakes was the manager of record for the business. Specifically, Bulger, Flemmi, Weeks, and Steve's brother, Boston police officer Michael, were observed having a meeting at the site on January 30. For several months thereafter, random surveillance was conducted at Stippo's, revealing criminal associates of Bulger and Flemmi showing up in the late afternoon.

On many occasions, Bulger would go to the residence of his Southie girlfriend, forty-three-year-old Theresa Stanley, spending evening dinner hours with her. At the end of a hard day of meetings, he would transit to his ninety-six-thousand-dollar Louisburg Square condo in Quincy, where his live-in paramour, the younger Catherine Greig, waited.

Flemmi was no slouch in the female department either. His philandering interludes had him juggling between Quincy and Medford, less than two years after killing Debra Davis. His address on Quincy Shore Drive, directly across the roadway from Bulger, was listed in the name of his girlfriend from the North Shore city of Medford.

Not only was Flemmi frequently meeting at Stippo's, but several times a week, he would meet with his cronies at the Marconi Club in Roxbury. During the daylight hours, a half dozen or so convicted bookies and their motor vehicles were observed in the month of February. On February 13, Bulger was observed at the club with Flemmi.

Toward the end of May 1984, Henderson and I met with the chief prosecutor for the Suffolk County Organized Crime Unit and his Boston police counterpart. We hoped to apply for an application for a court-ordered electronic surveillance directed at Bulger and Flemmi, for violations of the state gambling statutes. An assistant district attorney adopted the code name Pisces as an operational title for the combined investigation. After nearly a year of going it alone, Henderson and I conducted our first physical surveillance as part of a joint operation. However, Pisces was to be short-lived, like a fish out of water.

The following month, in discussion with a Suffolk County prosecutor about my zeal to pick up where the 1980 Lancaster Street investigation fell off, I was pleasantly surprised by the response; DEA in conjunction with a local police department (with a similar unit to that of the state police) were in the embryonic stage of constructing a plan to bring down Bulger, Flemmi, and others. Information was that an electronic surveillance in the form of telephone dial-digit decoder / pen register was being conducted on phones used by Bulger and Flemmi. At this point, the scenario produced a federal drug agency, the state police, and two local police department organized crime units focusing disjointed law enforcement efforts on similar targets for different reasons, albeit for the same purpose: the successful prosecution and incarceration of major organized crime figures. The fact that the assistant district attorney had enough trust in me to share his thoughts and confidential information about an ongoing operation emboldened me to reach out to the Feds.

An immediate meeting was set up with a representative from the Department of Justice, DEA agents, Boston police, Henderson, and me. The crux of the meeting was to try to have a cooperative effort targeting what at the time was the Winter Hill gang. Several weeks would pass when the Suffolk County DA's Office bowed out, leaving the state police to deal with the Quincy Police and DEA.

The month of August would bring more meetings, this time involving the heavies from the DEA and Quincy PD, and the usual state police participants: Henderson and me. Robert Stutman, the head of the Boston DEA office, emphatically pronounced that he had secured permission from Commissioner of Public Safety Frank Trabucco for the SSU to be working with the DEA and Quincy PD.

Unbeknownst to me, in early 1984 and months before the shotgun marriage of sorts began, while I was trying to tail the ever-elusive pair (Bulger and Flemmi), DEA agents and Quincy police officers were simultaneously watching me watch the targets, since May 1983. Sometimes this occurs in circumstances where earnest law enforcement officials want to get the bad guys, but as a courtesy, protocol would have dictated a heads-up. It never came.

Long hours and a daily trek to Boston was the norm going into the summer. A secretive office venue was established in the Barnes Building (formerly known as the Fargo Building) in the area that is now known as the Seaport in South Boston for administrative purposes and to monitor several already activated pen registers.

A pen register is less than electronic surveillance and has the ability to record outgoing and incoming phone numbers. Unlike state wiretap laws, which do not allow pen registers, only a court order signed by a federal judge is needed. They are used as probable cause and therefore a precursor for a full-blown wiretap. To make the matter more confusing, a device known as trap-and-trace can technically capture incoming impulses or phone numbers on the target's phone.

Affidavits were filed by DEA agents for digital analysis for eight phones, including Pat Nee, an Irish Republican Army henchman heavily associated with Bulger, and Flemmi confidant George Kaufman. Additionally, analysis was done on Flemmi's secret apartment phone in the name of paramour Loretta Finn and his mother's home phone, located in Quincy and South Boston, respectively. The South Boston package store and Bulger's in town day-hugger, Theresa Stanley, were monitored for three months. Weeks's apartment was across the street from Bulger at 165 Quincy Sore Drive in Quincy, in the same building as Flemmi's. Numerous telephone numbers and tolls were recorded and analyzed of which the most interesting and productive was garnered from the owner of the Lancaster Street garage, George Kaufman. The digital electronic surveillance and analysis of Kaufman's phone located at his residence in Brookline and Bulger's condo located at

101 Louisburg Square, Quincy, were in full mode for eight months beginning in April and ending on Christmas Eve 1984 the same day the DEA and the justice department applied for a warrant to wiretap Kaufman's home phone. All the applications were signed by Assistant US Attorney Gary C. Crossen.

Physical surveillance reports bolstering the pen registers were conducted for over a year beginning in December 1983. For the most part, they were a hodgepodge of Bulger meeting Flemmi, Flemmi meeting Weeks, and Weeks meeting Bulger. The surveillances were a microcosm of what previously existed at the 1981 Lancaster Street garage operation.

In the now distant '80s, electronic beepers were the norm. Everybody had one, especially the bad guys, most notably drug dealers and, without saying, Bulger, Flemmi, and Weeks. Flemmi listed his beeper under his missing girlfriend's name, the deceased Debra Davis. The state police even had an excellent undercover trooper whose nickname was "Beeper."

A main target of the pen registers (besides Flemmi and Bulger) was George Kaufman. By Flemmi's own admission, Kaufman's role was that of an information center. "He had contact with everyone. I had George Kaufman reach people," according to Flemmi's DEA debriefing. Kaufman still owned the Lancaster Street garage from which he was a visible presence, but now it appeared he relied more on telecommunication. His telephone toll analysis revealed that collect calls were being received almost on a nightly basis from the federal prison at Leavenworth, Kansas, wherein the titular head of the Winter Hill gang, Howie Winter, was incarcerated. (The gang was named after a section in Somerville known as Winter Hill.) The pen register on Kaufman's telephone revealed phone calls to approximately twenty phones listed to known Boston-area organized crime members. Dozens of calls were made to the consigliere for the Angiulo crime family, Larry Baione, as well as a phone listed to the Brookline home of the so-called fugitive, John Martorano.

Even front man for the mob and heavy gambler Ted Berenson made the list. Additionally, approximately one dozen organized crime businesses known to law enforcement, either owned or run by the same, were called from the Kaufman phone. These included but were not limited to the aforementioned Marconi Club and Heller's Café in Chelsea, owned and operated by money launderer for the mob Michael London. At the request of the SSU, several pen registers were requested for the Marconi Club with the intention of gathering probable cause for investigating illegal gambling—our core mission. The request was never honored. At least one call from the club was made to a number listed to Bulger's Quincy condo paramour, Catherine Greig, and to a number listed to the Randolph address of Olga Davis, the mother of Flemmi's girlfriend Debra.

In the early morning of August 9, DEA Agent Boeri, Quincy Detective Bergeron, and I had an informative but fun surveillance. Bulger's car was parked approximately fifteen feet from the side entrance of his condo, which was not the usual spot. It was also noted the sliding door to his third-floor balcony was fully open. Fearing Bulger had not yet bedded down, we secured the area. We then checked the whereabouts of Flemmi. At approximately 3:30 a.m., we found his car parked in front of the address of his Quincy girlfriend. One of us shook his car in an attempt to find out if it was alarmed, but no alarm sounded. We then returned to Bulger's car, which was still in place. One of the Quincy guys had already taken up a stationary surveillance from a rented condo within sight of Bulger's. It was now nearly 5:00 a.m., when the agent, the other detective, and I physically shook Bulger's car to determine if it was alarmed. No noticeable alarm sounded. A subsequent review of the pen register tape for Bulger's home phone number ending in 0007 for August 9 reflected that at approximately 4:54 a.m., the phone dialed Bulger's beeper. Not surprisingly, his car had a silent alarm, which transmitted to his telephone, which then dialed his beeper.

Bulger, Flemmi, and Kevin Weeks would habitually sit in Bulger's car in front of the newly named South Boston Liquor Mart (formerly Stippo's). This occurred five or six times a week after closing time. On many occasions, the three men would drive around Southie in Bulger's shiny black four-door

Chevrolet and did not return to the liquor store until well after midnight. They remained in the car for an hour or so and then separately departed. Late one night in August, Pat Nee had the honors of riding shotgun with Bulger. Boeri and another agent were parked at the intersection of Dorchester Street and East Broadway when Bulger pulled his vehicle alongside the agents and saluted them with a wave and smile. Neither agent mentioned such a foreboding gesture to their state police partners.

The summer and early fall of 1984 brought about the heaviest concentration of physical surveillance, which led to the prior mentioned observations of Bulger and Flemmi meeting in Bulger's car, which up until the previous April had been a 1984 Chevrolet Classic Caprice. In mid-September, it was discovered that Bulger had sold that car to George Kaufman's wife and bought the same exact Chevrolet, applying the same registration plates to the new car. Bulger was not only paranoid but cute as an outhouse rat. In all likelihood, he sold the car thinking it was wired, which translated into the second clue he had a heads-up on our investigation that was ignored by the DEA agents. Secondly, a projected affidavit in preparation for an application to secure a federal search warrant to place a bug in a car would have to include the correct vehicle identification number. Problematically, the incorrect number would provide a judge reason to allow motions by a defense attorney to suppress all conversations gathered as a result of the bug.

To my astonishment, DEA Agents Steve Boeri and Al Reilly confided they were bringing in three out-of-town FBI agents for technical assistance installing the projected bugs. I guess the DEA agents must have been under the mistaken opinion that the state police were in agreement, when in fact we had previously displayed our displeasure with any involvement by the bureau. To add insult to injury, the agents did not respect the fact the SSU had personnel who possessed expertise in all areas of electronic snooping, and we had already made known our desire to bug Bulger's condo and car. The state police were not aware at the time, but in early April 1984, FBI Special Agent Rod Kennedy had been the Boston office liaison with DEA and Quincy police.

He was placed in a precarious position of someday having to disavow a possible leak. In my opinion, Kennedy was a trustworthy agent who did not leak.

In the middle of September 1984, the DEA agents, without prior warning or attribution, requested the state police suspend physical surveillance, but Boeri and Bergeron (particularly Boeri) continued to perform spot checks. I thought this arrangement was odd, but never having worked with DEA before, I thought maybe it was standard operating procedure. Upon reflection, I gave them the benefit of the doubt thinking they didn't want to spook the already shaky partners, Bulger and Flemmi. As a result, more time was expended in the Barnes building plant gathering, collecting, and filing available intelligence on our subjects. Having read everything possible I could get my hands on about Bulger and Flemmi, I was somewhat taken aback concerning information I previously hadn't heard or read about. Where were they getting this stuff? At one point, the intelligence file I had taken weeks to compile was removed from the plant without my permission. The answer I got was the DEA was making a copy. Then came the hammer.

In the middle of a period of concerted investigative effort, in preparation for an application for a federal court warrant to intercept oral communications, as opposed to pen register information, Henderson and I met with DEA case agents in late November and were advised, without any hint of prior notice, all current activities would come to a standstill. Just before Thanksgiving Day, Carlo Bocci, the assistant agent-in-charge of the Boston DEA office, related that Operation Beans would come to a temporary halt, effective as of the meeting, and that the DEA, state police, and Quincy PD were to discontinue active investigations, intelligence gathering, physical surveillance, and pen registers on Bulger, Flemmi, and Weeks until further notice, possibly March or April 1985. The reasons given by Bocci were varied and wide ranging, running the gamut from no federal funding to a leak in the Boston office of the Department of Justice. For weeks thereafter, Lt. Henderson would listen to my protestations that the reasons for the unceremonious divorce from our shaky marriage with the Feds was a bold-face lie.

I gave him credit for one thing, he did not completely dismiss my skepticism.

As I was leaving the plant for what I thought was the last time, I questioned DEA Case Agent Steve Boeri, why the Kaufman pen register remained. He answered another DEA squad was going to utilize it for an ongoing case. He lied. Not only was the Kaufman pen register still in play but so was Bulger's phone, which was listed to Catherine Grieg. Strategically, the SSU's major intention was to concentrate our resources on Bulger and Flemmi, particularly the latter because of his illegal gambling involvement. Kaufman would have been integral, but pen register and telephone toll analysis did not reveal any calls to or from Bulger or any suspected or convicted drug dealers: drug investigations being the main mission of the DEA. Kaufman proved to be nothing but a middleman for Flemmi and his cronies. If given the opportunity, as difficult as it would have been, we collectively had to establish more concrete probable cause in the state police endeavor to pursue state gambling violations.

My disbelief heightened, so in the month of December, my former partners were themselves the subject of occasional physical surveillance at the plant. Christmas fell on a Sunday that year, and on a snowy Friday pre-Christmas eve, Boston was all but emptied out of celebrants heading home for the holiday. I headed for the plant. At approximately 5:00 p. m., spotted looking out a second-floor window talking on the phone was one of the Quincy detectives. I stormed into the plant and waited for someone to come out of the office. Within minutes, two Quincy detectives, whom I had worked hand in hand with for months, came out and saw me standing in front of them. The looks of astonishment on the faces of the pair were precious. After asking what was going on, I was told to wait in place while they returned to the office, leaving me standing in front of a closed door to an office that a month prior I had carte-blanche access to. Out stepped two puzzled DEA agents, Boeri and Reilly. Before they could respond to my presence, I stated to the unsuspecting agents, before I called my bosses, "What's going on?"

Reilly immediately retorted, "Call your boss."

The agent's arrogance and flippant dismissal was surprising but not completely unexpected.

My first call was to my first line supervisor, Lieutenant Henderson. The second was to the head of the uniform branch of the state police, Colonel James Canty, through the state police dispatcher at headquarters. Later that evening, Canty called me at home, setting up a meeting with Henderson and me for the next day at 10:00 a.m. On Christmas Eve morning, with coffees and doughnuts in hand, the colonel took the time away from his family to meet with Henderson and me at the State Police Academy then located in Framingham.

After an introductory recital of my concerns about an investigation DEA led us to believe the colonel and Commissioner of the State Police Frank Trabucco were familiar with, he interrupted, stating our situation sounded similar to an earlier publicized investigation another trooper was unjustly accused of compromising resulting in him being an unindicted coconspirator. To his credit, the colonel admitted knowing nothing about our disbanded operation. This truthful reaction proved the first of several fabrications by the DEA agents. Colonel Canty immediately grasped the volatile situation at hand and expedited our concerns to Commissioner Trabucco.

Colonel Canty and Commissioner Trabucco had our backs, which led to a sit-down with Bob Stutman, DEA Regional director, and his second in command, Carlo Bocci. Henderson and I would meet them in January 1985 at the old Howard Johnson restaurant in Newton, which sat over the air rights of the Massachusetts Turnpike. Before the meeting, Trabucco had already decided the SSU would not be returning to the operation, allegedly for the lack of funds. Henderson and I saw firsthand the prevaricators explain away why the state police were summarily dismissed from an investigation that would later fail because of what the state police feared most: a possible FBI leak.

At the conclusion of the meeting, Stutman admonished me for still being skeptical. I answered the query with a glaring look of disbelief along with a self-authored thirteen-page intelligence report written within a few days after the inconsequential get-together. The report spelled out not only my skepticism but an in-depth appraisal of the activities and connections surrounding Bulger and Flemmi et alia, extending over a year of physical and pen register surveillance.

At the time of our coffee klatch, Stutman and Bocci shared a secret—an embarrassing secret at that. An integral participant and DEA cooperating witness involved in the biggest arms shipment to the Irish Republican Army from the United States had been missing since Thanksgiving 1984. It was weeks after returning from the most dangerous illegal smuggle of John L. McIntyre's fifteen-year criminal career.

CHAPTER 15

The *Valhalla* and the Murder of John McIntyre

With several murders already notched on his belt, Johnny Martorano was gearing up to be an accomplished serial killer while a just released army veteran and lobster boat owner was arrested for manslaughter while operating a motor vehicle. The year was 1969 when charges were dismissed, and John McIntyre walked out of Quincy District Court a free man.

In 1973, police from a small Cape Cod department in Wareham stopped McIntyre for speeding and arrested him for illegal possession of a dangerous weapon. At his court appearance, an unknown person or entity made an unusual demand to dismiss the serious felony charge at the "Request of the Commonwealth," which was granted by the sitting judge in Wareham District Court. Weeks beforehand, McIntyre was in the same court defending his arrest by the Wareham police, again receiving a dismissal for possession of marijuana, a class D controlled substance. If you were a cop, given what can only be described as a pass, you knew this kid had juice.

The juice did not end in Wareham. The twenty-three-year-old McIntyre was arrested in 1975 for larceny of a motor vehicle, larceny over $250, possession of burglary tools, malicious destruction of property, and conspiracy to commit larceny. As recorded by the state board of probation, all charges were adjudicated and dismissed at a district court a hundred miles north of Wareham in Salem, the City of Witches. An invisible and mysterious influence was pressuring courts at the behest of a repeat felon. This guy was skating and scoring better than renowned Boston Bruins and Hall of Fame defenseman Bobby Orr. Simultaneously, the lobsterman accumulated a slew of civil fish-and-game infractions, all of which were dismissed after he paid a measly thirty-seven dollars in court costs.

Alcohol was getting the best of the eldest McIntyre son, who was born in Germany to his German mother and Irish father. The "curse" had gotten him arrested by the Quincy police in early 1975, only for him to be found not guilty in Quincy District Court with minimal court costs.

For the second time in four years, McIntyre took another arrest for alcohol-related charges. He was stopped for operating under the influence of alcohol, paid a two-hundred-dollar fine along with a gift of a continued without a finding culminating in another dismissal.

McIntyre spent nine days of a thirty-day sentence as a guest of Norfolk County for his third driving drunk offense after the Quincy police arrested him in 1980.

At twenty-nine years of age, the six-foot, two-hundred-pound McIntyre was working in Chelsea for J. F. Walton, removing asbestos for the marine construction company while living with his wife on Birch Street, Quincy. The newly married couple were attempting to make a go at life in a rough part of town, as evidenced by local teenage gangs who menaced the neighborhood. Late one night in July 1982, a Quincy police report stated McIntyre

> pulled up in front of his home and observed at least six youths directly in front of his home. At this time, they were acting

in a loud manner—possibly fighting and yelling obscenities. As he approached the gate in front of his home, he stated he told them to leave. At this point a group of them jumped him and he began to punch.

McIntyre then retrieved a fire department-type ax made of natural wood with a red steel head from his house, "in an attempt to scare off his attackers, but they continued to assault him."

As a result of the mayhem, McIntyre was subsequently arrested for assault and battery with a dangerous weapon. Copious notes made within his police file manila folder stated, "the defendant is not a maggot so perhaps the pretrial probation would be an effective resolution." McIntyre was declared not guilty after a bench trial in the district court. This particular adjudication, in all probability, is by far the single most glaring example of McIntyre being legally served by the judicial system rather than outside influences.

A feeling of invincibility must have grabbed hold of McIntyre as a result of his recent acquittal. It wasn't enough he was getting bagged for drunk driving and smoking marijuana, but he chose to continue in that vein with his arrest on multiple charges less than a month after walking out of Judge Goldblatt's Quincy courtroom. Besides drunk driving, McIntyre assaulted seven teenage boys, ranging from fifteen to eighteen, with his car, causing malicious damage to the bicycle of one of the victims. He was found guilty of the charges, along with admitting to four counts of assault and battery. He received a two-year probation sentence and restitution to each victim.

Ten years after McIntyre's 1973 arrest and dismissal for formidable felony charges, he *allegedly* appears in Wareham District Court as a result of an arrest on July 7, 1983, by an unidentified Cape Cod police department. A board of probation file for McIntyre states he attempted to "bribe a p.o." but does not make clear whether "p.o." stands for a probation or police officer, but a not guilty was recorded. According to a Wareham District Court employee, a driving under the influence and leaving the scene of property damage resulted in a fine and was filed respectively before a six-man jury in Boston Municipal Court, seventy miles north. A good friend who has knowledge of probation matters thought it strange that the case was transferred to the BMC and succinctly defined the judgments as "inconclusive dispositions."

Previous to the dismissal of the state police from Beans, unexplained behavior by the DEA agents and Quincy cops seemed to permeate the air in September 1984. Physical surveillance by the SSU was suspended, yet DEA maintained the status quo just prior to September 13, when a fishing vessel named the *Valhalla*, loaded with seven tons of firearms and munitions, floated out of Gloucester Harbor on a transatlantic trip to the west coast of Ireland on a rendezvous to meet an Irish Republican Army vessel.

The young rebel sympathizer to the IRA cause John McIntyre was engineering the *Valhalla* (previously named the *Kristen Lee*) when the shipment of arms was off-loaded in international waters to a waiting *Marita Ann* crew on September 27, the same day DEA agents Boeri and Reilly conducted a "spot" surveillance of Bulger leaving his Louisburg Square condo, "carrying a portable radio scanner." Bulger then "entered his vehicle and approximately twenty seconds later, a vehicle alarm was activated on the Bulger vehicle." In a three-page handwritten report authored by Reilly, he further notes,

> At approximately 5:45 p.m. the same day, the same agents observed the Bulger vehicle parked at the So. Boston Liquor Mart, 295 Old Colony Ave. So. Boston, along with the Flemmi and Weeks vehicles. At this time the agents obsed. [sic] Flemmi outside the above store talking to Kevin Weeks while pointing to the interior of the store.

Two days later, on September 29, the *Marita Ann* with seven tons of IRA-bound weapons was seized by the Irish police. According to former Assistant US Attorney Gary Crossen, upon hearing news of the seizure, Bulger was "overheard" to say from his Quincy condo, "That's our stuff." Bulger was presumably referring to the seizure of the *Marita Ann*. There is no official record, document, affidavit, application, search warrant, or court order signed by a federal judge to conduct electronic surveillance in September or October 1984 at Bulger's Louisburg Square condo in Quincy, other than a court-ordered pen register, also known as pen talk. In the lingo of savvy cops, there was no paper, reminiscent of the "black box" illegal six-year FBI wiretap of New England Mafia boss Raymond L. Patriarca Sr., in the 1970s.

The storm-ravaged *Valhalla* arrived back in Boston on Friday, October 12. The next evening, as soon as the thirty-two-year-old McIntyre recovered his sea legs, he tried to break into his former wife's Warren Avenue apartment, and at 10:32 p.m., McIntyre was arrested on a Quincy District Court probation warrant by Quincy police officers Anthony DiBona and Jack Kelly for assault and battery by means of a dangerous weapon, according to DiBona's red book diary. The arrest occurred two years after he pleaded guilty to drunk driving and malicious damage to property in 1982, for which he was previously arrested by DiBona. At that time, he noted in his diary that McIntyre "tried to run over kids on bikes" and "three months ago struck a kid with an ax." He violated his probation in that arrest because he failed to pay a hundred dollars' restitution to each of seven young victims and three hundred dollars for malicious damage to property.

While in custody for the probation warrant arrest, McIntyre was facing a two-year sentence that was originally suspended pending restitution in 1982, which went unpaid. He suddenly got diarrhea of the mouth, spilling his guts about criminal activities he had been involved in with drug dealers and a Southie guy who owned a liquor store named Whitey, as alleged by the Quincy police. Neither of the arresting officers, DiBona nor Kelly, could recall any talk about what McIntyre said about Whitey or drug smuggling. Although it has never been established otherwise, after having been tossed around the rough seas of the Atlantic Ocean for over a month, given his history of alcoholism, foremost on his mind was getting drunk once he made land. In a possible state of intoxication, he allegedly rambled incoherently about various partners in smuggling drugs and munitions, possibly prompting somebody at the booking desk to telephone Detective Bergeron. Boeri and Bergeron then raced each other to the Quincy police lockup on an early October 14 Sunday morning.

For a gunrunner involved in the largest shipment of munitions by Irish American supporters of the IRA, all McIntyre wanted to talk about was smuggling drugs. He stated that starting in 1982, he had made seven trips on engineering vessels loaded down with cocaine and three thousand bales of marijuana per trip. He told Boeri and Bergeron about sophisticated shipments of drugs in special containers you had to flip upside down to see what was inside. In April 1984, months before McIntyre went over to the shores off Ireland and back, a nondescript warehouse located on the edge of South Boston at 345 "D" Street, filled to the ceiling with bales of marijuana, was discovered "accidentally" by federal agents. Beside Boeri, Bergeron's boss, Captain Dave Rowell, listened intently about clandestine cells controlling everything in McIntyre's boss Joe Murray's operation. Murray's Charlestown organization, which lost the Southie warehouse, was divided into three distinct, autonomous areas of responsibility: intelligence, enforcement, and labor. Joe's brother Mike was the treasurer. Those who smuggled outside the Murray crew were known as renegades. And for the most part, they seemed to always get arrested, according to McIntyre.

Partway through the tape-recorded conversation, Boeri proffered, "Here's the deal."

Bergeron later wanted to know if McIntyre was going to play ball with us. He responded he wanted to straighten his life out. The three-way conversation turned to McIntyre's role as the engineer on the *Valhalla*. He was able to physically describe a guy named Kevin (presumably Kevin Weeks). In a forty-seven-page transcribed and unredacted debriefing, McIntyre dropped the name of Bulger's criminal associate Pat Nee but never once mentioned "Whitey."

On or about October 16, US Customs seized the eighty-foot stern trawler

Valhalla as she lay in disrepair in a Boston Harbor docking berth. McIntyre and the captain of the *Valhalla*, Robert Anderson, were detained after attempting to disembark the vessel but were later released. The following day, FBI Agent Rod Kennedy and US Customs officials interviewed McIntyre.

One month later, on or about November 16, the drug-laden mother ship, *Ramsland*, loaded with tons of marijuana, was boarded and seized by customs in Boston Harbor. Before McIntyre's arrest, none of these incidents was fodder for conversation by my partners, who apparently were conducting a parallel operation and wanted the state police out, which transpired after the *Ramsland* was seized and within days of Thanksgiving. During his plea for a deal with Boeri and Bergeron, McIntyre consummated his end of the bargain by giving up the *Ramsland* after bringing the prospective smuggle to the attention of his interrogators.

On or about November 29, McIntyre met Bulger criminal associate Pat Nee at the Victoria Restaurant located at the Fort Point Channel in Boston, for the purpose of engaging McIntyre as a partner in a twenty-thousand-dollar drug operation ostensibly involving Bulger and Flemmi. Nee fails to mention the meeting in his 2006 book, *A Criminal and an Irishman*. After the meeting with Nee, McIntyre allegedly told Custom Agent DeFago that he had just given Pat Nee the money. Shortly thereafter, McIntyre was led by Nee to 799 East Third Street, a nearby South Boston house where Bulger, Flemmi, and Weeks waited for an afternoon of torture and murder with McIntyre literally begging for his own demise. Flemmi says he was shot right away. The murderous group, with the possible assistance of FBI agent Connolly, correctly figured out McIntyre gave up the *Valhalla*, *Marita Ann*, *Ramsland*, and possibly a South Boston warehouse owned by Charlestown drug smuggler Joe Murray, wherein millions of dollars of marijuana was seized by the Feds in April 1984. Without the benefit of being wired up and no suitable backup surveillance by the Feds, customs provided McIntyre with twenty thousand to invest in what proved to be a subterfuge drug transaction allegedly orchestrated by Bulger and Flemmi in order to lure McIntyre to his death. For his part in the smuggling of munitions to Ireland and luring McIntyre to his death, Nee received less than five years in federal prison.

FBI, DEA, and customs finally realized McIntyre was missing on or about December 6. Unfortunately, he wasn't missing because the triad of federal law enforcement and Quincy detectives allowed a prime informant (with twenty thousand dollars) to fall prey to Bulger and Flemmi in the cellar of a South Boston murder chamber without the benefit and full protection of federal and local law enforcement. McIntyre proved to be an efficient international gun and drug smuggler, who turned down witness security protection and wanted to get out of the life, yet his ambitious federal handlers sent him into the lion's den one last fatal time.

Before he was a federal judge, Mark L. Wolf was a deputy US attorney under the tutelage of US Attorney for the District of Massachusetts, and its future governor, William F. Weld. Wolf sent Weld a confidential memo, of which the subject matter was Assistant US Attorney Gary C. Crossen stating in part, "In your absence, I took a telephone call on December 21, 1984, from Steve Trott, Assistant Attorney General in charge of the Criminal Division. He asked me about Gary Crossen's background." Wolf goes on about Trott's affidavit expert, Fred Hess, who proof-read the affidavit prepared by Crossen for a Title III (wiretap) in the Winter Hill case. Wolf writes that Trott and Hess, "Consider the worst [affidavit] they have ever seen…And much of the information in it was superfluous. When Hess discussed it with Crossen, Crossen was combative. The affidavit was reduced and revised, but Trott said that it remained 'awful,' with ten words often being used when one would do." The remainder of the letter was no less complimentary as paraphrased by Trott phoning Wolf stating he would approve the Title III, but he wanted Weld to know "of this problem." Boeri signed the affidavits, but Crossen had to approve them.

After eight months of pen register surveillance, the second-rate Boeri affidavit was presented and an application for a wiretap to intercept George Kaufman's home phone was signed by Judge Garrity on Christmas Eve 1984, three days after Wolf's memo to Weld and the day after a pissed-off trooper confronted his former partners. If you were from the neighborhoods of Boston, you certainly remember Judge Garrity for implementing forced busing in 1974 and the cause and effect of "white flight" to the suburbs. In retrospect—the judge signed bad paper probably justified by a rush to be with his family for Christmas Eve.

Boeri had the stones to plagiarize what essentially was stale state police informant information going back nearly five years; emphasizing in his affidavit that "This investigation has been a joint investigation participated by" DEA, Quincy PD, and Massachusetts State Police. This was true to an extent as far as the state police involvement was concerned given the fact troopers from the Special Service Unit were summarily dismissed months before the affidavit was presented to the judge and had no input in its composition.

In an attempt to bolster probable cause, Boeri revisited ancient history in terms of affidavits when he pointed out a 1974 application Judge Garrity signed seeking electronic surveillance to intercept conversations of Howard Winter and redacted others. He then neglected to cite the adjudication of the Title III.

With all due respect to Crossen and Boeri, the entire second half of the 104-page affidavit proved to be replete with redundancy to the extreme. How many times can you report Bulger met Flemmi, Flemmi met Bulger and Weeks, Weeks met Bulger at the liquor store and then met Flemmi, and they all drove around South Boston? On one such occasion, Bulger added a bit of a lighthearted moment into the otherwise monotony unnamed surveillance agents were experiencing on an August 1984 evening. Kevin Weeks was sitting in the front seat and Pat Nee in the rear seat with Bulger driving as usual. The agents passed Bulger's parked vehicle on East Broadway when he pulled out and began to follow the agents. Bulger then pulled alongside the surveillance vehicle at the intersection of Dorchester Street and East Broadway at which time, as stated in the affidavit, "I observed Bulger smile and wave to the occupants of the surveillance vehicle. Surveillance was terminated at this time."

One month after Judge Garrity approved the Crossen/Boeri affidavit, a Quincy police civilian clerk from the criminal records bureau requested probation records for John McIntyre via teletype (before computers)—two months after federal agents inexplicably sent him to his death?

Lack of technical expertise previously displayed by the DEA agents must have been solved because Judge Garrity signed the first official warrant to bug Bulger's condo and car on February 1 and a subsequent renewal on March 1. Eleven days into the second renewal, Agents Boeri and Reilly had to retrieve the discovered bug in Bulger's car.

Former federal prosecutor Gary C. Crossen gave an interview on condition of anonymity to a *Boston Globe* reporter producing a rough transcription in 1988. At the time, Crossen was in private practice working for a prestigious Boston law firm and did not want to be quoted because "the firm would be better served…" if he wasn't quoted. Crossen pontificated that when the *Valhalla* was seized,

> Maybe it's something of an anecdote is that there was a bug in his [Bulger's] condo at Louisburg Square, and when the Valahla [sic] seizure went down, the local newspapers did a big splash, of the guns being seized in Ireland, and the local television stations picked it up as well. He and his girlfriend, Bulger was in the aparemnte [sic] watching the news and that particular story come on and a voice it's very difficult to ascertain on the tape, but wh ich [sic] people believe is Bulger's voice, indicates that "That was our stuff" referencing the guns that had been seized off the Irish vessel.

Was it an *anecdote* or a fact that there was a bug in Bulger's condo in September 1984? It can't be both.

In December 2006, information was filed in the Supreme Judicial Court for the County of Suffolk by the Board of Bar overseers, wherein former

Assistant US Attorney Gary Crossen contested the filing with the court, which stated, "His part in an intricate plan to discredit a superior Court judge presiding in an ongoing matter in which he represented some of the litigants." Judge C. J. Marshall concluded on February 6, 2008, in a twenty-nine-page complex opinion that Crossen was, "unfit to retain the office of attorney," and he was then disbarred. (See IN RE: CROSSEN IN THE MATTER OF GARY C. CROSSEN 450 Mass. 533 SJC-09905.)

Quincy Detective Dick Bergeron retired from the department and in 1996 was appointed chief of police in a small central Massachusetts town. In 1998, he was interviewed by *Boston Globe* staff reporters Dick Lehr and Gerry O'Neill, on background for an anticipated book, eventually published, titled *Black Mass*. The April 8 meeting with Bergeron noted that a copy of McIntyre's confidential debriefing was pending. Not only did Bergeron tell the authors he was going to provide the debriefing, but he would attempt to get from Assistant US Attorney Gary Crossen the Boeri affidavit (which he did) and unindictable tapes and transcripts from the Kaufman wire and Bulger bugs.

As part of his 661-page encyclopedia report, Judge Wolf addressed the 1984-85 DEA and Quincy PD wiretap in 1999 when he ruled:

> For the foregoing reasons, the December 24, 1984 Order authorizing the wiretap on Kaufman's telephone was unlawfully contained. The motion to suppress the evidence obtained as a result of that Order is meritorious. Accordingly, neither the communications intercepted pursuant to that Order, nor any evidence derived from them, may be used at trial. 18 U.S.C. 2515 (1994).
>
> The fatally flawed December 24, 1984 Boeri affidavit was expressly incorporated in his February 1, 1985 affidavit, which resulted in the issuance of a warrant extending the tap on Kaufman's telephone and also authorizing bugs for Bulger's automobile and apartment.

Both of his prior affidavits were expressly incorporated in Boeri's March 1, 1985 affidavit, which prompted the issuance of a warrant authorizing the continued bugging of Bulger's automobile and apartment. Thus, suppression is required of all of the evidence intercepted as a result of the tap on Kaufman's telephone and the bugs in Bulger's automobile and apartment.

As described previously, the December 24, 1984 Boeri affidavit was not only false and misleading with regard to the need for electronic surveillance to assist the DEA in developing a prosecutable Title 18 case against Bulger, Flemmi, and others. It also was drafted in a convoluted and confusing manner which obscured the fact that there was not probable cause to believe that evidence of any Title 21 drug offense would be intercepted if a warrant to tap Kaufman's telephone was issued.

DEA Agent Reilly testified in 1998 at the Wolf hearings in *US v. Salemme*, prompting the *Boston Globe* to report on May 21 that Reilly wrote a November 1986 report stating, "There wasn't enough hard evidence linking the pair [Bulger and Flemmi] to the 1984 gun-running, just an agitated exclamation by Bulger that was picked up by a microphone hidden by the DEA in his Quincy condominium."

The *Globe* further reported,

> When Bulger heard a news bulletin in September 1984 that $1.2 million in guns and ammunition smuggled aboard the Gloucester-based *Valhalla* had been intercepted by the Irish Navy, "He jumped up and said, 'That's our shipment. That's ours.'" DEA agent Albert G. Reilly testified yesterday in federal court.

In the middle of the Wolf Hearings, a newspaper article appeared in the

Quincy-based daily newspaper *Patriot Ledger*, on July 3, 1998, making reference to DEA Agent Al Reilly stating, "A listening device planted by Quincy police and the DEA in Bulger's Quincy condominium recorded him explaining, 'That's our shipment,' when he heard a news bulletin in September 1984 that the *Valhalla* and its $1.2 million in guns and ammunition had been intercepted by the Irish Navy." (The *Marita Ann* was seized not the *Valhalla*.)

"Albert G. Reilly, a federal drug agent, testified at a previous hearing that, without witnesses, the information heard by the bug was not sufficient to charge Bulger."

Judge Wolf wrote,

> More specifically, at 12:30 p.m. on December 24, 1984—the verge of Christmas Eve—Crossen [assistant US attorney] submitted to United States District Judge W. Arthur Garrity Jr. an Application, incorporating a 104-page affidavit of Boeri, and a proposed Order authorizing electronic surveillance. Exs. [exhibits] 133, 138, 139. The order was, without notification, promptly issued. Ex. 139.

Further, page 180 of the Wolf report states, "More specifically, the electronic surveillance recorded that upon seeing a news report that the *Valhalla* had been seized, Bulger exclaimed: 'That's ours.' Id. [used to indicate a reference previously mentioned] at 74–75." In laymen's terms, Agent Reilly had prior testimony to that effect. Additionally, Judge Wolf missed the fact there was no "electronic surveillance" on Bulger in September 1984, unless of course an unknown bug or wiretap was illegally being conducted by nefarious agents of deceit. In other words, there was no good paper.

As noted earlier, the *Valhalla* was seized in Boston Harbor on or about October 16.

The closest anyone in the media or law enforcement ever got to discovering it was virtually impossible for Reilly to overhear a bugged conversation of Bulger in his condominium in September 1984 (unless he was present) was a reporter for the *Boston Herald*.

But one investigator familiar with the surveillance of Bulger said there was no bug in the apartment at that time and, while the quotes are accurate, they were in response to an IRA attack. "(The weapons) were seized before we started the wiretap." said the source.

According to records, the DEA received court approval to plant a bug in the Quincy home of Bulger's girlfriend, Theresa Stanley, on December 24, 1984, three months after the weapons were seized.

The first paragraph is fairly accurate when the extensive front-page report, entitled "Valhalla's Wake" on January 23, 2000, was written, although I am not familiar with what IRA attack he makes reference to. He failed miserably in the follow-up paragraph because no bug was authorized for Bulger's Quincy home until February 1, 1985, and his girlfriend living with him in the Quincy condo was Catherine Greig, not Theresa Stanley.

During the '90s, the tantalizing remark, "That's ours," allegedly spoken by Bulger was quoted in the *Boston Globe* no less than a half dozen times (by my count) with no official attribution excepting a quote by DEA Agent Reilly. As an example, "According to sources," "Sources familiar with," or "No source," was the basis for reporting either a figment of Crossen's and Reilly's imagination or an illegal wiretap reminiscent of the early '60s tap on Patriarca's and Angiulo's phones in Providence and Boston, respectively.

As mentioned earlier, after eight months of pen register surveillance, the flawed Boeri affidavit was presented and an application for a wiretap was signed three days later by Judge Garrity on December 24, 1984 for a warrant to intercept conversations on the phone of George Kaufman (not Bulger or Stanley), which occurred the day after the confrontation with my former partners in law enforcement.

The first *official* affidavit that allowed the Feds to bug Bulger's Chevy Caprice and Louisburg Square condo in Quincy was signed on February 1, 1985, nearly five months after DEA Agent Reilly quoted Bulger about the

Marita Ann being seized. Also, that same day, a renewal order for Kaufman's phone was signed.

• • • •

On February 28, 2000, one day after the *Boston Sunday Globe* printed an extensive article written by Dick Lehr titled, "Mob Underling's Tale of Guns, Drugs, Fear," Judge Wolf immediately volleyed with a three-page order, demonstrating his anger with the newspaper, which "reflects another apparent violation of this court's June 26, 1997 Order restricting the dissemination of documents and information disclosed in discovery in this case." (He was referring to the *US v. Salemme* 1997 case and an established protective order.) Wolf further elaborated that "Dick Lehr, may have obtained other information subject to the Protective Order from the government." Wolf officially summoned Richard Bergeron, his old boss Captain David Rowell, DEA Agent Steve Boeri, and FBI Agent Rod Kennedy to appear for a hearing to be held on March 2, 2000. For two days, Judge Wolf contemplated contempt charges against Bergeron but dropped them upon his admission he provided a copy of the 1984 transcript of the John McIntyre debriefing as promised to Lehr in 1998. Fortunately, Bergeron was able to avoid federal prison for his indiscretion, but he did accumulate eight thousand dollars in legal costs.

Bergeron fell on his sword for Lehr, "saving Dick from getting subpoenaed and asserting a confidential source privilege on that issue," as noted in a May 2, 2000, email from *Boston Globe* attorney Jonathan Albano to Louise Williams, the managing editor for newsroom administration. Lehr mentions Bergeron twice in the article but deflects away from him in such a way that the reader could not ascertain the real source of the information from McIntyre's debriefing. The authors of *Black Mass*, Dick Lehr and Gerry O'Neill, were concerned about protecting sources according to Albano stating in an email to Williams, "they are interested in whether the Globe would or should contribute to his [Bergeron] legal fees by paying 50% of the bill ($4,000). They see it as both an ethical issue and as a preventive measure to avoid sources running away from fear that the paper will not stick with them when times get tough." The issue of checkbook journalism was defined by Albano as "it should be clear that the fee was not paid as a quid pro quo, since he got no money as a result of or after giving Dick the transcript last year." Albano then formulated a plan to funnel the fee from a noted Boston law firm to Bergeron's lawyer, Janis Berry, thereby avoiding payment from accounts payable.

A cold phone call was made in midwinter 2019 to Dick Bergeron. Neither his failing health nor location in New Hampshire was known to me. He was surprisingly forthcoming and affable to my inquiry about the fact he was the source who gave Lehr a copy of the transcripts. He stated the *Globe* paid half his attorney fee to Berry. (Ms. Berry was a former *Boston Globe* attorney for the Spotlight Team before becoming a federal prosecutor and federal appeals judge in Massachusetts.) When asked how there was no publicity or media coverage, he just giggled a bit, laughing about friends in the media.

Not until I read his June 19, 2019, obituary notice did I realize Dick Bergeron was dying from cancer at the time of our earlier conversation. Because we were not close associates, I knew nothing of his distinguished army military career but then again, most Vietnam War–era veterans didn't vocalize about their experiences. His excellent investigative skills were certainly recognizable for the short time we worked together during Operation Beans in 1984. Peace be with you, Sarge.

To reiterate:

- DEA agents and Quincy PD detectives assigned to Beans never fully accepted the Massachusetts State Police participation.
- The Massachusetts State Police had minimal access to pen register analysis.
- The Massachusetts State Police respectfully disagreed that FBI electronic surveillance involvement was necessary

because of confidentially matters, when in fact the bureau was involved all along, in one form or another. Disgraced former FBI agent John Connolly (released from a Florida prison in 2021 for second-degree murder) has been a legendary suspect in compromising Operation Beans.

- Massachusetts State Police physical surveillance of Bulger and Flemmi was shut down from September 13 through 21, by DEA Agents Boeri and Reilly while the *Valhalla* set sail on September 14, 1984, from Gloucester Harbor to the western shores of Ireland. Why the shut down? Retrospective theory: the DEA along with customs had firsthand knowledge provided by John McIntyre of the *Valhalla* arms shipment to the IRA. The Feds then worked to minimize any inadvertent discovery or interference of the operation by working troopers. (Understandable, given the fact reducing the firepower of the IRA took priority over a yet-to-emerge organized crime investigation, notwithstanding the internal politics displayed by DEA officials that was bush league in dismissing the state police for purely speculative and fictitious reasons.)

- DEA Agents Boeri and Reilly conducted spot physical surveillance of Bulger et alia during four days in September, on September 20, 21, and 22, and the last on September 27, the same day the *Valhalla* off-loaded her munitions to the waiting IRA Marita Ann. Two days later, she was seized by the Irish Navy.

- I surmise Operation Beans transitioned into a clever farce to protect the IRA gunrunning operation from the FBI and Massachusetts State Police. After months of physical and electronic surveillance amounting to hundreds of man-hours, no DEA drug operation ever materialized

against Bulger or Flemmi (nor was the Massachusetts State Police given an opportunity to develop a gambling/loan shark case) as Judge Wolf correctly brought this fact to the forefront in his 2003, 661-page report.
- The Massachusetts State Police were summarily dismissed from Beans after Bulger and Flemmi concocted a ruse meeting with McIntyre. US Customs does not normally hand off twenty thousand dollars to a perceived rookie cooperating witness without being assured he can handle himself in a ticklish situation.

Point being, McIntyre was a longtime informant for either the US Customs, the DEA, or FBI Agent Rod Kennedy. If McIntyre hadn't been eliminated, he would have continued to be an extremely important source of intelligence for DEA and customs and a prime candidate for the FBI's Top Echelon program or at least a cooperating witness for the Feds. Neither was going to be an option due to the fact there would have been competing interests: Bulger versus McIntyre. Bulger won.

Ironically, many years later, Agent Boeri was quoted in Ralph Ranalli's excellent portrayal of the Top Echelon Informant Program in his 2001 book, *Deadly Alliance*, stating, "We had the utmost respect for those guys." Ranalli further wrote, "DEA agents said they never suspected that the State Police detectives they worked most closely with, Lancaster Street veteran Richard Fraelick and Joseph Saccardo, were anything but arrow-straight."

For the record, I never worked the Lancaster Street investigation.

A portion of Ranalli's book proved to be prophetic as relates to Boeri paraphrasing a conversation he and Reilly had with Bulger when the agents realized Bulger had discovered the DEA bug in his car and they confronted him in order to retrieve "government property." While Reilly worked extracting the bug, Boeri bantered back and forth with Bulger and Kevin Weeks in empty conversation.

"Two days later," Ranalli wrote, "Boeri and Bergeron were cruising South Boston again at dusk when they spotted Bulger, standing on the sidewalk and beckoning them over." Bulger queried the two about his car door panel falling off as a result of Reilly retrieving the bug. The group swapped bellicose remarks when Bulger said, "I think you guys were on my phone too."

Boeri responded, "No, we weren't on the phone. All we had were pen registers."

Bulger countered, "Bullshit. Oh, please, don't you guys think I know you can listen to those things?"

Boeri replied rather demurely without denying the affront, stating, "What good would that do? You couldn't use any of it in court."

There is no easy avenue to allege serious accusations against the previously named principals in the fiasco known as Operation Beans. The whole scheme was a straw, a farce in order to subvert any unwanted attention on the international gun-smuggling operation that may have been monitored by federal agencies not previously mentioned in cooperation with British and Irish intelligence, who were able to foil the delivery of arms and munitions to the Irish Republican Army allegedly with the cooperation of an IRA informant.

A commonsense approach would dictate that a person or persons strategically located within the cadre of federal law enforcement or the Quincy PD somehow couldn't resist the temptation to make a slight adjustment by simply hitting a toggle switch on a pen register machine, turning lawfully seized paper intelligence into an unlawful invasion of privacy by listening to the intercepted party's conversations, thereby abridging their civil liberties. Alternatively, the possibility exists that an illegal bug was planted in Bulger's condo or an illegal wiretap on his phone or both. On the surface, it appears major federal and state felony statutes were compromised by those sworn to uphold the very same laws they may have violated. Incidentally, Reilly could not bring criminal charges against Bulger as a result of his "That's ours" remarks because to do so would possibly incriminate Reilly in violation of wiretap laws. By the time Reilly testified in 1998, the statute of limitations had expired. Not one of Reilly's superiors or cohorts ever publicly came forward to discredit Reilly pertaining to his publicized statements. Reilly's boss, Robert Stutman, former head of the Boston DEA office, also testified at the same Wolf hearing that "The investigation [Beans] was compromised. But there is certainly reason to believe that the FBI might have burned us." Even Judge Wolf missed the moment.

The foregoing travesty of injustice and the unavoidable murder of John McIntyre, who I speculate was a deeply entrenched cooperating witness/informant for either the DEA, FBI, or US Customs, amounted to nothing more than a hill of beans.

CHAPTER 16

The Bad Apples: Corrupt Cops

Walking among Boston's criminals were several cops who would later earn reputations of disrepute within their organizations. In the debriefing of cooperating prosecution witness Steve Flemmi in 2003, he gave them all up, including a Boston police detective, William Wallace Stuart. Flemmi said that Stuart was on the payroll of a fellow thug, Edward "Wimpy" Bennett, for "a hundred dollars a week." In today's currency, that would translate into well over five hundred a week. When the Boston-born Stuart joined the police force in 1954, he was a navy veteran of World War II with a twelfth-grade education. Like most kids from the hood, he had street smarts, which he parlayed into a position with the elite intelligence unit. The Silver Fox, as he was known, would become the most corrupt of cops. Flemmi said he was aware that Stuart and Agent Rico were "very friendly." That would prove to be an understatement.

Two uninvited FBI agents started to come around the Roxbury neighborhood where some of the loosely affiliated gang conducted business, legal and otherwise. In 1958, FBI partners Dennis Condon and Paul Rico, who hailed from Charlestown and Belmont respectively, descended upon the den of thieves. This retinue of friends and foes, and others to follow, such as Detective William Stuart, would eventually meet at the intersection of cops and corruption.

Three days after Christmas 1964, an FBI informant was murdered, which precipitated an immediate dispatch by the Boston office to Director Hoover, reporting he "was stabbed fifty times and then shot…Vincent "Jimmy" Flemmi committed the murder." There is no way of deducing if the earlier Condon memo inadvertently precipitated or caused the murder of the informant, George Ashe, a forty-one-year-old ex-con whose body was found in his Chevy Corvair outside Saint Philip's Catholic Church in the South End. This information does not reference the source.

Again, Rico authored a memo that alluded to an informant hearing from Vinnie Flemmi that Patriarca wanted Teddy Deegan to be hit. It is presumed that Deegan had earned the wrath of Patriarca because Flemmi and Barboza were having an unexplained problem with him. Two days later, on March 12, 1965, Vinnie Flemmi entered the Top Echelon Informant Program under the tutelage of Agent Rico. On the same night, sometime between 9:00 p.m. and 11:00 p.m., Deegan was shot to death in an alleyway in Chelsea, a small city across the Mystic River north of Boston. Within days of the Deegan murder, a Boston police report contained information from a reliable informant naming seven prominent local hoods, including Barboza, as the killers. The report was "likely written by Detective William W. Stuart." In the years to follow, Barboza and two suspects made the gangland hit parade, and two others were erroneously charged and convicted. If Stuart wrote the report, he would prove to be terribly misinformed or had made it up out of whole cloth.

A counterfeiter of US currency and fraudulent government checks, Henry Reddington was found mortally wounded in his Weymouth real estate office in January 1965. He had previously been surveilled many times in the Dearborn Square neighborhood meeting with Steve Flemmi and other hoods. In 1963, Stuart had conducted a five-month-long investigation targeting Reddington and recommended the unknown results of his probe be turned over to the FBI. Whether he was charged with federal violations is unclear, but someone made damn sure he was sentenced to death.

Days before Rico had his first informant contact with Vinnie Flemmi, the Patriarca bug generated an FBI memo dated April 8, 1965, reporting Jerry Angiulo was of the opinion "that Edward 'Wimpy' Bennett and (Vincent) James Flemmi are 'stool pigeons.'" Additionally, the memo stated, "that Flemmi (Vincent) admitted that he was friendly with Det. William Stewart (sic)." Within days, the same bug produced a conversation by an unknown party who related Patriarca was told "that (Boston Police Department employee) Stuart must be getting info from the Feds." He is also told that Vinnie Flemmi and Stuart were at a New York grand jury. Angiulo was also informed (by an unknown source), that "Stuart + Flemmi went to NYC on $100,000 of AMEXCO [American Express] check (counterfeit) 5 or 6 months ago."

As the winter of 1969 was approaching, Suffolk County District Attorney Garrett H. Byrne sent a formal letter to the Boston police commissioner requesting the personnel record, the days and hours worked for the latter part of 1967, and any and all reports submitted during the aforementioned period of and by "Detective William Stewart [sic] of the Intelligence Division." The fourth and final requested item was "all reports by Officers involved in the investigation of the death of William Bennett, which occurred on December 23, 1967." The chief of the Bureau of Inspectional Services hand-delivered the file to the district attorney containing all of the requested information in November 1969, noting in a memo to the commissioner, "There were no reports submitted by Detective Stewart [sic] during the described period and this information was brought to the attention of the District Attorney."

Approximately three months later, after being indicted, Stuart surrendered to the DA in February 1970, accompanied by Attorney Frank Bellotti. He was charged with accessory after the fact for the first-degree murder of

William Bennett. He was released on a five-thousand-dollar bail and relieved of duty with pay the day before his arrest after pleading not guilty to four indictments. Remarkably, the month after he was indicted, the US Secret Service sent a letter to the Boston police commissioner expressing "personal thanks" for the "cooperation extended this service by Detective First Grade William Stuart...regarding counterfeiting information he had received from an informant," resulting in two arrests and ten thousand dollars in counterfeit currency being seized.

The *Boston Globe* reported in April 1970, "Det. Stuart testified in Suffolk Superior Court that Robert Daddieco, the key government witness, killed Richard Grasso who was driver of the car in which Bennett was killed." The paper noted, "Stuart was testifying in his own defense in the trial of Hugh J. Shields Jr., 3, of K street, South Boston, who is charged with being the triggerman in the Bennett murder." Daddieco was unable to remember the name or identify "the other man" involved in the Bennett homicide in his 1969 statement to the Boston police and FBI. Shields was later identified by the prosecution witness, Daddieco, as "the other man," but Stuart turned the tables and accused Daddieco of being the killer. The following month, Stuart and Shields were acquitted in the gangland murder of William "Billy" Bennett. Steve Flemmi likely got the word about the verdict by his handler, Agent Rico, while still a fugitive from justice for the murder of William Bennett.

The Congressional committee report directly quotes Vinnie Teresa's book *My Life in the Mafia* (1974) as follows: "it was a cop that was responsible for the murder of Wimpy Bennett." The report further quotes Teresa, saying Henry Tameleo told Teresa that Wimpy was a stoolie:

> We got the information straight from our man on the Boston Police Department...Then in November 1967, Wimpy disappeared. Steve Flemmi and Frank Salemmi [sic] handled the job. They're a couple of assassins for (Raymond) Patriarca.

Both of them are missing, either whacked out or in hiding. They're wanted in a murder case, for killing Wimpys brother, Billy. They hit Wimpy and dumped him in lye in a construction site that's now part of Route 93. After the mob hit Wimpy, they tried to hit his three brothers. Walter ran a nightclub in Boston, and when Wimpy disappeared, Walter began talking about hitting Patriarca. He disappeared, too, without a trace. They found Billy in the Dorchester section of Boston on December 23, 1967. They indicted Daddieco, Salemmi [sic] a kid named Peter Poulos, and another kid named Richie Grasso for the murder. Grasso was talking, so he was hit about six days after Billy Bennett got his. They found Poulos' body at a later date in the desert in Nevada. After that they whacked out the two other Bennett brothers. That's six guys that died all because a cop on the take fingered one man for the mob.

One may infer Teresa is fingering BPD Detective William Stuart as the "cop on the take" who was responsible for at least three of the six guys who got whacked.

A week after William Bennett was murdered, as reported by the Brookline police (a western suburb of Boston), Richie Grasso was found in the trunk of his car fully dressed except for his trousers with two bullets lodged in his head. Brookline Detective Charles Simmons said, "Bennett was the brother of Edward and Walter Bennett, also members of the Boston Underworld, who are missing and assumed to be dead."

Neither Flemmi nor Salemme were charged with the disappearance or murder of two Bennett brothers. Nor have the Grasso and Poulos homicides been adjudicated.

In July 1970, an article appeared in the *Boston Globe* saying that "Peter Limone files a motion for a new trial. Accompanying the motion is an affidavit signed by police detective William W. Stuart of Mattapan, stating that he (Stuart), 'has information that Limone and three co-defendants are innocent of the Deegan killing.'" The next month, Stuart was reduced in rank and transferred to uniform duty assigned to the Traffic Division.

Patrolman Stuart continued his crusade in defense of the July 1968 conviction of the Deegan killers. The *Peabody Times*, a suburban newspaper north of Boston, reported in April 1971,

> Boston Detective William W. Stuart swore in an affidavit that he gave evidence to John Doyle, Chief Investigator for the Suffolk County District Attorney Office, that Louis Greco, Peter Limone, Henry Tameleo and Joseph Salvati were innocent of the Edward Teddy Deegan murder. Doyle, however, did not care, saying the men were probably guilty of other crimes. Stuart's affidavit states that Edward Wimpy Bennett told him an account similar to Joseph Barboza's trial testimony, but with different participants.

As mentioned, Wimpy had been missing since 1967 and obviously could not corroborate the affidavit.

To put all of this into perspective, Barboza and Vinnie Flemmi sought out and got permission from Patriarca to kill Deegan. Armed with knowledge obtained from the illegal FBI electronic surveillance that Deegan was scheduled for elimination, Vinnie Flemmi became Rico's informant on the same day as the hit.

Two days later, March 14, 1965, a Boston police report of information received, presumably authored by Stuart, detailed a reliable informant naming Barboza, Romeo Martin, and four known police characters as the hitmen. It is my contention that the Machiavellian Rico manipulated Stuart to write the report in order to insulate his prized puke, Vinnie Flemmi, from suspicion. I also believe Rico was instrumental in steering FBI intelligence information in the form of throwaway cases or leads in Stuart's direction, thereby compromising him to do Rico's bidding, not to mention elevating his status within the police department along with promotions.

What is puzzling though is that Rico knew Barboza and Flemmi were the real killers of Deegan, yet Stuart was trying to deflect suspicion away from the indicted killers, Limone et alia, while simultaneously avoiding public speculation he had knowledge of whether Barboza and Flemmi were suspects. Why? Although I hypothesize Rico was playing Stuart, it is my further contention that Stuart, for some selfish motive, was undermining Rico in the game of who killed whom. Essentially, they were both protecting killers for all the wrong reasons. Rico was protecting his informant Vinnie Flemmi and the illegal Providence and Boston bugs, while Stuart was carrying a huge pail of water for Patriarca underboss Jerry Angiulo, with whom, shall we say, he had a certain fascination and working relationship.

And just to make matters even more confusing, a onetime cellmate of Barboza wrote to him saying that Stuart "gave a police report to Gerry [Angiulo] on Romeo Martin giving him information on the Deegan murder; Gerry then ordered Romeo killed." The letter writer stated he got his information secondhand from another wise guy, professing, "I can pass a lie test on it." Romeo Martin took four fatal shots to the head in 1965, four months after Stuart wrote his report fingering Barboza and Martin as Deegan's killers. I cannot confirm Stuart was aware of who Rico's informants were, but on the other hand, Rico had to have some intuition as to Stuart's veracity and honesty by virtue of intelligence provided to him by his star snitches, the brothers Flemmi.

James "Whitey" Bulger is opened and closed as an informant by Special Agent Dennis Condon, all within a five-month period in 1971, "due to unproductivity." Prior to closing Bulger, the FBI Boston office stated in part in an earlier 1956 memo to headquarters, "We knew of his [Bulger] extremely dangerous character, his remarkable agility, his reckless daring in driving vehicles, and his unstable vicious characteristics." I'm sure the Boston police detectives did not have much forewarning about Bulger before filing the following report.

> We had conversation with someone we know and were informed Bulger was driving past the Normandie and spotted Frankie Jazz (Mazarella) he stopped to greet Frankie and invited Frankie to join him in a drink which he did. We were also informed Bulger has never been in the Normandie before. We noted at this time Dave Gearty's Cadillac Mass. Reg. 641-451 was parked unattended across the street. We inquired if Gearty was inside and were advised he was.

The preceding quote was taken from a report written by two cops, who for all intents and purposes, lived their job twenty-four hours a day. Boston Police Intelligence Division Detectives Chenette and Bulman authored the preceding in August 1972, in a three-page memo to Sergeant Detective Frank L. Walsh. The following is excerpted from the last page and a half:

> We sat on the car. At 2:05 A.M. when it was obvious Bulger knew we were outside and waiting and wasn't going to come out we pulled around the corner entered the parking lot adjacent to the Normandie Lounge from Harrison Ave and drove to the sidewalk right near the front door. Sure enough, at 2:10 A.M. this fellow came out casually, completely ignored the Oldsmobile and cut through the driveway of the parking lot. When he reached Harrison Avenue, we approached him after watching him constantly so he couldn't dump anything. We identified ourselves, displayed the badge and asked for identification. He produced same indicating he was James Bulger and at the same time commented "You know what my name is." He was right. But, we had never laid eyes on

him before. We searched for weapons and he was clean. He was fondling a handful of 50's. We asked him to accompany us back to the vehicle which he did, and we then searched the car which was also clean. However, the other man who was with him whoever he was never showed up. He was surprised when he learned from our conversation that we were interested in the other man and he never enlightened us on this score. While we were searching the car David Gearty left the Normandie, entered his car and drove off. We had conversation with him (Bulger) and he was in no hurry to leave. Strangely enough he knew both our names. He also mentioned that he knew Eddie [BPD Det. Walsh] was travelling all over town asking about him because as he put it "There are no current photographs of me in circulation." He was gentlemanly and well spoken.

We asked him who he used for an attorney and he said his brother [William] because it was economical. He also stated his brother had supper at his house tonight. He admitted he has been a will of the wisp and said he prefers it that way. He said he has no problems and doesn't anticipate any therefore never carry's and will not carry. He also said McNamara [former FBI agent and Boston police commissioner] and he went back a long way to the "Reef." [Possibly Alcatraz where Bulger spent his formative years.] He appreciated the necessity of our work and now we could make out our F.I.O. [field interrogation form] on him. He stresses the fact he is a bachelor and foot loose and fancy free and if the heat gets too bad he can go to New York or Chicago or the cape. He blames his current car for his recognition and referred to it as an Albatross around his neck. The car is outstanding, black and extremely well simonized.

He discussed politics stating although his family were lifelong Democrats they were now Nixon men and would never vote for that fool McGovern. (Amen)

He spoke of everything and nothing for 20 minutes. He had been drinking heavily and was thick tongued. They say he don't drink?????? Why not a photo from the Registry of his license. He was about 5'9–10 well tanned receding hair, blond, blue eyes, about 165 slim, thin face, Lemon colored sport coat, blue bell bottom slacks, blue sport shirt open down the neck and no undershirt (Naples style).

That's about it any questions feel free to call. We left the office at 3:55 A.M.

Respectfully submitted,
Det's. Robert L. Chenette and Gerald R Bulman.

The aforesaid was quoted word for word including grammatical discrepancies. This unnoticed insight into Bulger by a couple of savvy street cops and the documentation reveal a side of Bulger not seen since.

The following August, FBI Agent John Connolly got a belated Christmas gift when transferred from New York to the Boston office in February 1973, as a result of apprehending fugitive Frank Salemme the year before. With less than a half dozen years on the job, Connolly was able to convince Bulger to rejoin the team.

• • • •

Flemmi skipped town in 1969 after he was indicted for murder and attempted murder. FBI Special Agent Paul Rico arranged his return five years later, promising the indictments would be dropped. Twenty-five years after the return of Flemmi in 1974, it came to the attention of FBI agents in Boston that Boston Police Detective Stuart had visited him in Montauk, Long Island.

The relationship had to have been special because Flemmi was on the lam for his involvement in the Bennett murder, and Stuart beat the rap for being an accessory after the fact in the same murder due to excellent representation of then defense attorney Francis X. Bellotti.

William Wallace Stuart coincidentally retired the same year Rico did. After twenty-one years of service, he was approved by the Boston Retirement Board for an Accidental Disability Pension allowing him 72 percent of his yearly salary.

The first year into his retirement, the *Boston Globe* headline for April 26, 1976, read, "Canton Man Slain when He Answers Door." Thirty-three-year-old George S. Hamilton was felled by a volley of shots to his chest at 4:00 a.m. the day before on a Sunday morning. The former owner of Hamilton Furniture in the South Shore town of Braintree, which had just been sold to the international furniture Scandinavian Design company, was facing bankruptcy and was heavily insured by his partners, to the tune of one million dollars. A Boston newspaper reported the Norfolk County grand jury had subpoenaed witnesses to testify, writing, "Another witness, who appeared two weeks ago, was William W. Stuart of Dedham, a former Boston detective who left the police department in 1975 and operates a security company associated with Groper's firm and a number of other liquor distributors. Stuart also handled security at Hamilton's."

Earl "Pat" Groper was a partner and investor in the Hamilton furniture store and executive of Branded Liquors, Inc., Westwood, Massachusetts. He testified before the grand jury investigating the Hamilton murder. Stuart died a painful death in 2000 of cirrhosis and renal failure, among other ailments.

Several years after the death of Stuart, Flemmi had made allegations about him in his 2003 debriefings. He remembered former Republican Massachusetts Attorney General Elliott Richardson was a political rival to Democrat Frank Bellotti—who successfully represented Stuart in his criminal trial in 1970—also was elected AG in the early '80s. According to Flemmi, Stuart had planned to run over Richardson with a stolen car after he left the gym at the South Boston "L" Street bathhouse. There was no mention of a motive, but Flemmi said, "the plan faded when STUART couldn't find a good location from which to park the stolen car, while waiting for Richardson."

Steve Flemmi also asserts in his 2003 debriefing that "George Hamilton was murdered as a favor by Bill Stuart for his (Stuart's) employer, Ray Tighe [sic], the owner of Allied Liquors. Tighe [sic] supposedly had a problem with Hamilton and Flemmi added, "Tighe [sic] did not ask STUART to kill HAMILTON, but this was the solution to the problem that the former Boston Police detective chose."

According to the filings at the Corporations Division of the Secretary of State for Massachusetts, A. Raymond Tye had been affiliated for many years with various liquor-distributing businesses including Branded Liquors where Groper was an executive. It is perfectly conceivable that Flemmi misidentified Allied Liquors and his interrogator phonetically misspelled Tye. At the age of eighty-seven, Tye died in 2010 after making "his fortune building United Liquors into a wholesaling empire" as reported by the *Boston Herald*.

Retired State Police Detective Lieutenant Joe McDonnell recalled the Hamilton homicide as if it happened yesterday. When interviewed in 2011, he was still bitter as hell about being replaced as an original investigator by then Norfolk County District Attorney Bill Delahunt. McDonnell said he interrogated Bill Stuart at the Backside Restaurant in Dedham about the Hamilton murder. Stuart told him he once owned a thirty-eight-caliber special gun but said he gave it away. He believes at one time Stuart fired the gun in the back area of Hamilton Furniture. According to police reports, Hamilton was shot with either a thirty-eight-caliber revolver or a .357 Magnum handgun. McDonnell never got to testify at the trial of four men who were indicted, according to the *Boston Globe*, for "alleged insurance fraud involving an $800,000 policy on slain furniture executive George S. Hamilton." All four were acquitted, and the Hamilton murder remains unsolved.

FBI Special Agent Rico, Massachusetts State Trooper Schneiderhan and

Boston Police Officer Stuart formed a loose trifecta of once highly respected law enforcement officials who surreptitiously led double lives, degraded and disgraced every person who proudly wore the badge, and in the process, left a lasting legacy of destruction and deceit. These men and others to come were the first generation of ethically deficient cops who came on the scene in the turbulent '60s and '70s. During that period, the likes of the Flemmi brothers, the Martorano brothers, Bulger, Frank Salemme, and Barboza murdered well over fifty men and women. Many in Massachusetts law enforcement circles never recognized the absurdity of the situation.

Jai Alai and the Canada Murder

In 1982, Brian Halloran, a Boston hood who was talking to the FBI before he was murdered on the Boston waterfront by Whitey Bulger (and an alleged accomplice of heavy Irish descent) told FBI agents that a Boston accountant named John Callahan had connections with the chief executive officer of World Jai Alai, L. Stanley (Buddy) Berenson. Callahan was hired by Berenson in 1974 as president, and he in turn hired retired FBI agent Paul Rico as head of security.

In March 1976, Callahan, known as a fixer with an accounting degree, resigned his position because of pressure relating to his connections to mobsters Steve Flemmi and the Martorano brothers. Berenson then recommended his former associate as CEO. Halloran stated Callahan had invested money for the First National Bank of Boston, the "principal investor when WJAI (*World Jai Alai*) started in Hartford, Connecticut." (In 1985, the First National Bank of Boston pled guilty to money laundering for the Boston branch of the Mafia led by Jerry Angiulo.)

In an earlier press release, Callahan denied any involvement with the First National Bank financing the acquisition of WJA in 1978 by Roger Wheeler.

An undated request from John Ragazzi of the Connecticut State Police directed to the Boston police sought a background check on Callahan. He noted Callahan was president of WJA in Connecticut and had hired a computer expert from January through March 1976, stating, "during this time, operation suffered financial losses in handle." Additionally, "both were involved in "skimming" and could be a possible factor in the murder of Wheeler in Tulsa, Oklahoma." Berenson had bought the Hartford, Connecticut, from Wheeler in 1981. Parking lot revenues from the Miami fronton were going to be the source of skimming and money laundering under new mob ownership if Wheeler sold out, which he refused to do.

Wheeler was murdered after he finished a round of golf at his country club in Tulsa in 1981 by John Martorano in conjunction with his allies, Bulger and Flemmi, in the process notching his eighteenth murder. Prior to the murder, Agent Connolly allegedly warned Martorano for the second time, the FBI knew his whereabouts in South Florida. A little over a year later, Callahan, a potential executive at the Miami Jai Alai fronton was found in the trunk of his Cadillac at the Miami-Dade International Airport, shot to death. Callahan knew too much, and it was feared he may talk under pressure. Per a police report, "a dime was placed on his chest by the killer."

The Wheeler and Callahan murders were Martorano's last admitted hits during the period he was enjoying freedom as a fugitive from justice. Or were they?

Numerous emigrants from Calabria, Italy, settled in Canada from the late 1800s and well into the next century. Calabria is surrounded by water, is incredibly mountainous, and is situated below the big toe of Italy's boot, which points directly toward Sicily. The Calabrian element of the Canadian underworld made the city island of Montreal the face of the Mafia in the northern hemisphere. As separated as Sicily and Italy are by the Tyrrhenian and Ionian Seas, so too were the Sicilian and Calabrian clans each vying for power and money in the New World.

When first-generation Italian-American gangster Steve Flemmi beat feet out of Boston on the heels of a pending indictment for the 1967 murder of his associate, William Bennett, he ended up in Montreal. He said he had a job at a local newspaper, the *Montreal Gazette*, as an offset machine operator. It is uncertain which Mafia clan took him in, if any.

Four days before another of Boston's notorious serial killers, Joe Barboza, was assassinated (US Marshals had relocated him to San Francisco as part of the Witness Security Program), Pietro Sciara met the same fate three thousand miles away in Montreal. While his wife looked on, the Sicilian consigliere to the local Calabrian godfather lay mortally wounded in the street from a gun blast just after watching the Italian version of *The Godfather II* on Valentine's Day, 1976.

The La Cosa Nostra branch of the Montreal Mafiosi had struck three times within four years, killing two brothers of Calabrian underboss Paoli Violi. On February 8, 1977, Francesco Violi was shot to death, and four years later, his brother Rocco met the same fate in 1983. The hits have never been solved, nor has Sciara's, but that was not the case with Paoli Violi. In between the shootings of his brothers, the acting boss was fatally shot while attending a card game in 1978. Three members of an opposing Sicilian clan were later found guilty of conspiracy to murder him.

Volpe in Italian means fox, and Paul Volpe certainly depicted his criminality while literally living the meaning of his surname. Volpe's home in the northwest Toronto suburb of Schomberg was called Fox Hill, but in retrospect, Fox Hole would have been more appropriate for the Volpe compound. To the consternation of his companions, Volpe dug into every illegal money-making venture he could find from casinos in Haiti to the union machinations of James Hoffa. Volpe was a member of the Buffalo crime family who had extensive ties to Toronto's construction unions.

According to James Neff's 1989 expose of Hoffa's teamster union pension fund, "Volpe was believed to have developed a close relationship" with Hoffa confidant Gil Davis, who was laundering money from the fund.

Evidently, Gil Davis went missing after the revelation, but Hoffa has been missing since 1975 and is presumed dead. But Volpe's biggest mistake was interfering in the Philadelphia mob's control of Atlantic City gambling casinos. As noted in *Iced: The Story of Organized Crime in Canada* (2009) authored by Stephen Schneider, Volpe "had to go to the airport where he would be meeting with people 'from over there.'" This was most likely a reference to American mobsters, either from the Magaddino or Scarfo Mafia family. Magaddino was the hierarchical name affiliated with the Buffalo crime family as was Scarfo with the Philadelphia family.

On November 13, 1983, Volpe was found dead by gunshot in the trunk of his BMW at Toronto International Airport, reminiscent of the Callahan hit by Martorano.

In his 1999–2000 debriefing, Kevin Weeks recounted a conversation he had with the jailed Steve Flemmi shortly after John Martorano found better living and housing conditions due to his realization Flemmi had been cheating on him. The state police transferred the forlorn Martorano from the jail he and Flemmi had shared to another facility so he could better rat him out.

Flemmi asserted his former partner in murder had killed fifty people. A DEA debriefing report indicated, "Flemmi further stated that in the 1970's MARTORANO was involved in 5 contract murders in Laval, Quebec, Canada." Laval is the largest suburb of Montreal with a population of over 400,000.

A later debriefing (which is bureaucratic phraseology for deposition) of Flemmi in 2003 amplifies his 1999 conversation with Weeks.

Flemmi fingered his close associate George Kaufman as being the source for Martorano's alleged murderous foray into Canada, ostensibly because "in the late 1980's, John MARTORANO contacted George KAUFMAN and asked if KAUFMAN could obtain a clip for an Uzi machine gun." Kaufman told Flemmi that MARTORANO was friendly with an individual from Laval named "Andre" LNU Kaufman later told Flemmi, that Martorano did find a clip for his new toy.

In July 2010, *Toronto Sun* reporter Rob Lamberti wrote a column about a decades-old mob hit. "Although 27 years have passed since (Paul) Volpe, 55, was found Nov. 14, 1983, in a fetal position—dead of gunshot wounds to the head, in the trunk of his wife's car at the then-named Toronto International Airport—Maurice is keeping as many secrets as he can."

Maurice is J. P. Maurice, a homicide detective sergeant with the Peel Police Department near Toronto. Lamberti describes Maurice as "the keeper of murder file 83-055131, the region's oldest cold case: Toronto mobster Paul Volpe." Granted, Toronto is a six-hour drive from Laval, that is but one distinction between the murders of Paul Volpe and Miami World Jai Alai businessman and Boston native, John Callahan.

Compare the Callahan and Volpe murders:

- Callahan traveled to Fort Lauderdale International Airport for a meeting with mobster John Martorano.
- Volpe drove himself to the then-named Toronto International Airport for a meeting with alleged American mobsters.
- Callahan was killed at an unknown location.
- Volpe was too.
- Callahan was found shot to death in the trunk of his Cadillac at Miami-Dade International Airport.
- Volpe was found shot to death in the trunk of his leased BMW at Toronto International Airport.

According to Martorano, he shot Callahan in the back of the head with a twenty-two-caliber handgun. Volpe was also shot in the back of the head with a small-caliber handgun.

- According to Martorano, he had an accomplice.
- According to Toronto police speculation, Volpe may have been killed by more than one person.
- There is no doubt the Callahan murder was a contract hit.
- The Toronto media speculated the Volpe hit was

    committed by a professional outsider.
  - Martorano *had* been a fugitive for five years with several aliases at the time Volpe was killed.

J. P. Maurice, the homicide investigator, elaborates whether the Volpe hit was professional when he was quoted in Lamberti's article, "I'm not suggesting it is. It certainly has the aroma."

PART 5

EVERYTHING GETS WORSE

CHAPTER 17

Olga's "Mother"

Dating a mobster may seem glamorous to young women. Your man showers you with expensive gifts and takes you out to expensive restaurants. But beware if you—or anyone in your family—crosses your guy in any way. Debra Davis and her family learned this the hard way.

In 1969, Steve Flemmi fled to Montreal to avoid a federal arrest warrant for the murder of William Bennett. On his triumphant return to Boston five years later, after the warrant was dismissed with the assistance of FBI Agent Paul Rico, Flemmi romanced Debra, one of the four daughters of Olga and Edward Davis.

Flemmi knew Olga (Sciulli) Davis years before when she was dating a guy named Jack Morris. She later married Ed Davis, and the couple reared ten children in Brookline, Massachusetts, where Ed owned a gas station for many years. One day, Debra showed up at her father's work to show off a Jaguar XKE to her dad, a gift from Flemmi.

Ed knew of Flemmi's reputation; he was so angered by the glitzy gift, he proceeded to try to destroy the car with a sledgehammer to the dismay of the new owner.

When she told Flemmi of the destruction, he told her—according to Debra's sister Eileen—"You are lucky he is your father."

Six months later, her father had an accident.

Ed Davis and his longtime friend and drinking buddy, Bob Youngsman, had moored their boat because of mechanical problems at the nearby Dorchester Savin Hill Yacht Club overnight on June 19, 1975, planning on returning the next day when Davis would pilot the boat over to the nearby Boston Harbor Marina in Quincy. As planned, Youngsman dropped Davis at the yacht club, and he then drove to the marina.

Youngsman waited patiently for four to five hours for Davis at the dock. Eventually, a Quincy police officer came to him with bad news. His friend had apparently drowned. Davis, who was a strong swimmer, was found facedown in Dorchester Bay by the US Coast Guard, who recovered the body. A single log entry by the Quincy Police Department is the only official police record of the incident. The forty-eight-year-old Davis was laid to rest shortly thereafter without the benefit of an autopsy. While viewing his father lying in the casket, Steve Davis remembers noticing a visible bruise on the side of his father's head.

Yes, Debra Davis stuck with her new man. She had already married and divorced a fellow named Latournia. Before she reached the age of twenty, she moved in with the forty-year-old Flemmi.

They lived together in Brookline and other nearby communities for seven or eight years. Debra continued to work at Taylor's Jewelry store in Brookline.

Even without the benefit of legitimate employment, Flemmi lavished his girlfriend with expensive gifts, things she could never afford. She eventually quit working, allowing the couple to travel frequently. Sparing no expense in responding to her needs. Flemmi provided Debra with fancy cars, or maybe one of her brothers, who was in the stolen car business, handled the assignment.

In 1978, federal, state, and local law enforcement in Massachusetts became aware that more than sixty thousand cars had been stolen during the past several years in the state. According to the FBI, 40 percent of all cars reported stolen were not recovered and assumed to have been taken by professional thieves. This means that about twenty-four thousand cars were stolen for resale, to be resold for parts, or to defraud insurance companies. To handle these illegal activities, there were facilities ranging from a location to store a car short term to a fully equipped garage and salvage yard capable of quickly and efficiently dismantling or destroying stolen cars.

A gas station located on Harvard Street, Brookline—owned and operated by the Davis brothers—came to the attention of troopers assigned to the attorney general's organized crime unit. In the midst of the 1979 investigation, Corporal Schneiderhan was involuntarily transferred from the unit; I replaced him. I had such respect for him at the time, I called the corporal to explain I did not request the transfer, although I was not unhappy about my new assignment. Later that year, the secretary of public safety formed a task force targeting cities throughout the Commonwealth to investigate auto-theft rings.

"Burners," "beaks," "clips," and "chop shops" are examples of slang attributed to car thieves and to be learned by troopers investigating auto thefts. Thieves would purchase burned cars for the title and VIN (vehicle identification number). A beak was the front end, or nose, and the clip the rear end of a car. A body shop, where stolen cars were dismantled for parts, was commonly known as a chop shop, or sawmill. Integral to the success of the illegal operation were corrupt insurance company motor vehicle damage appraisers who worked in conjunction with auto body shops and who were either connected with chop shops or involved in criminal operations themselves. Certain individuals within the Davis family of ten siblings were suspected of dealing in the stolen car conspiracy, prompting physical surveillance of the Davis Bros. garage in Brookline.

For the better part of 1979, the garage was sporadically surveilled for illegal activity, but none was observed. Because a Buick dealership was situated across the street from the garage, the troopers were briefed to be aware of a possible sighting of Flemmi, as he was an alleged frequent customer. Several of the Davis brothers, who had serious police records, were observed at the location from time to time, but Flemmi was not seen.

Then in 1981, Debra Davis vanished without a trace. That same year, her older brother Ronald was stabbed twenty-nine times while serving a prison sentence in then Walpole State Prison. Steve Davis, Ron's brother, is convinced Flemmi arranged his brother's murder. His death goes unsolved.

A sorrowful twenty years passed.

Olga Davis became a plaintiff in a wrongful death lawsuit against the federal government in 2002. In a statement of material facts, Olga testified, "Approximately one week after Debra Davis' disappearance, [on Sept. 17, 1981] Olga Davis received a phone call from a person who identified himself as an FBI agent. The individual asked Olga Davis if she would like the FBI's help in finding her daughter and a meeting was scheduled for the following day."

According to the statement, she met with FBI agents several times during the fall of 1981. These were clandestine meetings, including one in a hotel where she was questioned and audio-recorded by the agents. As stated in the material facts, "Olga Davis became upset and angry with the FBI agents when she realized that they were more interested in discussing Olga's knowledge regarding Stephen Flemmi's activities than in her daughter." She said, "You're not here to help me find my daughter. You're here to find out information of Steve. And I don't know nothing about Steve and I don't like what you're doing."

One of those agents had recently been transferred to the Boston office a year before Debra went missing. The son of an Irish bar owner in Bloomfield, Connecticut, a graduate of Providence College, and the happily married father of four children, he had more compassion for Mrs. Davis than she would ever realize. His brother was a Catholic priest who was even more rugged than the handsome six-foot agent. As a statement to his fidelity, Special Agent Matt Cronin volunteered to become the employee assistance officer for the Boston bureau office.

He had plenty of empathy, but his professional instincts told him Debra was dead and Flemmi may be a suspect in her murder. As a normal course of investigative procedure, Agent Cronin requested permission to wire Olga's home or if she would participate in a potential recorded conversation with Flemmi. She refused. Unbeknownst to her, the telephone in her home was already being tapped as a result of an ongoing case involving her sons. In reality, Cronin had no conclusive evidence of what had happened to Debra, and her mother was not cooperating.

Decades later, this experience led Olga to file a wrongful death lawsuit, although it would take a heavy mental toll on the aging mother. She sued the federal government contending the FBI protected Bulger and Flemmi, therefore allowing them to kill innocent victims, including Olga's daughter Debra. Her strong Italian heritage was no match for the details of her daughter's death. In her deposition, she noted how Debra "treated her as a daughter and she was my mother." In her perceived metamorphosis state, the daughter (Olga) had a stable mother (Debra) resulting in a flourishing relationship.

But the eight-year love affair Debra had with Flemmi presented another problem not readily apparent to Olga. For he had been in a life-or-death allegiance not only with the FBI but with his sociopathic partner since 1975, James Whitey Bulger.

From all appearances, the fact Debra disappeared and could not be found by any of her family or friends was surprising because she led a fairly austere life before meeting Flemmi. She had a responsibility to take care of her "daughter" and would not abandon her. The last person she was scheduled to meet and the first one who called Olga, ostensibly looking for Debra, happened to be Flemmi, the man responsible for her fate.

Agent Cronin and others were onto something, but all they got was the back of Olga's hand. Why was she blinded by the chameleon bearing gifts? Was she unaware that her six sons were up to their neck in illegal activities? Did she ever wonder what really happened to her husband? The insightful Cronin at least made the attempt to pursue Flemmi.

Years had passed when Olga finally found out what happened to her "mother." The young and attractive blonde was killed in the future home of Flemmi's aging parents, a modest house in South Boston, purchased by Flemmi. The front door of 832 East Third Street faced the front door of Bulger's brother, then Senate President William Bulger, and his family of ten. The duplicate white Cape Cod–style houses shared a mutual twenty-foot-long asphalt walkway stretching from the sidewalk, creating an unusual entrance by Southie standards.

Debra Davis was asked to come to the house. As she was walking down the cellar stairway, a noose was thrown around her neck, cutting off her breathing. Her eyes rolled into the back of her head. She would reflexively kick for leverage while trying in vain to grapple with the rope and the strong hands of her killer. Her body was eventually buried in a roadside grave within walking distance of Bulger's Quincy condo.

Why did Debra have to die? And who killed her?

Although Flemmi told Debra he had connections with the FBI, she thought he was cheating on her because of his many phone interruptions with Agent Connolly. In a weird juxtaposition of events, Flemmi was definitely deceiving John Martorano about his connection with the bureau, but Debra thought there was another woman. She paid dearly for her curiosity. The real cause of her death, Flemmi would later testify, was the uproar from Bulger when he learned that Flemmi had confided in Debra about his relationship with Connolly and the bureau. Flemmi further would allege that Bulger killed Debra—Bulger would blame Flemmi.

Two years after Debra was reported missing to the Randolph Police, Flemmi was spotted standing in a Dorchester coffee shop overlooking the

Edward Everett Square traffic in 1983. He was tanned and looking fit for a man pushing fifty. An attractive young lady stood a foot away, slightly over Flemmi's right shoulder as he spoke, and she attentively listened. She was heavily made up, appearing to look much older, when in fact she bore a remarkable resemblance to Michelle Marie Davis, Debra's younger sister, who had just turned fifteen.

Turns out Debra was not the only Davis daughter that Flemmi preyed on. Beginning when she was a minor, from 1981 to 1990, Michelle was assaulted and battered by Flemmi. This would be alleged in the wrongful death action brought by Olga Davis in 2002. Michelle died as a result of acute intoxication of cocaine in 2005.

The estate of Debra Davis was awarded $350,000 by the federal government in the wrongful death lawsuit.

Retired FBI Agent Matt Cronin testified for the defense in the 2013 racketeering trial of Bulger. He openly rebuked the FBI for allowing the death of Debra and many other victims at the hands of Bulger and Flemmi. He professed remorse for being unable to stem the deceit and destruction by certain agents in the bureau.

To the surprise of every person following the trial, the jury found Bulger not guilty in Debra's death, but he was guilty of eleven other murders.

Olga Davis would not live to see the killer of Debra be captured, sentenced, and imprisoned for life. Seven horrible years after the discovery of her daughter's body, the once hearty mother of ten died in 2007.

CHAPTER 18

Guns, Roses, and the Hussey Family

As weddings go, my attendance in the early '90s of the wedding of a son of a good friend was interesting not in of itself but because of who was also in attendance.

That particular guest and his family would reinforce my theory of one degree of separation particularly as relates to Dorchester natives. As an example, when I was working with FBI Agents Nick Gianturco (Oreto wire, 1984) and Matt Cronin (Heller's Café wire, 1986), I made a point of mentioning I was familiar with the wedding guest years before the wedding. He was not my friend or informant, of which I did not have many because I did not trust them to hold up their end of the bargain. Case in point, state troopers were working a Peruvian informant out of the AG's office drug unit in the late '80s. As the unit commander, it was part of my responsibility to maintain good relations with our federal counterparts at the DEA and FBI drug squad C-2. Word got out to me our Peruvian snitch was getting down and dirty with the very subjects of our cocaine distribution investigation. Against the advice of certain troopers in our unit who had been handling the Peruvian, he was booted from the office after being photographed and fingerprinted.

First to come by my table to exchange greetings were the Hussey brothers, William and Stephen. Two decades after young Stephen was born, we met for the first time. He introduced himself with the greeting, "Hi, Uncle Buddy." We immediately made a connection even though it had been twenty years since I transported his mother to the maternity ward.

During those many years, tragedy had befallen the children of Marion Hussey. Marion had thrown Steve Flemmi, the father of their three children, out of the family home in Milton because her daughter Debbie told her mother her stepfather was molesting her. Now that daughter was missing. Stephanie, the youngest child and only daughter of Marion's common-law marriage was dealing with her own drug-related problems. Even though Marion's children carried the surname of her first husband, she would pack up her kids and visit their fugitive father, Steve Flemmi, in New York State. He had been on the lam from 1969 to 1974, avoiding arrest warrants for the murder of his one-time criminal associate William Bennett and the car bombing of Joe Barboza's attorney, John Fitzgerald. Now he had been back in Boston for nearly twenty years after the warrants were dismissed with the help of FBI Agent Paul Rico.

Marion looked stunning as she walked toward my table with Steve Flemmi a few steps behind. She exchanged personal greetings with the guests at our table, which was adorned with a centerpiece vase of red roses. As the band played on, Flemmi and I were soon standing on the edge of the dance floor, having an animated conversation about his messenger and confidant George Kaufman making accusations against a trusted state trooper. He threw out all pretensions of small talk and got right into my face. I should not have been surprised given his criminal reputation. He began to verbally attack my fellow trooper accused by Kaufman of stealing twenty thousand dollars during a recent state police raid at his Brookline residence while searching for illegal gambling evidence. An allegation made by a convicted felon was cause for a review by the state police internal affairs unit. Captain Nelson Ostiguy and I investigated the Kaufman complaint and exonerated the trooper. My immediate response to Flemmi was "Tell Kaufman he is full of shit…The trooper did not take any money." Flemmi lightened up a bit and dropped the subject. Internal affairs never heard from Kaufman again. The Flemmi/Hussey family eventually returned to their table. We all met again at the after-wedding party and shared a drink and polite conversation before leaving the venue together.

It was a surreal experience spending part of a beautiful wedding ceremony and reception with a man I suspected of foul play in the disappearance of Debbie Hussey. (Far be it from me to question why Flemmi was a wedding guest. I am not judging, but I did have the opportunity to square him away about the Kaufman accusation.)

Months after I verbally sparred with Flemmi at the wedding, John Martorano was arrested in a Del Ray Beach, Florida, restaurant parking lot. He identified himself to the Massachusetts State Police troopers and Boston based FBI agents as Vincent Joseph Rancourt. Given he *ran* from a superior *court* warrant in 1979 and was arrested in January 1995, Rancourt was a fitting alias.

While a federal fugitive at the time of his arrest, Martorano had for years been operating a lucrative gambling and loan-sharking business in absentia through his underling Joey Yerardi. Joey Y, as he was known, came from Newton, a born and bred kid from the predominately Italian lake section of the suburban city west of Boston. In April 1994, Yerardi was arrested in Deerfield Beach, Florida, by the same troopers who later arrested Martorano. Then Trooper Tom Duffy was assigned to the Special Service Section. He turned John Kelly, a Yerardi codefendant in an earlier illegal gambling case. Kelly then became a cooperating witness and at the direction of Duffy began recording incriminating bookmaking conversations with Yerardi.

Combined with Kelly's grand jury testimony as to his involvement in

Martorano's loan-sharking activity, the Winter Hill gangster house of cards was in the embryonic stages of crumbling.

The fifty-four-year-old father of five children with four different women, John Martorano, spent six months incarcerated on a 1979 statewide horse-race-fixing indictment before being dismissed because of speedy trial violations. He screws for sixteen years to avoid a trial and somehow a federal judge decides the defendant got screwed. He still had to answer to the original complaint of loan-sharking charges that got him arrested in the first place, which he did in July 1995 at the old Post Office Square Federal Courthouse in Boston.

He was being held by the Marshals Service late into the afternoon, awaiting a prosecution detention order until Judge Reginald Lindsay could wait no longer. He dismissed the charges without prejudice, releasing Martorano to the street over the objection of the government. The prosecutors belatedly arrived with the order, but it was too late because the last a pursuing deputy marshal saw of Martorano (alias Rancourt), he was driving away in a taxicab. The next day, he surprisingly surrendered on a warrant on the original complaint issued by a magistrate judge the previous evening. Martorano apologized to the Boston native and newly arrived deputy marshal who had just transferred from Baltimore and had pursued him telling Joe Saccardo (my son) that it was not his fault that the judge set him free. At a different courtroom and a different time in 1976 at the Plymouth County Superior Court in Brockton, it would be the first time the marshal's father interacted with Martorano at his sentencing for state gambling violations. He was not so apologetic to the state troopers who knocked him from his bookmaking perch and for the first time was imprisoned with a minimum sentence of three to six months in the Plymouth County House of Corrections. In September 1995, a federal magistrate judge detained Martorano pending trial.

Don't ever play with guns was the theme when famed country singer Johnny Cash wrote his 1955 hit song "Folsom Prison Blues." The song did not reach the Billboard Top 100 until 1968, the year after Steve Flemmi was suspected of killing three of the Bennett brothers. And they were his friends and criminal partners, not a man shot in Reno as portrayed in the Cash lyrics.

Flemmi shot the third surviving brother, William, in Boston with his friend Frank Salemme, who made certain Bennett was dead. Guns to Flemmi became an obsession. He could not get enough weapons. His stint as an army paratrooper and Korean conflict veteran won him the moniker "the Rifleman." Cadillacs were Salemme's obsession.

At the age of thirty-three, Salemme was arrested twice in 1965 by the Boston police for suspicion of violating firearm laws. Less than thirty years later and a week from Salemme's sixty-first birthday, the less-than-stellar Mafiosi stewardship, as demonstrated by an old-time wise guy, came to an abrupt end without him being carried away in a body bag, which nearly occurred in a 1989 botched attempt at Salemme's life.

Francis Patrick Salemme, the maternal son of Irish ancestry, was experiencing the summer heat of West Palm Beach, Florida, when arrested in August 1995 by the FBI as a result of a RICO warrant. He was captured only miles from where Martorano had been apprehended months earlier.

Flemmi was arrested without incident in the area of the downtown Boston restaurant owned by his son William weeks before Christmas 1995 by DEA agents and Massachusetts State Police troopers assigned to the Special Service Section, who had been toiling for many years for just such a moment. He and Bulger were indicted by a federal grand jury for various RICO charges. Bail was denied Flemmi because he was deemed a flight risk.

While returning to Boston from an extended cross-country road trip with Theresa Stanley, Bulger officially learned of his indictment and the Flemmi arrest. Stanley objected to life on the road with the likes of the novelist Jack Kerouac of South Boston, demanding she be returned to her humble family home on Gold Street, thereby cutting herself loose from a nomadic existence with the now fugitive Bulger. The turnaround of companions was almost immediate. In a preplanned meeting at a shopping mall parking lot south of Boston, Bulger's younger Louisburg Square Quincy condo paramour,

Catherine Greig, would sacrifice her life for the man she had to love more than herself. That December meeting could be worthy of a country song Dolly Parton would be proud to record about James Joseph Bulger Jr.

> *Jimmy Joe: My Beau*
> *The law men have risen, they say your gonna go to prison.*
> *The lies that they spread won't mess up my head.*
> *Those piercing blue eyes keep my heart on your side.*
> *Don't lead me astray, just show me the way,*
> *for the love I have for my man, I will forever pray.*

For years, Flemmi kept a sizeable number of weapons in George Kaufman's home in Brookline. The Kaufman house was up for sale sometime in the mid-'80s, prompting Bulger and Flemmi to direct Kevin Weeks to remove the guns to the backyard cabana of Flemmi's parents' South Boston home at 832 East Third Street. Weeks and Flemmi bundled nearly half a dozen bags of machine guns, silencers, shotguns, and handguns, secreting the weapons behind a false wall in a one-room building adjacent to the home of Bulger's younger brother, then Massachusetts State Senate President William Bulger.

After Flemmi's parents passed on, their home went into a real estate trust naming his youngest son, Stephen Hussey, a trustee. The father of two children was unable to enjoy the Cape Cod–style home for long. In an unsuccessful attempt by the Feds to squeeze information from Hussey concerning his father, he was sentenced in 1997 after being convicted in a complicated case where he was accused of filing a false affidavit in a federal racketeering case targeting his father.

Bulger, Flemmi, and Salemme were indicted in 1995 as a result of federal racketeering charges resulting from years of intense investigations by the state police and DEA. The roles were reversed: this time, the state police became the lead agency.

Unlike Boeri and Reilly, DEA agent Dan Doherty turned out to be a formidable and reliable partner for Troopers Tom Foley, Tom Duffy, Steve Johnson, and John Tuntigian and other state police officers in their successful pursuit of the three elusive hoods.

Hearing of the indictments, Bulger and Salemme fled, leaving Flemmi to his own devices, which led to his arrest in December 1995. The sixteen-year federal and state fugitive John Martorano was finally arrested by the Massachusetts State Police and FBI agents from the Boston office in 1995. Salemme was captured the same year. What followed was three years of protracted court proceedings presided over by Judge Mark Wolf (the Wolf Hearings, as they came to be memorialized) that produced a 661-page encyclopedia of the decades-long life and times of partners Bulger, Flemmi, Salemme, John Martorano, and FBI agent John Connolly.

CHAPTER 19

The Drug Trade and Its Impact

As a young kid growing up on the third floor of a three decker in Dorchester, I and my friends occasionally heard rumors about a drug you smoked called marijuana. We could hardly pronounce the word, let alone spell it. It wasn't long before my dad caught me smoking cigarettes. I will be forever grateful to him for a tongue lashing instead of a backhand to the head, imploring me never to smoke anything.

Four decades later, Southie drug dealers dressed in fancy jogging suits that never saw a bead of sweat with nicknames such as "Polecat," "Red," "Rocky Boy," "Gucci," and "the Fireman," ravaged South Boston and environs with kilos of cocaine.

George Hogan, a suspect in the homicide of Frances Mansfield would step out from behind the counter of his "D" Street Deli store to become a head honcho, lording over several dozen street dealers and enforcers.

Meanwhile, across Boston Harbor, a fifteen-minute boat ride from South

Boston, was an East Boston drug trade quite unlike the burgeoning coke epidemic that Whitey Bulger was profiting from.

The *Boston Globe* page 9 headline for May 6, 1985, read, "Mass. Raids Show a Rise in the Illegal Sale of Drugs." According to the article,

> An affidavit filed by State Police Officer William G. McGreal named owner Anthony R. Barrasso as head of an organization that distributed Pacs. McGreal stated that he had arrested a drug distributor who told police he had purchased 4,000 Tylenols with codeine and Doridens, (a hypnotic sedative) from Barrasso on 30 occasions in the last two years. Barrasso's lawyer, Joseph T. Traveline, had no comment.

Boston Police Superintendent Anthony DiNatale had originally launched an investigation after Eastie residents complained about the drug store activity. The Boston PD had two of its best detectives from District 7, Joe Fiandaca and Joe Mugnano, working the streets of East Boston already fighting the scourge of illegal drugs. McGreal, also known as Beeper, was working undercover with the State Police Diversion Investigation Unit, or DIU, with an office in the North Station area of Boston. He made acquaintance with a local hanger-on who told McGreal he was a ticket scalper who had access to the sale of pills from a drug store in East Boston. He reported that only four people dealt with the owner and proceeded to give McGreal the name and phone number of one of the unidentified pill pushers.

McGreal, the 1981 Massachusetts State Police Trooper of the Year, arranged a loan from a local pharmaceutical company for fifteen to twenty thousand pills that would form thousands of so-called "pacs." Each pac consisted of eight Tylenol codeine and three glutethimide pills (hypnotic sedative) worth thousands of dollars on the street. With this product, McGreal was ready to contact one of Barrasso's guys. A meeting between Troopers McGreal and John Curtin was set up at the downtown Boston tourist attraction known as Quincy Market. Numerous follow-up phone calls between the buyer of the pills and McGreal led to a meeting at the former Southie Pier 4 Restaurant parking lot overlooking Boston Harbor, which provided a scenic view of the East Boston waterfront.

Arrangements were made to sell the pills. The buyer was immediately arrested after handing over $16,000 to McGreal. By the end of the deal, he had become McGreal's informant, telling the trooper that the Bennington Street business and apartments owned by Barrasso in East Boston were going to be torched for the insurance money. Evidently, the druggist had money problems due to a gambling habit. He was calling Las Vegas bookies at an alarming rate as his telephone toll records later revealed.

Within days, McGreal was sitting in front of Suffolk Superior Court Judge John Irwin with an affidavit requesting an application for a search warrant for the premises of the East Boston pharmacy. When McGreal, armed with the warrant, proceeded to arrest Barrasso, the dealer told him, "I've been waiting for you a long time."

Anthony Barrasso was indicted, found guilty, and sentenced to nine years in state prison. As of this writing, he sells pizza in Portland, Maine.

On the other side of town, across the waters of the Atlantic Ocean flowing into Boston Harbor, detectives assigned to the Suffolk County Organized Crime Unit were investigating Charlestown's progeny of the enormously successful 1979 major hijacking investigation known as Operation Lobster. Tailgater William "Beaver" Cavanaugh would come under the scrutiny of Boston police detectives Jim Carr, Ken Beers, and Frank Dewan.

Detective Carr was very familiar with Cavanaugh because they both hailed from the Brighton neighborhood of Boston. Sometime in the mid '80s with the help of a long-standing informant, Carr put together an affidavit securing a warrant to tap the home phone of the "Beave." Cavanaugh had transitioned from tailgating to illegal drug distribution and was making a lot of calls to a South Boston pharmacy. As the *Boston Globe* reported in 1985, many drug addicts addicted to habit-forming painkillers filled prescriptions from a Brookline doctor at "The Apothecary on West Broadway, South Boston. Owner Emanuel Rosengard charged exorbitant prices for the drugs, which he sold only between 4 and 6 p.m., according to pharmacy board documents. Rosengard carried a gun while filling the prescriptions, according to police testimony."

Carr and his BPD cohorts, along with the DEA, raided The Apothecary in 1988, and they discovered hundreds of grams of cocaine, ten pounds of marijuana, and dozens of marijuana plants, along with sixty thousand diazepam pills (also known as Valium) with an estimated street value of one million dollars. In the process of surveilling Cavanaugh, the Boston police detectives assigned to the Suffolk County Organized Crime Unit, recognized some of Southie's finest hoods frequenting the pharmacy. It wasn't long before mobile surveillance by the Boston cops picked up fellow tailgater Pat Linskey and other known drug dealers.

Time and again informants for Boston Police Detectives Carr, Ken Beers, and Frank Dewan, were told that if you wanted to sell your drugs in Southie or if you ran an illegal cash business, you invariably had Bulger and Flemmi as partners. It was the 1984 operation Beans all over again.

Sometime in 1988, Carr maneuvered his informant into introducing a young, attractive female with a hankering for "snow" to a fifty-year-old mid-level drug dealer named Tommy Cahill. She was buying the good stuff by the ounce and allegedly smacking down the crap. Cahill was also selling as much bull as he could lay on her. Whether it was to impress her or not, Cahill told her, according to Carr's affidavit, "he was a part of an established, extensive and ongoing cocaine organization based in Boston with ties to Florida." Cahill further bragged he was a "member of organized crime in Boston." The older Cahill fell prey to an age-old demon: he fell for a woman decades younger than he was. Due to his infatuation in the one-way romance with a woman he thought was a drug dealer, Cahill surrendered a lot of inside information regarding who-was-who in the Southie drug trade to Bonnie Alexander, a DEA undercover agent.

So in February 1989, as a result of hours and hours of monitoring the South Boston cocaine organization along with painstaking and laborious street-level investigations conducted by the Boston police and DEA agents of illegal drug distribution by a large contingent of Southie residents, a federal judge signed off on a 118-page affidavit prepared by Carr, chronicling numerous intercepted conversations and seeking permission to electronically monitor the cell phones of Bulger and Kevin Weeks. Agent Alexander simultaneously submitted an affidavit in support of the same application.

BPD Detective Carr recounted in his 1989 affidavit that John "Red" Shea and Hobart Willis "must pay a percentage of the profits from their cocaine business to James Bulger in order to continue to operate." As an example, undercover DEA Agent Alexander questioned Cahill about paying Bulger. Cahill responded, "You either pay "Whitey Bulger or you don't deal or you end up dead." DEA Agent Sean McDonough noted in a 1988 meeting with a reliable informant that Willis was charging too much for a kilo of coke because of the rent money Bulger and Flemmi extorted from Willis.

During the fall of 1988, members of the coke ring started to get a little edgy about being followed. John "Red" Shea commented in a recorded conversation with a street-level dealer "that if [Polecat] Moore was caught with a 'big one' (a reference to an amount of drugs) he was likely 'to sing to the day he dies.'"

Several months later, in January 1989, "Red" Shea went to Florida with Cahill to "replenish his cocaine supply." The tables were turned on Red when he was robbed of $120,000 of buy money. Red called Walter Bagley, the same person he predicted that Moore would sing about (which he did). Let Red tell his predicament from a condensed version of the affidavit:

> John "Red" Shea: Just got ripped off.
> Walter Bagley: Who's this, Red?
> S: Yea.
> B: Where are you?

S: Florida.

B: No shit.

S: Um, at gunpoint.

B: Wow!

S: They pulled us over in the police car: I thought they were cops ya know? Two of them pulled in, which, four, two cars, four guys jumped out, okay?

B: Yea

S: In daylight! Just happened! I was with my friend too, ya know? I was with my other friend…

B: Yea, Yea. I know.

S: So anyways, ah, I had, we didn't have anything but the money in the car, ya know? Took all the money. $125,000.

B: Ooh boy!

S: So I think, ah, things are gonna be ah, I'm gonna try to get something, ya know, from cuff, but I don't know how good I'm gonna do, maybe two kilo, I don't know…

A long, protracted conversation continued with Red Shea telling Bagley more about the rip-off and that he believed his source, Jesus Nodarse, "burnt him," so Shea intended to burn Nodarse for two to three kilos.

Shea returned to Boston on January 15 with the cocaine but discovered that Nodarse had given him "powder," which was highly diluted cocaine. In a recorded conversation with Nodarse that evening, Shea complained about the "re-con," or diluted product, adding that he wanted to kill Carlos, who supplied cocaine to both Nodarse and Shea.

Toward the end of 1988, while Detective Beers was performing a late-evening December mobile police surveillance, Red Shea and a couple of his cronies attempted to intimidate Beers by chasing him through some South Boston side streets, trying to force the detective off the road. Beers drove to the old District 6 police station on "D" Street, where he flagged a pedestrian to summon the police inside. Shea then parked his car next to Beers's cruiser, probably realizing he was not going to be the subject of another rip-off.

In another part of town was George Hogan's deli located at 165 "D" Street. On a regular basis, he and his cronies, Red Shea and Paul and Jimmy Moore, to name a few, would be seen in front of the deli huddling around a sidewalk postal mailbox. From the middle of April until June 1989, a listening device had been placed inside the mailbox. An antenna was situated across the street atop the Condon Community School to monitor whoever decided to talk business around the mailbox. At one point during the two months of surveillance, the mailbox was replaced with another. A postal worker was making regular rounds retrieving the mail when the electronic equipment was discovered. Thinking it was some sort of explosive device, the worker literally blew the whole bug up.

One of the most aggressive law enforcement efforts—to stem illegal drug distribution in an otherwise close-knit and proud neighborhood of South Boston—came to a head with the August 1990 federal grand jury indictments and arrest of fifty-one men and women. Numerous counts of federal violations, particularly relating to distribution of cocaine, were recorded against defendants with diminutive names: "Rocko," "Moscow," and even "Andre the Giant." In this case, no indictable cell phone conversations were recorded of Bulger and Weeks, not to mention Flemmi, who completely slipped under the radar screen. However, George Hogan was sentenced to a measly fourteen months for his involvement in the cocaine drug distribution ring.

CHAPTER 20

The Murder of Frances Mansfield

As far back as the '70s, hijackers, otherwise known as tailgaters (theft from trucks), had a habit of hanging around John Rooney's bar in Dorchester at Neponset Circle. After Rooney's was torched in 1976, they could be found at Barney Grogan's, "B," and Broadway, South Boston, owned by Jimmy Kearns, a suspect in the shooting death of Kathryn Murphy in 1966.

Another joint not far from the South Boston waterfront was a place called The New Deal II, where Hobart Willis, an active hijacker, bank robber, and drug dealer was the proprietor. A South Boston bar and restaurant, Kelley's Cork and Bull, on Old Colony Avenue, was the hangout for owner "Mutt" Kelley, a low-level bookie and former owner of the Big M, a dive bar notorious for providing buckets of blood to its patrons along with a cold beer. It was located on Massachusetts Avenue in the South End of Boston. The old Howard Johnson's lounge just off the former southbound expressway exit at Andrew Square was a regular hangout for future Florida death row inmate "Big" Billy Kelley, who spent his formative years residing in the area of South Boston and Dorchester.

I could go on and on, but I just want to point out it took a lot of Boston bars for over three dozen bank robbers, hijackers, and assorted tough guys to satisfy their parochial thirst for not only a boilermaker (whiskey with a beer chaser) but everything they could steal.

These thieves stole from trailer trucks, warehouses, museums, and ships docked at the receiving point of their contraband, Castle Island in South Boston. The movement of the stolen goods was handled by a fence, whom Charles Dickens characterized in his nineteenth-century *Oliver Twist* novel as the middleman who then resells the loot. A tailgater can't survive without the fence, and in many situations, they are one and the same.

The most prolific fence at the time, who was a receiver of stolen goods and had the added ability to sell those same goods, was Gerard Ouimette, a Frenchman from Rhode Island who had the respect of every thief from Maine to New York. In retrospect, Ouimette theoretically could have been a prime fence for the five-hundred-million-dollar theft of irreplaceable art stolen from the Isabella Stewart Gardner Museum in Boston. The thirtieth anniversary of the theft was celebrated in 2020. But the majority of larcenies, armed robberies, drug deals, and stealing and receiving of stolen goods was perpetuated by the criminal element from the Boston neighborhoods of South Boston, Charlestown, and Dorchester.

One of the gang leaders of the Charlestown crew who lived in Canton, a suburban town south of Boston, was George McLaughlin. A reliable source reported to the Canton police in October 1964 observing McLaughlin driving his red and white Oldsmobile accompanied by two local thugs, Ed Gabree and Lenny Bickford, who were well acquainted with the Boston police.

Eddie Gabree was one of the most proficient thieves during the gang wars of the 1960s. Gabree was arrested at midnight May 23, 1973, in the rear parking lot of Eddie Connors's Savin Hill bar, known as Bulldog's, as he and five other thieves surrounded three cases of stolen tuna. (Connors was a Marine so he obviously named the bar after the Marine Corps mascot: bulldogs.) Two years later, Connors was assassinated by Bulger, Flemmi, and John Martorano a little over a mile from where he viewed his stolen loot. The prospect of selling hot tuna also fizzled for "Big" Billy Kelley, who has spent his adult life on death row in Florida. The owner of the tuna stolen from a warehouse on Dorchester Avenue in South Boston was unable to identify the property as his, after being visited by two private investigators of unknown affiliation. The defendants were found not guilty.

In October 1978, at the age of forty-two, Ed Gabree became the father of a baby girl whose mother was twelve years his junior. She signed the birth certificate as Mrs. Frances Gabree. Nine years later, Frances Mansfield Gabree's daughter, Danielle, would be without a mother.

Although Mansfield signed her daughter's birth certificate as Mrs. Gabree, she never married the father. She had been friendly with a convicted felon who had just been released from federal prison. The two shared an apartment in the western suburb of Waltham, several miles from South Boston.

On a cold, cloudy, windy thirty-degree November day in 1987, while the nation was celebrating Veteran's Day, Boston Police Officer Gus Frangie had been several hours into his day shift when he was dispatched to respond to a woman sleeping in a car. Frangie was assigned a one-man cruiser working a uniform patrol out of South Boston District 6 when he got the call at approximately eleven o'clock.

Arriving in the area of 11 Baxter Street, Frangie recalled, "I pulled up alongside the car and observed her head down in the driver's seat. She was sitting straight up and her chin up against her chest. I couldn't see her eyes. I never touched the car door. I said to myself, 'This is not good.'" He then called his patrol supervisor.

He further related, "She may have been in the car possibly since the night before. When I got to the scene nobody was around the car. It was a

911 call of unknown origin made to police headquarters at Berkeley Street. A woman identifying herself as the sister of the victim arrived on the scene within a half hour of my arrival along with her husband. She was trying to get into the car, but I wouldn't allow her to do so." According to Frangie, normal procedure with regards to a 911 call would be for the caller or another party to meet the police officer, "but not in this call. To me it sounded unusual that somebody would call for a party sleeping in a car." It was rumored the woman had been missing for a day or two.

Slumped over the driver's seat of her brand-new white 1987 Nissan Maxima with the key still in the ignition, the motor turned off, and the all the doors locked except for the front passenger door was a thirty-nine-year-old mother dressed in an ensemble of green. Frangie remembers, "a couple of teeth that had broken off were laying on the dashboard" as a result of multiple gunshots to the rear of the head from a small caliber handgun. No personal belongings were taken from the victim.

The victim was identified as Frances Mansfield. Shooting a defenseless woman in the back of the head must have taken a lot of guts…

On Christmas Eve 1989, Mansfield's roommate and parolee from Plymouth, Massachusetts, was arrested by Boston FBI agents with five other professional thieves attempting to burglarize a bank located in a Cambridge mall.

Mansfield's murderer would be tentatively identified in 2001 by Kevin Weeks. He was a confidant of Bulger's and Flemmi's for many years commencing in the mid-'70s and ending with his arrest in 1999, whereupon he began cooperating with the DEA and Massachusetts State Police. Weeks's debriefing resulted in a Report of Investigation about his knowledge and participation in murders committed by Bulger and Flemmi. And a few more.

Mr. Weeks was not an innocent bystander. Before he hooked up with Bulger, he was a part-time bouncer with a full-time hack job at the MBTA, the state public transit system commonly known as the "T." His brother Jack, a Harvard graduate, excelled as a Democratic political operative not only within Massachusetts politics but on the national stage, having been involved in presidential elections.

In the report of the debriefing prepared in 2001, Weeks proclaimed, and I quote,

Weeks further related that George HOGAN was contracted to kill Frannie MANSFIELD by Hobart WILLIS. WEEKS reported that WILLIS paid HOGAN $20k to kill MANSFIELD because MANSFIELD owed WILLIS a large sum of money from cocaine that WILLIS had fronted to her and she was neglectful in her obligation to pay. According to WEEKS, Jimmy MOORE was with HOGAN and MANSFIELD just prior to HOGAN leaving with MANSFIELD and meeting her demise.

Unlike many other assertions made by Weeks, his information on the murder of Frances Mansfield was not corroborated when Flemmi was debriefed by a DEA agent and state troopers several years later. Nor did Weeks reveal much in his autobiography *Brutal*.

In a July 2000 plea agreement with Weeks, US Attorney Donald Stern spelled out Weeks's terms of cooperation by stating,

> He [Weeks] must provide complete and truthful information to all law enforcement personnel. Defendant must answer all questions put to him by any law enforcement agents or government attorneys and must not withhold any information. He must not attempt to protect any person or entity through false information or omission, or to implicate falsely any person or entity.

He was also required to testify in front of any grand jury but with a stipulation his testimony had to occur within three years of the signed agreement.

Weeks's defense attorney Dennis J. Kelly signed a proffer dated July 6, 2000, from subsigner Suffolk County Chief of Homicide David E. Meier, indicating he, Meier, "agrees not to prosecute Mr. Weeks for any crimes arising out of five murders he was implicated in Suffolk County with Bulger and Flemmi nor prosecute for any crime based upon, 'information, materials or evidence that he provides to the United States Attorney's Office.'"

Weeks was also implicated in the murders of Brian Halloran, Michael Donohue, Arthur Barrett, John McIntyre, and Debbie Hussey. Weeks spent five years in prison or one year per murder.

It is not confirmed if Mr. Meier had firsthand knowledge or was ever allowed to read Weeks's debriefing, particularly as relates to the 1987 murder of Frances Mansfield. I'm sure he would have vigorously attempted to interrogate Weeks about his incriminating statements made against the alleged suspects mentioned in the report. (Mr. Meier was contacted via voice mail and a letter but never responded.)

You can't convince me that the men Weeks gave up consulted with Bulger about the plan to kill Mansfield. My reasoning leads me to an example, when in 1979, Bulger killed a low-level Southie bookie Louis Litif because Litif killed Jim Matera, his partner in a Boston bar called Haps Lounge and to make matters worse, Litif killed the witness, whose body has never been found, all without the permission of Bulger. The misogynist Bulger did not decree a death sentence for whomever murdered Mansfield, because at the time she was just another shoplifter boosting stolen jewelry for Southie thieves. Conversely, he and Flemmi were collecting so much tribute money from drug dealers that Bulger did not wish to bloody his already bloody hands anymore. Bulger had lost control. Southie bank robbers, hijackers, and thieves were now riding the white powder horse pretending to be cocaine cowboys.

The man Weeks fingered for hiring Southie hood George Hogan to kill Mansfield, the now deceased Hobart Terrell Willis Jr., had a long history of misbehaving, starting with his two years of service in the US Army. In spite of a court-martial in 1954 for being AWOL (away without leave) and for careless discharge of a forty-five-caliber service pistol, he was honorably discharged in 1957. Five years after leaving the service, his fascination with firearms brought him five years of probation and a dismissal for various dangerous weapons violations in Suffolk County. Willis was not so fortunate when he was secretly indicted, arrested, and convicted in the western Massachusetts county of Hampden for armed robbery of a bank while carrying a firearm. He received a sentence of twelve to fifteen years to be served at the state prison in Walpole (now known as Cedar Junction), commencing on September 11, 1969, all while being on bail for four federal charges of robbing four separate banks in 1968.

The five-time loser bank robber was weighing in at nearly three hundred pounds in the mideighties when he broke into the tight-knit South Boston drug business. Legendry Southie thugs allowed Willis to move easily among the street dealers of kilo amounts of cocaine. But his big mouth matched the size of his girth. An unknown party told the Boston Italian mobsters that Willis disparaged them with a derogatory ethnic insult to Italian Americans, calling them "fucking guineas." The slang term was derived from "Guinea Negro," thereby creating the hypothesis that dark-skinned Italians were of African descent. A small street located between East Second and Third Streets in South Boston was called "Guinea Emmet," presumably because of its large Italian presence and a local favorite neighborhood Italian American restaurant. Then again, a Southie native who was the daughter of Irish-born parents married a first-generation Italian whose parents were from Avellino, Italy.

As my dearly beloved maternal grandmother, an immigrant from Ireland, Mary Collins Gillen, used to say, "There is the right way, the wrong way and the Galway." In spite of the fact Willis was a Flemmi guy, he found out the hard way not to insult Italians, paying a $250,000 fine to Bulger and Flemmi for his ethnic indiscretion of which Mafia hitman Ilario Zannino (also known as Larry Baione) received half.

The unsolved Mansfield murder was not without a town full of Southie suspects. The demographics of the crime scene, the Lower End, did not lend themselves to the tonier City Point patriarchy, juxtaposed to six people being murdered by Bulger and Flemmi and temporarily buried in the cellar of a home situated in the heart of the "lace curtain Irish."

Weeks excelled at keeping his mouth shut until his ass was on the line. The 1985 death of Debbie Hussy was one of five murders and the third woman killed that he either had participated in or had firsthand knowledge of, as told by Weeks in his official debriefing. He had women all around him. His mother, sister, wife, daughter, girlfriends, and many more. Would he have been so circumspect if, out of necessity, Bulger decided to kill one of them? That's a rhetorical question, Mr. Weeks.

CHAPTER 21

Linskey's Lottery or How "Whitey" Become a Millionaire

In 1964, fire swept through Bellflower Street in one of Dorchester's worst conflagrations. Dozens of homes were destroyed, and three hundred people were left homeless. Metaphorically speaking, in the late 1980s to early 1990s, Southie was burning like the Bellflower Street fire as Bulger and Flemmi continued to operate their crime network with near impunity.

Rent (i.e., extortion) was treated as a four-letter word among the indolent cocaine salesmen who as convicted felons would pay a higher price of imprisonment if they did not accept the "protection." Newly inducted Boston Mafia don Frank Salemme was up to his ass in a gang war reminiscent of the Irish Mob War of the '60s, but this time, Italians were killing rival Italians instead of Irish hoods slaughtering each other. Salemme's rival was Vinnie Ferrara, who had been a second-tier member for the now-defunct Jerry Angiulo criminal organization. Ferrara and his minions killed a handful of

Salemme sycophants while Salemme's crew polished off a dozen or so overrated Ferrara soldiers.

Meanwhile, Flemmi was buying up property all over Boston despite a shaky real estate market and in the process become a millionaire in his own right. The less astute Bulger owned a condo in Quincy and Clearwater, Florida, along with a few fancy cars. By conservative estimates, both criminal entrepreneurs each illegally obtained well over twenty million dollars before Bulger went on the lam and Flemmi was arrested in 1995. One thing they both had in common besides boodles of cash was world travel and a liquor store in South Boston.

One of the worst blighted areas during the early '80s in Boston was scheduled for urban renewal. The Boston Redevelopment Authority's main target was the Combat Zone. Porn theaters, strip clubs, and raunchy bars shuttered their doors because of redevelopment bulldozers, creating slow business for a small liquor store just off Washington Street and within walking distance from the Intermission Lounge. Dewey Square Liquors went into bankruptcy in 1983, and later that year, Stephen and a South Boston woman named Julie Rakes were able to get the retail liquor license for 215 Essex Street transferred to an empty storefront in the Preble Circle area of South Boston. Less than a hundred yards from the new "packy," at 295 Old Colony Avenue, was Saint Monica's Church, which served for years as the Bulger family parish church.

Stephen Rakes was a longtime Southie native who was related by marriage to a large family originally from Upstate New York who had settled in South Boston. He was married to Julie Ann Miskel, the sister of a Boston cop and niece of Boston Police Detective John Lindbohm, who was convicted on three counts of a five-count indictment of aiding two illegal Flemmi gambling businesses while performing his police duties. With the unorthodox nickname (by Southie standards), Mr. and Mrs. Stephen Rakes named their joint enterprise liquor store Stippo's in 1983.

Rakes had long wanted to get into the liquor business. As late as August

1983, Rakes was trying to buy J&J Liquors at 285 Dorchester Street just around the corner from the future Stippo's. The seller was asking $185,000. Rakes' counteroffer of $50,000 less did not fly.

Now he owned his liquor store—and some unsavory partners with it—who soon made Stippo's their new base of operations, now that they had abandoned the Lancaster Street headquarters. Eight months later in April 1984, Bulger and Flemmi were surveilled by the Quincy police, comfortably entrenched in their new base of operations.

The next month, Kevin Weeks became the approved manager of the store after purchasing the property for $40,000—at least that was the official price. Stippo's was renamed the South Boston Liquor Mart, becoming the most popular legal and illegal distributor of booze in Southie under the helm of Kevin Weeks, who represented the epitome of self-preservation.

After being in business for a year or so, Rakes allegedly succumbed to extortionist Bulger and Flemmi to force the sale of Stippo's for a price that has ranged from $60,000 to $100,000, depending on whom you wish to believe: Bulger or Rakes.

Next to the retail liquor store was a room located at 305 Old Colony Avenue, which was designated by the Alcoholic Beverage Control Commission as a room not to be used for storage of liquor. For most of 1989, that area, known as the can storage room, illegally supplied beer and liquor to a dozen Southie entities, including the Columbia Yacht Club, Teamster's Pub, Sullivan's Tavern, several veterans' posts, and a *Boston Herald* newspaper truck delivering booze to Connolly's Bar. Boston police detectives assigned to the Organized Crime Division of the Suffolk County District Attorney's Office, the DEA, and the IRS Criminal Division executed a search warrant for the premises of the liquor store and storage room in January 1990. No evidence of value was found except for a relic of the times: a liquor store receipt with the name of an FBI agent who presumably purchased the booze at a discount for a recent FBI Christmas party.

By the time Boston police from the district attorney's office caught up with Weeks's Prohibition-era-style illegal sales and storage of liquor, Bulger was the sole owner of 295 Old Colony Avenue, the location of the liquor mart. Bulger bought the building on paper for $400,000 and immediately conveyed it to the trustees of Shamrock Realty Trust, who granted him a mortgage to ensure "payment." The affiant for the liquor store search warrant, Sergeant Stephen Murphy, correctly surmised the "sale" was to show a "legitimate source of income."

In 1990, for the first time in forty years, a Republican was elected to the Massachusetts Treasurer's office. Robert Crane, longtime Democratic party ally of Senate President William Bulger, did not run for reelection after holding a decades-long death grip at the treasurer's office. After running unsuccessfully against Senator Ted Kennedy for the US Senate in 1988, Joe Malone, a 1978 Harvard graduate and Republican political operative, beat his Democratic opponent for treasurer by twenty points in 1990.

Malone would soon be mired in an infamous incident that is still talked about in Boston today when somehow one of Boston's most notorious criminals managed to win the lottery's popular Mass Millions game.

Treasurer-elect Malone was several days away from taking his oath of office when a Bulger underling and native South Bostonian named Mike Linskey received a Mass Millions 1991 season ticket as a Christmas gift. Seven months later, the titular head of the legal state lottery system, Malone, oversaw four lottery winners unwittingly posing for a candid camera video on July 29 at Lottery headquarters in Braintree, cashing the winning ticket for their share of the $14.3 million prize of the July 26, 1991, Mass Millions draw.

Dressed in a dark golf shirt, matching sunglasses, and a white baseball cap, the unemployed James "Whitey" Bulger was one of the winners. He had muscled his way into a legitimate source of income.

The odds of winning the Mass Millions Draw were nearly as high as the purse ranging from 13.9 million to 1, according to lottery officials.

Whitey Bulger, the killer of many; Kevin Weeks, his short-tempered gravedigger; Pat Linskey, a convicted felon; and his brother Mike Linskey shared the ticket bought from the Weeks-owned liquor store lottery machine. Weeks and the Linskey brothers split the winnings. In reality, Mike Linskey had the winning ticket as a result of brother Pat purchasing eighteen season tickets in December 1990 as a Christmas gift for liquor store employees. Mike played the numbers: 8-15-32-35-40-42 / bonus number 46.

It was understood by the employees that "we're partners, if you hit." Pat Linskey's wife, his son, and his brother Mike were employed at the liquor store at the time the lottery ticket was bought. The younger Linskey had the winning ticket and walked off with half the money while his brother Pat, an ex-con, had to share the other half with Bulger and Weeks. It would guarantee the Bulger trio approximately $84,000 after taxes for twenty years. Flemmi was not included in the scheme so Bulger and Weeks came up with a cover story, telling him they were going to use the money as a tax dodge without Mike Linskey really having to share the prize with them. Bulger told Weeks that Flemmi had agreed, but Flemmi was still pissed off.

Why would Pat Linskey hand over his winnings? To understand that you need to know his history.

Patrick Linskey was fourteen in 1959 when he began his long criminal career. He had an extensive juvenile record including charges of habitual breaking and entering. Through the years, his family bounced from South Boston to Dorchester while he bounced from courtroom to courtroom. At the age of twenty-three, Pat Linskey, now in the merchant marines, and another hood killed a black man in a street fight and spent thirty-five days under psychiatric observation at the Bridgewater State Hospital while awaiting trial.

The merchant marine beat the first-degree murder charge in 1970. Before he achieved a modicum of wealth, Linskey was a Bulger cohort, supporting his family by becoming a proficient burglar and hijacker in the late '70s with a small group of Charlestown natives.

Massachusetts State Police Lieutenant Colonel Jack O'Donovan and his Major Crime Unit were affectionately described as "the Flying Wedge" because they were famous for going into a city or town, making a few arrests, and then blowing out without giving the local district attorney a heads-up. Such was the case when they arrested a Charlestown crew in 1977 for receiving $300,000 worth of hijacked goods from a truck terminal. Pat Linskey and the other tailgaters then defaulted on $60,000 cash bail before being brought to justice and sentenced to three to five years at Walpole State Prison.

You can take the hood out of Southie, but you can't take Southie out of the hood, not even in a nice neighborhood in a small town south of Boston called Hanover. One December night in 1985, Pat Linskey had a midlife crisis in criminality. For no apparent reason, according to a seventeen-year-old male victim, Linskey beat up the kid pretty good, right in front of the police station. Several Hanover officers responded to the scene and had to pull a drunken Linskey off the kid as he was kicking him. Unsteady on his feet, he tried to flee the scene on foot, complaining that the teenager hit him. In a struggle with the pursuing police, he continued the rage, assaulting them, which resulted in an arrest for assault and battery on two police officers, assault and battery with a shod foot, and operating under the influence of alcohol according to Hanover PD.

Linskey would have no problem making bail. In his right front pants pocket was a roll of bills totaling $5,000. An inventory search of his car produced another $5,000 from the front seat, and a bag in the trunk of his car contained $6,200.

In an ironic 2001 twist, the license for South Boston Liquor Mart was transferred to Julie's Liquor Mart at the same location. From 2002 to September 2004, the former wife of Stephen Rakes, Julie Ann Dammers, was the manager of record and owner of the liquor store.

But here's the real question: were Pat and Mike Linskey able to rig the lottery system?

Numerous countries that are in the lottery business are located in five continents, including America and Canada, all of which have at one time or another dealt with a French-owned company that manufactures the finest lottery equipment in the world. Established more than seventy years ago in France, Ryo-Catteau supplied the terminal system that the state of Massachusetts bought in the late '80s, which was in operation when Linskey et alia won their millions.

Sixteen years after Linskey won Mass Millions, blogger Wintariofan, who signed off as Derek, posted the following on January 6, 2007 concerning a Ryo-Catteau-made machine, stating, "The machine which ironically the public can buy is about $90,000."

Ryo-Catteau touts itself as the specialist of gravitational technology. The company supplies both solid and composite lottery balls with diameters ranging from 40, 50, 70, or 83 millimeters, each measuring one thousandth of a meter or 0.04 inch. The solid balls consist of plain natural rubber and the composite balls have an external envelop in plain natural rubber with each featuring vulcanized figures or symbols such as a number. A human being known as a controller can instruct the lottery machine on how many balls are wanted or needed for a game. The claims Ryo-Catteau make concerning mixing and dispensing the random device are far more technical. The point is the central focus of possibly corrupting the lottery draw rests with "somehow" manipulating the balls.

There is no confirmation whether or not any of the four newly minted lottery barons, Linskey and company, ever purchased a Ryo-Catteau lottery machine as partially described above. In some instances, used lottery balls can be purchased at a cost well into the thousands of dollars. A public records request via email was made to the lottery in 2018 and 2019, inquiring the make, model, manufacturer, age, cost, and patent number for the lottery machine and what type of balls were used in the Mike Linskey Mass Millions winning lottery drawing for July 26, 1991.

The lottery provided limited information stating, "No lottery records exist in response to your request. However, the terminal system from 1991 was manufactured by Ryo-Catteau." Additionally, the lottery could not provide records of lottery security officials assigned to the drawing in question but stated, "drawings were witnessed by independent witnesses, not state police troopers." In an attempt to dig deeper into the weeds about who performed security functions before and after the drawing and if there were any peculiar actions related to the drawing not publicly known at the time, the response was "no lottery records exist."

The lottery did offer they had the Numbers Game and the Ryo-Catteau draw game equipment for the Megabucks, Mass Millions, and Mass Cash located at the WHDH, Channel 7 television Boston office, and the machines had not been in service since 1997, "because it was not reliable mechanically." Ryo-Catteau lost the bid to a company that was "more effective." With regards to a bid or no-bid contract for the machines, the lottery stated, "Our contracts are awarded through a procurement process, where we award to the bidder that is the best overall value to the Commonwealth. Again, we don't have records from 1991, so I am not aware of the cost of the contract. I hope this helps."

Blogger Wintariofan was far more circumspect in 2007 than lottery officials were forthcoming in 2018 with the obligatory no records exist mantra although the person I corresponded with was very professional and attentive to my requests. Whatever his expertise was then, the blogger scripted a believable scenario on how the national lottery in Ontario, Canada, secures its use of the Ryo-Catteau machine. He stated the Ontario lottery machine "is always under heavy lock and key and so are the balls that are locked and stored in cases." The case of balls is then sealed with a plastic security tag with a serial number "that is recorded/checked whenever the sealed cases are opened." He goes on to describe the forty-nine solid India rubber fifty-five millimeter balls are all similar in weight, diameter, density, and resiliency with the number embedded into the rubber.

Given the cast of characters who walked away with the second-highest Mass Millions jackpot at the time, balls would not have been the problem.

CHAPTER 22

The Tragedy of Debbie Hussey

Debbie Hussey spent her early childhood visiting her aunt who occupied an apartment above my family's in the same three-decker in Dorchester. She was nine or ten years old at the time and on occasion would play with my wife's younger sister Jean.

I had known Debbie's mother, Marion, since taking her to the wrong hospital in 1967, where she gave birth to her son Stephen because the prospective father, Steve Flemmi, was missing in action.

In the twenty-year span since the hospital run, we would reacquaint at a family function or maybe a wake. And of course, Marion had to bust my chops for either my Italian heritage or being a state cop. How could my wife have married the likes of me? She used to say the only difference between Flemmi and me was that I was a cop.

That was harsh! None of it fazed me because I genuinely enjoyed her company, but at the same time, I understood her personality. After all, such traits were endemic to those of us who were OFD, or originally from Dorchester. Her son Stephen even took to addressing me by my nickname, Buddy—Uncle Buddy, no less.

I always thought he possessed his father's looks, but, more important, he was a good kid and a gentleman. Her other son Billy was more standoffish and sort of played the role of tough guy, more in tune with his father's persona. I never met Stephanie, who was Marion and Steve's middle child.

The parents of Marion (Murray) Hussey were natives of Canada. Her dad, Michael, was a fisherman, and her mom, Elsie, was a housewife, producing up to ten children with six surviving birth. Marion left high school and was married at an early age to Thomas Hussey, the father of Deborah Ann. The couple had two boys who died in infancy previous to the birth of Deborah. Just before Deborah's first Christmas in 1958, the Husseys separated, presumably because of her husband's excessive alcohol problem, which led to their divorce in 1962 according to Marion.

Marion and her girlfriends then started to frequent a bar in Dorchester where another sister worked. It was here at a place formerly known as Sonny's Café, located on Columbia Road, on a Memorial Day weekend in 1959 that the owner of the bar gave her a ride to another club where she was supposed to meet a friend who never showed. Marion had heard various rumors from her girlfriends before she was about to have dinner and drinks with the man who gave her a lift. The attractive nineteen-year-old and the sociable nondrinker, who was six years her senior, became constant companions.

Those first dates were memorialized with the birth in October 1960 of William, the first son of Marion and Stephen Joseph Flemmi. Debbie was two years old.

In those days, Flemmi owned rental properties, a grocery store, and a bookstore (not to be confused with a bookie joint) and was part owner of a bar with Edward "Wimpy" Bennett (Flemmi was strongly suspected of being instrumental in his disappearance in 1967). Marion had heard rumors that Flemmi was a bookie but rarely inquired any further. She understood that he bet horses and took numbers, but she never gave it any thought.

Eleven months after William, Marion gave birth to Stephanie, whereupon she moved to another Dorchester apartment where the unmarried couple lived for nearly five years. Flemmi would become a part-time resident and sometime father.

Marion was working part-time as a waitress in a bar partly owned by Flemmi when he started to physically abuse her, possibly causing her to suffer two miscarriages. It became a point of contention with Marion that Flemmi would not marry her, foreclosing her desire for her and their children to assume his surname. In the summer of 1967, that and other issues drove Marion to take a potshot at Flemmi with his own gun while he was leaving their new Dorchester apartment on Newhall Street.

He fled the area, ducking the shots while hastily steering his black Pontiac and attempting to avoid the irate mother of his children. The Boston police responded, but the incident went unreported.

Before the family moved out of yet another modest Dorchester apartment to the tony Boston suburb of Milton, Marion bore her last child with Flemmi. He was not available to drive Marion to the hospital, but I was. Stephen was born in June 1967, the third child Flemmi had with Marion, yet not one of their offspring carried his surname, nor was he listed in any of the birth certificates.

By this time, Deborah was nine years old and by all accounts a sweetheart of a girl.

Young Stephen was two years old when Flemmi fled Massachusetts for Nevada and then Canada on the heels of a state indictment for the murder of William Bennett and the attempted murder of Joe Barboza's lawyer, John Fitzgerald. Marion and her kids visited him in New York several times during his absence from 1969 through 1974. She was a single mom with four young children surviving on welfare, a menial job, and money given to her from family and friends.

But that didn't stop Flemmi from throwing a huge welcome back party in May 1974 at their Milton home. The guests included celebrity hoods, such as the titular head of the Winter Hill mob, Howie Winter; the Martorano brothers; Whitey Bulger; Flemmi confidant George Kaufman; and assorted paramours.

Upon Flemmi's return, Marion had to endure the company of a man she disliked. She described Whitey Bulger as "argumentative" and "a chauvinist." Marion stated, "He was very demeaning to women. Always tearing you down, you know. You were like, like, different things that he said. I was always bickering back and forth with him. Him, I never liked."

Flemmi's parents lived next door to them in Milton, where his mother cooked a traditional Italian meal nearly every Sunday afternoon with him and his South Boston hugger, Theresa Stanley, in attendance.

Flemmi had been back at the Milton home for less than a year when in 1976, Debbie got in trouble with the law. At sixteen, she was arrested for larceny over a hundred dollars, and an operating under the influence charge followed a little over a year later. Both charges were dismissed as was a 1978 charge for prostitution. As she entered her twenties, several drug and prostitution arrests would haunt her mother along with speculation she was working for a pimp.

Within two days in September of 1981, she was arrested by the University of Connecticut Police Department in Storrs for larceny and being a fugitive from justice. The next day, two larceny charges were dismissed in Woburn District Court at the request of an unknown commissioner. Debbie's half sister, Stephanie, may have used Debbie's identification in the Woburn case, according to Marion. The last year Debbie filed income taxes was 1982, using her father Tom's Florida address.

In the fall of 1982, Marion came home from her banking job and found Debbie arguing with Flemmi. Marion remembers her twenty-four-year-old daughter being on "drugs or drinking" when she blurted out that she had been providing oral sex to Flemmi for years. "And I passed out when she said it. And I mean, I was just beside myself." Debbie told her she was not lying. Marion reassured her that she believed her.

Naturally, Flemmi denied the accusations, stating Debbie was drugged up. Marion then unceremoniously threw Flemmi to the street, knowing full well that he was more than capable of harming her if she went to the police. Although Flemmi says, "I wasn't thrown out. I left."

Within months of Debbie accusing Flemmi of sexually abusing her, Stephanie, the middle child of the separated couple, began nearly two decades of illegal drug use several years after dropping out of high school.

Lacking an education and jobs skills, Debbie had difficulty holding down a steady job. Without any firsthand knowledge, I can speculate Stephanie looked at her father in a different light upon learning he was accused of molesting Debbie. She herself had two children by two different fathers. Marion took her grandchildren into her own home because of her daughter's problems. It is unclear if Flemmi gave Stephanie any moral or financial support.

Debbie tried to escape the predatory Flemmi sometime in 1982, traveling to Los Angeles, where she continued her drug addiction with an arrest for possession of a controlled substance. During the next several years, Debbie would drop in and out of Marion's life. Debbie's last recorded Massachusetts probation entry was for a 1983 surchargeable accident in Revere. Subsequently, there were no other probation notations chronicling any arrests.

In the fall of 1985, Marion's sister mentioned to me that Marion hadn't seen or heard from Debbie in quite a few months. She asked if I would please contact Marion and talk to her because she was heartsick and didn't know which way to turn or, even worse, whom to trust. She had my attention. I wondered to myself, *How is this going to play out?* since I had been involved with the state police in several attempts to put Flemmi in jail. Past physical surveillance concluded Flemmi was keeping company with several women, none of whom was his longtime paramour Debra Davis, but he utilized a beeper listed in her name. If Flemmi was still dating Davis, that fact was not brought to my attention during the 1984 Operation Beans, nor immediately thereafter. The Hussey family was living in a huge house in Milton, provided by Flemmi, and from all indications, he did not spend very much quality time there. Those who were in the know were so preoccupied with enhancing professional creds (including myself), we missed the obvious. Where was Debra Davis? Now the script would read, "Where is Debbie Hussey?"

It was unilaterally decided by Marion to meet at the Quincy doughnut shop where she worked part-time in October 1985. Her Milton home was unquestionably not a good choice due to who knows who was surveilling the Flemmi-owned home and could speculate what I was doing there. I came at dusk when business was slow with just a few customers. She hadn't lost her ability to bust my chops, and on this occasion, things were no different. Right out of the box, she questioned if I was wearing a wire. My protestation not only invited a profane rebuttal but a free cup of coffee, sans the doughnut. Marion and I obviously had a special dialogue, but the coffee counter meeting would begin with small talk. Specifics about why she wanted to talk to me would understandably become more difficult for her as she was initially hesitant to explain her dilemma, invariably due to the fact she was fearful of what Flemmi would do to her for talking to me.

For years, the Hussey/Flemmi family traveled to central Massachusetts for a joyful day of apple picking. The fall of 1984 would be no different, excepting for the fact, as described to me by Marion, that outing was the last time she had contact with Debbie. Several months later, the Christmas holidays would come and go without the ever-present Debbie. Birthdays, holidays, and sporadic drop-ins by her were nonexistent for the following year.

Short of reporting Debbie missing, I reached out to several trustworthy state troopers. On a confidential basis, I asked if they could squeeze their sources for any information as to the whereabouts of Debbie. Within weeks, they reported nothing reliable but did encounter some surprisingly hostile reactions to the inquiry. Not to be daunted, I continued with a teletype search, exhausting all platforms of resources along with several interviews. One such interview involved a person who had been arrested with Debbie for illegal drug violations. Even though I had an acquaintance with her and had met the young lady years before, the mere mention of Flemmi and the possibility Debbie might be missing did not bring hostility, only disclaimers. Her body language and facial expressions told me all I needed to know, not to mention her lack of any valuable information. Nothing. The search slowed to a trickle.

The soon-to-be born infant that I brought to the hospital in his mother's womb was now eighteen and fighting for his life with severe head injuries in an intensive care unit. The year was 1985, and Marion had not talked to Stephen's father in quite some time. She beeped him, and when he called her back at home, she had to tell him his son was dying as a result of a serious car accident. Marion said she got into "a confrontation" at the hospital. "I said something to him about, 'Where is Debbie? You killed her didn't you.'" If one can believe it, he professed his innocence to Marion on bended knee.

It was now 1989, and Marion had not heard from Debbie in years. I proposed contacting Flemmi to see what he had to say, but that was nixed by Marion. What I didn't know and was not mentioned by Marion was he had been having sexual relations with Debbie since she was a teenager, as told to Marion by Debbie. Later that same year, a private conversation with FBI Special Agent Matt Cronin prompted a resurgence of interest. We had been preparing for trial in the Mike London money-laundering case when I casually mentioned the Hussey situation. Without hesitating, he responded Debra Davis had been missing since 1981. Half a decade later, we both learned about women who were close to Flemmi and were missing (at intersecting periods). Matt didn't know about Hussey nor I about Davis.

Without any evidence of Flemmi's complicity, circumstantial or otherwise, I enlisted the services of Trooper Jack Henley. He and I were stationed at the AG's office together, where he had a reputation for being a bulldog of a worker. Trooper Henley conducted a tedious digital search for Debbie, resulting in the discovery of a California woman whose driver's license photo fit Debbie's description. Ironically, her name was Debbie Ann, and her month and year of birth was the same as William Hussey's. At the time, California driver's licenses contained a thumbprint of the licensee. The girls' prints were compared, but they did not match. Marion handled the disappointment well but wanted to contact the California woman just to be certain it wasn't Debbie, confirming how closely the license picture matched. She was disappointed once again.

The fact Debbie wasn't Flemmi's natural daughter, she obviously came from a broken home, as did two daughters from his first marriage. Flemmi insisted the birth certificates of his three children with Marion carry the Hussey surname of her first husband. Flemmi frowned on his boys smoking, drinking, or doing drugs. He was moderately successful. What parental discipline Flemmi contributed to the adolescence of Debbie was minimal. His and Bulger's motive for killing Debbie—because she was besmirching their reputation—is laughable in light of his suspected involvement by law enforcement in murder and mayhem.

As the story goes, the hoodlums orchestrated the premeditated slaying of a weak, defenseless, drug-addicted twenty-six-year-old woman. Ironically, Flemmi couldn't countenance Debbie possibly dealing with a pimp, but he had no problem with being best buddies with one of Boston's most prominent pimps, John Martorano. Flemmi said Bulger made the decision Debbie had to go two weeks before killing her. They induced Debbie into what became a triple grave in the basement of the same cellar where the decomposed bodies of John McIntyre and legendary thief Arthur Barrett already lay.

Flemmi confessed to Debbie's murder prior to testifying at Bulger's 2013 trial, saying Bulger strangled Debbie with the same grubby hands that caught Debra Davis off guard, although a federal jury exonerated Bulger for that murder. The strangulation of Debbie Hussey had the inglorious distinction of making her the last *known* female who was sacrificed for the misguided benefit of indirectly keeping alive the FBI's Top Echelon Informant Program. Debbie Hussey was collateral damage.

Within two months after Stephanie Hussey had lost her life to drugs, the turn of the twenty-first century brought the families of John McIntyre, Arthur Barrett, and Debbie Hussey more tragedy, when they learned the state police discovered graves containing the decomposed bodies of their long-missing relatives. The three had been transported in sacks, after being dug up from a makeshift grave in the cellar of 799 East Third Street, the then South Boston home of the brother of Pat Nee. Bulger and his cadre—Flemmi, Kevin Weeks, and Pat Nee—irreverently tossed the remains in the trunk of a car, followed by a postmortem funeral procession through the streets of South Boston to the new burial site in Dorchester. The degradation of the dead ended adjacent to the embankment of Boston's busiest expressway and across the street from the Boston firefighter's union headquarters. Coconspirator Weeks was not looking forward to an indefinite prison sentence for crimes he would be charged with due to his years-long close surrogate association as Bulger's South Boston son of Erin. After his arrest in 1999, he committed the worst sin one Irishman could commit against another: he informed. The FBI, or first-born Irish, destroyed forever the fabled myth of noncapitulation in less than two weeks among the boyos, which kept Kevin Weeks from a long stretch in federal prison, but in doing so, he significantly assisted in the reinternment of the dead.

CHAPTER 23

The Criminal and Fugitive Investigation of Bulger (It Is a Bit Confusing)

Right from the outset, Assistant US Attorney Fred Wyshak kept the FBI in the dark as he was building a Racketeer Influenced and Corrupt Organizations, or RICO, case against Bulger and Flemmi, but in December 1994, former FBI agent John Connolly tipped off Flemmi about the forthcoming indictments Wyshak had secured without the assistance of the premier investigative body in the nation, yet the Boston FBI office managed to enforce Wyshak's exclamation point of confidentiality. Bulger was returning from a long road trip with his day paramour, Theresa Stanley, when he allegedly got word of his indictment over his car radio. Bulger had been on an extended road trip with Stanley possibly preparing for just such a moment of retreat. He then made arrangements to drop her off at a restaurant parking lot in a town south of Boston, exchanging Stanley for his nighttime hugger, Catherine Greig. The two wasted no time in disappearing.

Steve Flemmi was unarmed the night of his arrest by the DEA and state police troopers in January 1995; except for the mistaken belief his psyche demanded that he had immunity from prosecution, hoping retired agent Connolly would ride in on a white horse to his rescue, otherwise, he would have screwed.

The fact that Bulger was on the run and Flemmi had been incarcerated prompted a seasoned ex-con drug dealer to make an anonymous phone call to Assistant US Attorney Fred Wyshak. The former DEA defendant aroused such curiosity a meeting was arranged sometime in 1996 in a room at the Parker House Hotel in Boston with the caller, a federal drug agent, and state troopers inside the rented room with FBI agents outside in the adjoining hallway. A DEA agent and several Massachusetts State Police troopers from the Special Service Section, or SSS, formed the nucleolus of the Strike Force within the justice department's Organized Crime Strike Force, or OCSF, answerable only to justice in Washington, DC. The Boston FBI agents were a precursor of what would become the Bulger Fugitive Task Force, or BFTF. (Hereafter, in most instances, MSP and FBI will be used in reference to the disparate criminal and fugitive investigative bodies, respectively.)

What happened in 1996 and for the next ten years between the MSP and the FBI was a road race based on a rivalry of which agency could capture Bulger first. A DEA Report of Investigation dated December 20, 2004, refers to the 1996 hotel meeting with the source, stating,

> The initial information was extremely vague and the SOI [source] appeared mentally imbalanced and somewhat questionable. At the time, the FBI was working independent of the other agencies and disregarded the SOI's intelligence as lacking credibility. At the conclusion of the above initial interview the SOI was instructed to make available proof of "its" ability to create false identification.

The source of information, or SOI (hereafter referred to as "the source"), stated he was "recruited by Kevin WEEKS to create false identifications for 'fugitive' BULGER." A second meeting was held in the source's psychiatrist's office with two MSP troopers but without the alleged disinterested FBI agents, per the 2004 DEA report. The source may have been a bit unsteady in his mental capacity, but his expertise in producing false identifications was not.

By whatever means the source inserted himself into the inner circle of the MSP, it became incidental because of his rising stature upon implicating Kevin Weeks in the scheme days after MSP members met the Vietnam vet at his psychiatrist's office. "At about this time WEEKS gave the SOI [source] two complete sets of biographical identifications for BULGER, in the name of Mark SHAPETON and Harold W. EVERS." It was further reported "that MSP and DEA investigators traveled to Chicago (Circa 6-29-96) for the purpose of conducting surveillance on Kevin WEEKS. Pen register information at the time indicated that WEEKS was reportedly attending a paintball tournament in the greater Chicago area. The cited surveillance met with negative results."

Weeks then gave the source two complete sets of biographical identifications for Bulger. Subsequently, photos of Bulger were created to match the bio info, which produced false Massachusetts driver's licenses in the names of Harold D. Evers and Mark Shapeton, which were provided by Weeks. The photo renditions supplied by the source to the MSP were blurry and produced a poor image of an unrecognizable mustached John Bulger posing as his brother "Whitey."

MSP members were losing confidence in the informant although "the source never, requested anything except a guarantee the 'it's' would not be compromised." It is alleged the source originally wanted the reward of $250,000. "The source was told that in order to collect any reward additional people would have to be told of 'it's' identity." At the time, the source was controlled by the state police, according to the 2004 DEA report.

As the fall of 1996 was approaching, the criminal case heated up again when Weeks requested the source obtain additional false IDs for Bulger. New photos of Bulger were provided by Weeks along with holographs of the seal of Massachusetts with the already procured names of Shapeton and Evers. Two deceased individual identifications, Ernest Beaudreau and Robert W. Hanson, were provided by the MSP to the source for the brand-new false Massachusetts driver's licenses containing a photo of Bulger's false New York license in the name of Thomas Baxter, which he already had in his possession. (It was later learned that Theresa Stanley had already told Weeks and the FBI of Bulger's Baxter alias.) The DEA further stated, on "8-30-96 the SOI turned the new BULGER ID's over to Kevin WEEKS in South Boston." The source hand-delivered four false Bulger license identifications with Social Security Cards and actual birth certificates to Weeks while the federal strike force enlisted the aid of all the troopers assigned to the Special Service Section to surveil the exchange.

Bulger went from an FBI Top Echelon informant to a Top Ten fugitive in 1999, the same year Kevin Weeks was arrested and immediately began cooperating with the MSP. During the intermediate years of 1996 through 1999, every conceivable means of digital data surveillance was instituted by SSS troopers assigned to the MSP, in spite of the fact the false licenses had expired; a weekly check was conducted of all fifty states and Canada in the hope Bulger may have applied for a new license. Credit card and passport applications were also queried, all with negative results.

> "I'm here to tell you we are out to catch him."
> —Barry Mawn, special agent in charge of the FBI's Boston office
> *Boston Globe* on August 21, 1999—reprinted above statement

It wasn't until the millennium year 2000 that the MSP learned the FBI had been putting the peek on the MSP source. By this time, both entities had previously debriefed Weeks, who had laid out the entire false identification scheme. As a result, several MSP members met with a Boston police officer assigned to the FBI task force to discuss mutual interests concerning the effort the MSP had put into getting false IDs to Bulger. The FBI representative requested a picture of Bulger only to be denied because "he could not guarantee what would happen when he returned to the task force." Because of the perceived affront, the criminal and the fugitive investigators were called into a meeting with US Attorney Don Stern. The MSP investigators expressed a concern that the FBI databases were being queried by folks in the bureau to the determent of the MSP criminal investigation. An accusation was also made by the MSP that Bulger still had friends within the Boston FBI office, projecting the insinuation that the FBI was either going to go public with the false ID issue or protect Bulger. Stern later called a follow-up meeting with the investigators and the respective heads of the designated agencies in attendance, where he decided the Bulger photo would remain with the MSP for the safety of the source who was well known within the Boston Irish community for making false identifications for illegal aliens.

> Nov. 20, 2000
> "Our duty is to do whatever it takes to bring Whitey Bulger to justice."
> —Charles Prouty, special agent in charge of the FBI's Boston office
> *Boston Globe* on June 21, 2011—reprinted above statement

Boston-based and out-of-town FBI agents then immersed themselves in the search for Bulger in January 2003, seven years after the FBI was refused false driver's license photos and identifications of Bulger. The same month, C-7 agents interviewed the recalcitrant veterans of the MSP Bulger criminal investigation seeking the same information in spite of the fact the four or more fake licenses had expired without renewal. The agents were politely told by the interviewees that they would contact the holder of their request: Massachusetts State Police Colonel Thomas Foley. A four-page working copy authored by C-7 agents contained "information from their [MSP members] memory adding that more specific information such as exact dates could be obtained from their investigative files: SF [MSP] investigators also obtained the biographical information of three females…in anticipation of a request for identifications to be made for Catherine Greig."

The MSP pretty much reiterated the DEA 2004 report, which obviously was not available to the FBI at the time. The interview ended with the FBI agents requesting the MSP representatives "to produce the Bulger photograph and copies of the identifications for review by the FBI." The MSP's opaque response was "We'll think about it and get back to you."

> May 2003
> "I will do whatever it takes to get this guy [Bulger]. I don't care who catches him;
> I just want it over and done with. My goal is to have him caught and move on."
> —Kenneth Kaiser, one month after he was made special agent in charge of the Boston office.
> *Boston Globe* on June 21, 2011—reprinted above statement

Kevin Weeks's earlier debriefing in 1999 revealed to the MSP that another individual was involved in the final product of the four false identifications that were copied by the MSP before delivery to Bulger by a third party because Weeks correctly assumed he was being watched. During Weeks's cooperation, he admitted meeting Bulger in Chicago. At a later date, a road trip was arranged by the rivaling state and federal organizations. They flew Weeks's girlfriend to Chicago, hoping she could recall the hotel where Weeks passed off the false Bulger identifications.

Presumably, the MSP members did not physically surveil Weeks because they were relying in part on electronic pen register information for intelligence purposes.

The FBI Interviews the Source and Lead DEA Agent

Bulger had been a fugitive for nearly ten years when in March 2004 the FBI wrote the new US Attorney Michael Sullivan requesting an interview with the original MSP source seeking a subpoena for the purpose of facilitating what was now a harboring-a-fugitive conspiracy grand jury investigation. A Department of Justice bureaucrat responded, phoning Wyshak, who allegedly told the caller the FBI misrepresented their attempt to interview the said source. The DOJ attorney stated Wyshak told him the source first contacted one of the FBI agents who had met with MSP in the Parker House Hotel room years ago to discuss the production of the Bulger IDs. If true, this is in conflict with what was originally reported by the MSP that the source first contacted Wyshak, and he "reported that the FBI was fully informed regarding the [source's] ID production operation since 1998," as related by the C-7 FBI agent who wrote the memo. The year 1998 could not be confirmed, but Wyshak's statement is in conflict with the FBI memo. The original FBI agents who attended the Parker House clandestine meeting denied ever meeting the source, and one said they were only there at the request of the MSP in case the source would be eligible for the Witness Security Program, which never occurred for lack of viable information. The agent's partner reiterated the same account.

FBI agents from the task force attempted to put the aforementioned early stages (circa 1996–1998) of the Bulger chase into historical perspective by reporting an interview in 2003 with the lead DEA agent because FBI "interviews of Kevin WEEKS had resulted in conflicting accounts." Weeks had given the FBI agents another story. Well over a half dozen years had passed since the DEA agent had been interviewed when he recalled the source first came to the MSP, FBI agents were not involved, and the lead DEA agent "stated that the photographs were not recognized by the Strike Force investigators and no further action was taken." The FBI agents also asserted the MSP personnel and Weeks failed to mention a second source who told the agents Weeks approached him first for the Bulger IDs. Got it? (I completely understand this story can be confusing, but please bear with me.)

In a bit of a stretch, the FBI accused the MSP subjects of the interview of flinching on reports promised but never received by the agents. The real purpose of the back-and forth bickering between the competing parties was the FBI wanted to interview the source and review the reports and notes of the MSP personal, including Wyshak, but was told by the deputy section chief of DOJ Organized Crime and Racketeering, Ken Lowry, that the reports did not exist. The FBI claimed, in laymen's terms, that the DEA and state police team lied at the February 2003 interview, claiming they would review their file for accurate reports.

In an effort to disprove the FBI was informed of the Bulger ID machinations as alleged by the MSP in 1998, the FBI agents internally accused Wyshak of "discontinuing" a US Customs investigation involving the maker of the false Bulger licenses, theorizing it hampered the bureau's future efforts in the case.

The same agents claimed they were unaware of the criminal investigation being conducted by the MSP until June 2000, claiming the strike force was not cooperative given the following reasons:

- When a strike force member was questioned by an FBI agent sometime in 2000 about whether Weeks provided accurate false alias names, the member allegedly replied that Weeks had used the alias Shackleton. [The FBI agent may have confused the answer as being an alias for Weeks and not Bulger because a similar name, Shapeton, later turned up on a list made available to the FBI by the MSP.]
- After three previous attempts, the actual maker of the Bulger false IDs requested and was given immunity. In the process, the FBI gave a presentation to MSP investigators and prosecutors in a successful attempt to solidify the immunity request.

- According to the FBI team, during the presentation, a high-ranking state police officer told an FBI agent and a DOJ staff member the reason the MSP investigators and prosecutors concealed their 1996 investigation from the FBI was Weeks confided that "corruption existed within the FBI." It was noted by the FBI it was three years later in December 1999 when Weeks started cooperating with the federal government.
- The representative FBI agents complained that no Bulger aliases were entered into the nationwide National Crime Information Center, or NCIC, database by the MSP, therefore endangering law enforcement safety and leaving the FBI unaware of those very names.

The FBI agents attached to the task force were not satisfied with the MSP's perceived contradictions. They surmised they got screwed because of MSP interference from 1996 until 2000 and couldn't understand why, thinking the MSP should have pressed for a conspiracy investigation thereby precipitating Bulger's capture. The agents also accused Weeks of not being forthright with his information.

In concluding the March 2004 memo, the FBI's role in trying to interview the source amounted to "a pattern of interference by the Strike Force [MSP] in any effort to investigate the conspiracy to harbor Bulger."

Circumstances surrounding the 1996 initial MSP source were getting perilous. At the outset, all the source desired was anonymity, which then escalated into a piece of the Bulger reward money. According to several untitled FBI working copies of the Bulger fugitive case, a telephone interview with the source was conducted relative to his upcoming scheduled federal grand jury appearance on September 1, 2004. In a startled response to the prospect, the source used a common four-letter expletive, expressing fear Bulger's brother, John, would find out. But at the same time, he was comfortable exposing the names and photographs for Bulger's aliases as long as it would not jeopardize his safety. He feared retaliation by the Bulgers more than being prosecuted by the Feds.

Within weeks of the phone interview, the source and his attorney met with FBI agents and an assistant US attorney at the Moakley Courthouse in Boston for the purpose of signing a proffer agreed to by the source prior to his interview. The newly initiated cooperating witness or source literally joined Weeks in a litany of undated chronological events occurring in 1996 in securing false identifications for Bulger, for whom no fraudulent names were mentioned in the report. Following is my version of a synoptical interpretation of the FBI working copy of the bullet points dated September 14, 2004.

The law enforcement source was approached by a friend, whom I will give the fictitious name of Lenny, asking if IDs for Bulger could be made. The report reads that Lenny stated, "I need IDs (identifications) for Jimmy; this is a personal thing." Evidently, the source was not enthused, responding he would think about it. A day or two later, the source tells Lenny "his guy" (whom I will call Guy) can make IDs. Lenny then receives a camera from the source, and within days, he gives the source an "envelope containing four photographs and a slip of paper with alias names, dates of birth (DOB) and social security cards," as stated by the bullet points. The source believed the photos were Bulger but was not made aware until much later it was Bulger's brother, John.

Kevin Weeks had a friend whom I will name Squiggy who acted as go-between but may have been the photographer for the false IDs. (Lenny and Squiggy, Michael McKean and David Lander, respectively, were oddball fictional characters in the long-running '70s situational comedy known as *Laverne and Shirley*, starring Penny Marshall and Cindy Williams.)

The source provided Guy with a Massachusetts Registry of Motor Vehicles "machine," but they eventually scrapped it. The source then contacted the DEA prior to obtaining IDs from Guy, which resulted in the 1996 meeting the same day at the Parker House where the IDs were viewed by strike force members. (There appears to be a conflict in this statement in that the DEA asserts the source first contacted Wyshak.) Guy and the source had met while serving federal prison time, and Guy was proving to be an invaluable asset to the source. When they next met, the source was handed two Massachusetts driver's licenses, two Rhode Island birth certificates, and two Social Security cards. The next person to handle the fraudulent Bulger ID documents was the lead DEA agent, who made copies in his car, according to the source.

Back to Weeks's friend Lenny, who then arranged a meeting between Weeks and the source at the South Boston Stop & Shop food market in the South Bay Plaza adjacent to the Southeast Expressway. The source delivered the IDs, and Weeks delivered $750.00 in cash for the source of which $350.00 was given to Guy. Two weeks later, Lenny told the source they needed more IDs, and once again, he provided him with a camera. A quick turn-around performed by Lenny delivered an envelope with four more photographs and alias names, dates of birth, and Social Security cards to the source, who immediately supplied them to the lead DEA agent, who presumably made copies. In the final step of the recurring procedure, the source then met Guy at a Boston neighborhood Hyde Park house for the transfer of the envelope containing the fraudulent material for Bulger's false licenses. The source told the FBI he was "packing" (armed) when he met with both Guy and the DEA agent thinking he was being "set up."

Without mentioning from whom, the FBI stated the source received two more Massachusetts driver's licenses, two Rhode Island birth certificates, and two Social Security cards, which were given to the lead DEA agent, who the source "believes" made copies. Four additional photographs were not utilized, but allegedly the source told the FBI agents he had no knowledge of their whereabouts.

The final meeting between Weeks and the source was arranged by Lenny, at Weeks's request, at the same Stop & Shop where they had previously met. The source received one thousand dollars after he handed over the completed false IDs and his own unused, out-of-state Veterans Administration card. The source said he did not know what Weeks did with the IDs, nor did he recall getting IDs with female names for Weeks or Lenny. Guy later received a few hundred dollars from the source.

The Massachusetts Registry of Motor Vehicles plastic laminating sleeves containing the state seal hologram were provided by Squiggy. The FBI said, "he had someone on the inside of the Registry" who provided the plastics to them. The source was so impressed with the craftsmanship, he requested more from Squiggy. According to the source, other than his deceased father, there was no family history with any of the Bulgers.

MSP Version of Events

A trooper in the Special Service Section authored a to-from memo through channels to his commanding officer dated April 26, 2005. The subject: the 1996 James Bulger identifications. Large portions of the report were reflective of the 2004 DEA missive in response to a lack of cooperation as perceived by the FBI. The memo emphasizes the protection of sources, informants, and confidential information being paramount within the criminal investigator's (MSP) scope of managing the pursuit of Bulger.

The trooper conveyed this concern, stating,

> The informant's information was brought to the attention of then Lieutenant Thomas Foley, the commander of the Special Service Section Organized Crime Unit, and the architect of the criminal investigation into James Bulger. Lt. Foley determined that because of the numerous leaks in the current, as well as in prior investigations of James Bulger, and the gang's known proclivity towards violence, this informant's information was to be held within a very tight circle.

In the final paragraph of the report, the trooper reiterated a meeting he and the lead DEA agent had with a Boston police officer assigned to the FBI task force in 2000. The task force had just been made aware the Bulger identifications existed, and the trooper and agent gave "all the information concerning the identifications that we had" to the task force member. Additionally, the trooper met twice "with various task force agents to answer any question they had." As noted in the 2004 DEA report, a meeting was also held in the US attorney's office to settle the issue of inclusion of information among the competing agencies. One area the FBI task force agents would not be privy to was written reports by the strike force because there were not any. The trooper respectfully submitted his report ending with, "No reports on this matter were written, and this was done at the direct [sic] of Colonel Foley, for the protection of the informant and the security of the information."

The same year Bulger became a top-ten fugitive, 1999, former FBI Special Agent John Connolly was arrested for various RICO violations. The axiom "What's past is prologue" resonates in regard to Connolly, who in his career, personified the prologue and Rico the past. Connolly made the same institutional informant misgivings, allowing his snitches (Bulger and Flemmi) to control the supervisor (Connolly), as Rico and Condon did when dealing with Barboza and the Flemmi brothers.

The retired agent was convicted of alerting Bulger and Flemmi of upcoming criminal indictments. Kevin Weeks, upon his arrest for similar charges in 1999, wasted no time becoming a cooperating witness preceded only by John Martorano in 1998. Weeks's veracity proved to be the smoking gun witness the criminal investigators (MSP) needed against Bulger and Flemmi for convictions. His historical perspective alerted and formed the skepticism the MSP members formed in their distrust of the FBI's possible leaking confidential information concerning Bulger, thereby threatening his capture.

From 1995 until 2002, there were eleven confirmed sightings of Bulger, and all but one were within the States, according to a 2007 *Boston Globe* article. FBI headquarters in Washington, DC, finally put a full-court press on in 2011, featuring national and international newspaper and TV ads seeking the capture of Bulger and Catherine Greig. In October of the same year, the renegade couple, who had been living as senior citizens for years in a Santa Monica, California, apartment, were found.

For years, the Bulger family were parishioners at St. Monica's Catholic Church in South Boston, where in January 1980, Trooper Ed Whelan and I, assigned to Attorney General Frank Bellotti's office, tried to get a photo of reputed underworld figure James "Whitey" Bulger possibly attending the funeral mass for his deceased mother, Jean (McCarthy) Bulger. We did not have any idea what Whitey looked like, so Eddie took numerous photos of those in attendance. Our work was in vain because we later learned Whitey may not have attended the service, although rumors circulated for years that he did but in disguise. The point being he was successfully incognito at St. Monica's as he had been for sixteen years a fugitive. Ironically, he was captured in a California town known as Santa (Saint) Monica. St. Monica is revered by the Catholic Church as the patron saint of wives and abuse victims.

INDICTMENTS AND IMMUNITY

CHAPTER 24

Guns for Immunity / Money for Marion

Bulger had been a four-year fugitive as another local hood descended into the federal prison system. "Cadillac" Frank Salemme pleaded guilty to racketeering and extortion charges in 1999 in the same federal courthouse where Flemmi was still fighting an immunity defense that he thought was bequeathed to him by the Feds.

The so-called Winter Hill members were falling like ten pins at the old Lucky Strike bowling alley in the Fields Corner section of Dorchester. Kevin Weeks was arrested in November 1999 at the pleasure of the DEA, the IRS Criminal Investigation Division, and the Massachusetts State Police. Noticeably missing from the well-publicized event were FBI agents from the Boston office. Murder charges were hanging heavy over Weeks's head with the noose tightening around the ex-boxer's thick neck. No FBI Agent John Connolly, Bulger, or Flemmi to the rescue.

Flemmi asserted correctly that Kevin Weeks, Bulger's surrogate son, was ratting him out while he sat helpless in the Plymouth County House of Corrections, awaiting trial for his 1995 arrest. He needed outside help. Flemmi enlisted his son William St. Croix (who had taken his maternal grandmother's maiden name) when he visited his father at the Plymouth federal prison facility in January 2000 with Flemmi's brother, Boston patrolman Michael. Daddy told his son to get the guns the hell out of Grandma's pool house without the pool. Johnny Cash would have had another hit portraying Flemmi's younger brother, his oldest son, and his son's friend Michael Allen schlepping what remained of the arsenal just two days before a federal search warrant for the "detached sunroom" was executed on January 13, 2000.

Flemmi was correct: Weeks led the DEA and state police to the guns. St. Croix and company buried some of the guns in a Somerville backyard and the rest somewhere near Orlando, Florida. Flemmi originally told his son to throw the guns into the ocean. All that remained of the cache was some ammunition clips, several boxes of ammunition, a revolver, handcuffs, brass knuckles, and silencers—basically, a beginner's kit for Winter Hill wise guys.

The annals of Boston organized crime history will record that on the same day as the search for the guns came up short, three bodies of people who had been missing for nearly two decades were found. Weeks was the gift that kept on giving. An embankment of the Southeast Expressway southbound lane in Dorchester was the burial ground where Weeks had previously helped bury the missing persons: John McIntyre, Arthur "Bucky" Barrett, and Debbie Hussey.

The loyal son of a hood who was in the midst of an apprenticeship to emulate his father was emotional and very angry at the discovery of Debbie's body. William wanted an explanation from his imprisoned father. Like Flemmi had done with me in the alleged missing Kaufman money, he got right in the face of his son through inch-thick plexiglass in the prison family visiting room. All he wanted was the truth about Debbie, and he got it in spades. He had to kill her. She was a hooker working for a black pimp, chimed in Flemmi's brother, Michael, who had driven down to the jail with

William. Seven months later, on a warm July day, William and Stephen were sitting on the rear deck of my home trying to be circumspect about what they wanted to talk to me about.

It all started with a June 2000 phone call. William wanted to meet in person because he wished to speak in confidence to somebody who could help him make decisions about a family problem. Once again, Marion's sister played a major role in persuading the brothers to talk to someone they could trust even though I had been retired from the state police for five years. Without mentioning any names, I advised retaining former federal prosecutors who were then in private practice. But at the time, I was not made aware that Uncle Michael had testified that month in front of a federal grand jury investigating Bulger and Flemmi.

Mid-July, I called William from his aunt's house. I was more concerned about the brotherly Boston cop than some hotshot from Southie or Winter Hill making a move if they knew what was transpiring. For the first time, he stated he had information on his father. Immunity was my response. I gave him the name of a few former federal prosecutors who once worked with Assistant US Attorney Fred Wyshak and Brian Kelly, the lead Bulger and Flemmi prosecutors.

After several more phone calls, William and I met at a local Howard Johnson's restaurant in mid-July. "Guns! Bulger and Flemmi's guns?" I quietly shouted. I was blown over. He then went into detail about retrieving a small arsenal of guns from within an interior hidden wall in his grandparents' South Boston cabana house. Without disclosing where, he said he was still in possession of the guns, including one he thought may have been used in a homicide, but he didn't know which one. All I could think before advising he needed a lawyer was, *What the hell!* My second and third thoughts again were immunity. He told me how in the past he held up drug dealers and that he was worried about Jimmy Bulger. To be honest, so was I even though he had been gone for five years. William was awaiting an operation in a Boston area hospital for a cancerous tumor while dealing with his father's and Bulger's cache of weapons. We ended the meeting agreeing not to contact a lawyer until I heard from him.

Eight days later, on July 23, William, Stephen, and I met where William took the lead laying out his criminal liabilities. He said the most recent involvement was fencing a half million dollars in stolen jewelry and ripping off a drug dealer who gave him ninety thousand dollars, which he spent in Florida. Stephen was somewhat reluctant to go against his father, stating the South Boston house he was living in was in trust to him. Strategically, the brothers decided not to contact a lawyer until their father's federal court appeals were exhausted. These two kids were more educated about court proceedings than many attorneys. It was a fascinating three hours.

The decision was made that the former justice department attorney who had successfully prosecuted Michael London for money-laundering and racketeering charges would represent William. I had worked with Michael Kendall hand in hand for several years in preparation for the London trial. He was diligent and top notch. On a Sunday Labor Day weekend morning, William and I met Kendall in his downtown Boston State Street office. Imminent attorney fees, safety and security issues, and immunity provisions were discussed. Kendall would designate me his paralegal. The following Saturday, William was introduced to Assistant US Attorney Fred Wyshak. Within a month of the meeting, the DEA and the state police executed a search warrant at a Somerville home where an arsenal of firearms, including a machine gun, were confiscated. Shortly thereafter, a storage facility outside of Orlando, Florida, was searched, and many more weapons of the Winter Hill gang were recovered.

Within months of William St. Croix receiving immunity from prosecution, retired Boston Police Officer Michael Flemmi was arrested in November for perjury, obstruction of justice, and his part in allegedly helping his nephew remove his brother's weapons. It wasn't until a detention hearing was held several weeks later that it was reported by the *Boston Globe*, "The chilling confession was revealed yesterday in federal court, along with the startling news that William Hussey [St. Croix] is now cooperating against his father and was the one who recently led investigators to a mountain of weapons that allegedly belonged to Bulger and Flemmi."

The competing *Boston Herald* newspaper quoted prosecutors, "Based on information from an unidentified informant [Weeks], they allege Michael Flemmi provided the bulletproof vests that were recovered in 1984 along with seven tons of weapons intended for the IRA." Weeks was an accessory before and after the fact of murdering John McIntyre, the engineer of the *Valhalla*, which was the vessel that transported the weapons and vests to an IRA ship off the Irish coast.

Boston Police Officer Michael Flemmi's son and namesake fought for the thirty-two-year veteran cop at the detention hearing for low bail because Dad was not a flight risk. Michael, an assistant chief inspector for the US Immigration and Naturalization Service, was successful. William St. Croix, who did not want to be a Flemmi in name, was in the process of solidifying a life sentence for his father. In the theater of the absurd, the dichotomy of events of an accused corrupt Boston cop who allegedly was complicit in his brother's notorious criminality prompted his son to literally fall on a sword for him, while the son of a killer was stabbing the same sword into his father.

Another Flemmi brother was going to jail, but this time, it was a decorated Boston cop who spent much of his career in the bomb squad. Dealing with Bulger or Flemmi was tantamount to touching the third rail of electrified rapid-transit tracks. If the third rail did not kill or injure you, Bulger or Flemmi did. After three days of deliberations, Michael Flemmi was facing up to a ten-year prison sentence after a guilty verdict was rendered on May 3, 2002, for perjury, obstruction of justice, illegal possession of his brother's cache of weapons, and being the middleman in fencing stolen jewelry valued over a hundred thousand dollars. Four months later, he began prison life as another corrupt cop.

The twenty-first century, otherwise known as Y2K, immediately brought heartache to the Hussey family. The inaugural month of January was an inauspicious beginning with the discovery of the decomposed body of Marion's daughter, Debbie Hussey, followed by her stepfather admitting to her stepbrother that he had killed Debbie. It would take months before forensic experts positively identified her skeletal remains.

As a response to the jailhouse contrition that Flemmi killed Debbie, it was seven months before William St. Croix was able to get his head around the fact that a father he honestly admired and loved could commit such an atrocious homicidal act. Finally, after numerous discussions with his mother, her sister, his brother, and this writer, he capitulated and agreed to retain an attorney who legally saved him from himself and a life of crime.

Over twenty years of grief had already taken a toll on Marion and her sons when Marion and Flemmi's daughter, Stephanie, succumbed to years of drug addiction in 2007.

In preparation for a 2009 wrongful death lawsuit in the US District Court of Massachusetts by Marion's lawyer against the federal government in the death of Debbie, a file I had compiled as a result of her decades-old missing person investigation was turned over to State Police Detective Lieutenant Steve Johnson and Marion's attorney Ann Donovan. It wasn't until then that evidence contained in the file was presented at trial, disclaiming the opposing government's contentious claim that Marion had not filed the lawsuit in a timely manner. Aside from my file, testimony was needed to prove Marion made an effort in prior years to find Debbie, which would have satisfied the federal statute of limitation laws. In fact, a Californian named Debbie Ann was located who had the same date and month of birth as William, but her driver's license thumbprint did not match Debbie Hussey's. Desperate and unconvinced, Marion contacted the young lady in 1998 in a futile attempt to locate her daughter, who had been rotting for five years in a shallow grave before being found in 2000 by the DEA and the state police with the invaluable assistance of Kevin Weeks.

Under cross-examination by no less than three very aggressive justice department lawyers, who pressed the witness on the stand, asking, "Who did the retired state trooper trust when he opened the secret inquiry into the Debbie Hussey disappearance?" I responded, "It was very difficult in those times to trust anyone in law enforcement from the FBI on down," as quoted in the *Boston Herald*. The paper further stated, "there was one truth about Flemmi Saccardo dared not leave to chance: Knowing who Marion was living with and who he was—Stephen Flemmi," he said, "It became a well-known fact that he had friends in law enforcement."

Upon reflection, my statement "on down" also encompassed certain members of not only the FBI but the state police as well. The so-called "Boston 7" were Boston police officers who in 1988 were found guilty of various federal racketeering charges. The FBI supervisor of the investigation was an admitted recipient of gifts and seven thousand dollars in cash he took from Bulger and Flemmi. Special Agent John Morris confessed to the crimes after he was immunized, but serious jail time was handed out to the Boston cops who were far less gifted. Retired State Police Lieutenant Richard Schneiderhan was convicted of obstructing justice in 2003 and spent several years in prison for his misdeeds.

The government defense lawyers were relentless in trying to prevent Marion from claiming the FBI was responsible for the wrongful death of her daughter at the hands of Bulger and Flemmi. An example of how ruthless one of the government lawyers was in defending their argument showed when the *Boston Globe* quoted the lawyer saying Marion "lived on 'blood money' from Flemmi for years and cannot blame the FBI for her daughter's death."

Debbie Hussey was murdered by Bulger and Flemmi approximately five years after Flemmi's girlfriend Debra Davis. Her estate and the remaining family members were colitigants in the same trial as the Husseys, but the judge did not find enough evidence to award them a winning verdict. In retrospect, if Olga Davis had years earlier cooperated with a couple of sincere FBI agents investigating Flemmi, the terrible ordeal she suffered could have been avoided.

Judge Young eventually awarded Marion a three-hundred-thousand-dollar settlement for the loss of Debbie essentially because FBI Agent John Connolly lost control of the master manipulators, Bulger and Flemmi. Marion passed away as a result of brain cancer in 2019.

During the Hussey trial, I was having a conversation outside the courtroom with DEA Agent Dan Doherty. Standing nearby was a fellow I never thought I would shake hands with. Dan asked if I would like to meet Kevin Weeks. I introduced myself, immediately blurting, "Twenty years ago, if I had to, I would have shot you." He did not blink an eye. Once I got by that pleasantry, I queried him about a Southie kid who was found shot to death off Route 93 in Manchester, New Hampshire, back in 1984. At the time, *Boston Globe* columnist Mike Barnicle speculated in his column that a kid who had just robbed a South Boston liquor store owned by prominent local hoods (inference being Bulger et alia) was a dead man. A month later, the bullet-riddled body of Southie native Bryan Watson was found in New Hampshire. Weeks deflected my question, proposing the homicide victim came into the then South Boston Liquor Mart trying to sell a sawed-off shotgun, which Weeks claims he declined. He then named a couple of drug dealers as suspects in the unsolved murder of Watson. On May 31, 2022 Michael Lewis, 61, pleaded not guilty in Suffolk Superior Court for the murder of South Boston native Brian Watson.

CHAPTER 25

Ivan

He looked terrible, even though it was the best he had looked in years. The diamond stud earring and his long-standing goatee were gone. His neatly starched white dress shirt and bright-colored necktie were well coordinated with the dark, neatly tailored business suit that no one could remember seeing him in before. Detracting from his sartorial splendor were tears of fear rolling down his large, puffy jowls with bloodshot eyes to match his tie.

Massachusetts State Trooper John Zannon Naimovich, #754, also known as Ivan, was by far the most unorthodox and nonconformist undercover trooper the job had recently experienced. For two decades, beginning in the 1970s, he investigated illegal gambling and organized crime from the Berkshires to Cape Cod.

But now, Naimovich was on trial at the old Post Office Square federal courthouse in Boston for allegedly passing confidential law enforcement information to his longtime informant "Sammy," also known as Fran Mac.

The humiliation and stress of this state trooper facing ten years in prison for five counts of federal charges had met its tipping point this solemn day in the spring of 1989.

Trooper Naimovich, forty-seven, was displaying all the emotions a man could display as he was sitting nervously on a hard wooden bench outside the courtroom where jurors were preparing to hear further testimony from prosecution witnesses. Halfway through the trial, fellow troopers were waiting to testify.

The most notable defense witness was a no-nonsense, stand-up trooper who had worked side by side with Naimovich in a recent illegal gambling wiretap in Norfolk County, south of Boston. Trooper Steve Lowell would have no problem defending his friend. Also waiting to lend credence to Naimovich's innocence was Matt Connolly, a noble and brave Norfolk County assistant district attorney. Because the trial witnesses were sequestered, they were not privy to what Federal Prosecutor Gregg Sullivan was presenting as evidence and testimony against the defendant. The emotions subsided a bit as Gerry, John's wife of twenty years, stood at his shoulder trying to console him.

What must have been going through the mind of this robust, middle-aged man who was being reduced to a dish rag of psychological upheaval? How did an otherwise stellar career get to this point?

Long before the trial started, Ivan had three strikes against him formed by a troika consisting of a misguided federal prosecutor, an FBI agent known as the "Shah," and an ambitious state police captain.

What happened to Ivan, my fellow trooper and good friend, should not have happened. Sometimes in the zeal to weed out the bad eggs, some of the good eggs get broken. And while men of the criminal and law enforcement world battle daily, a female employee of the FBI will play a role, unseen until too late.

I will try to tell this story as dispassionately as I can, letting the facts speak for themselves. I based this narrative on my own experience and many hours reviewing the transcripts of Ivan's trial.

Ivan, as he was known to his close friends on the job, was born in Chelsea, Massachusetts, to Zannon and Assunta (Scopa) during World War II. He spent most of his early childhood like any kid from the neighborhood. After graduation from Chelsea High School, he landed a meat cutter job at one of the many processing plants in the city. When he entered the State Police Academy in 1964, he had already become familiar with many prospective bookies and wise guys from the Chelsea area.

Walking through the streets of Chelsea, Ivan would pass the home where lived two future FBI agent brothers whose mother was a nurse married to a practicing family physician who regularly made house calls in the less distinguished areas of the city. FBI Special Agents Nicholas and Charles Gianturco, sons of unselfish servants of health care, went on to have stellar careers in the bureau.

Upon graduation from the State Police Academy, Ivan spent several years as a road trooper before being transferred to an assignment where he had an opportunity to display his street smarts. Working out of the Plymouth County DA's Office in an undercover role as a bookie, in 1976, he infiltrated an illegal gambling operation in the small seacoast town of Scituate just fifteen miles south of Boston. At the time, I was a member of the state police illegal gambling enforcement unit known as the Special Service Unit, or SSU, and was temporarily assigned to assist Ivan in the investigation.

A convicted bookie and blood relative to a prominent Boston politician, Weymouth resident James Timilty, also known as "the Fox," practiced his trade in a rented South Shore apartment. He was under physical and electronic surveillance as a result of intelligence Ivan provided in his capacity as a local bookie. The unlicensed Timilty always drove his big white gas-guzzling Lincoln Town Car (with a politically acquired four-digit vanity license plate) under the speed limit in the right lane to his out-of-town bookie office.

Independent bookies like Timilty were forcibly being taken over by members of the Winter Hill gang. Timilty had been monitored for several weeks taking mundane sports bets over his rented apartment and home phone. Almost by accident or fate, John Martorano called Timilty at home. A five-minute one-way monitored conversation produced direct evidence that the caller was instructing Timilty in certain aspects of sports bookmaking. This incriminating call provided fodder for the rumor that suburban bookies south of Boston were being extorted in the form of paying "rent" to Martorano, Bulger, and Flemmi, who were the leaders of the Winter Hill / South Boston gang.

Led by Ivan, days before Christmas 1976, the principals of the illegal gambling ring, Martorano, Timilty, Richard O'Brien, James Matera, and several dozen bookies, were arrested for various state gambling violations by troopers from the Plymouth DA's Office, the SSU, and the Quincy Police.

In the mid-'80s, the SSU was the premier organized crime investigative body in Massachusetts, rivaling the FBI section known as C-3. Undoubtedly, agents from C-3 were provided with many more resources than the state police, such as personnel, wiretap equipment, informants, and money. Along with the external rivalry between the agencies, an internal one among SSU troopers was festering.

A soon-to-be superintendent/colonel was promoted to captain and transferred from the SSU to internal affairs. Several other troopers, along with Captain Charles Henderson, who had successfully led the SSU for many years, were also transferred. Simultaneously, organizational restructuring occurred, transitioning the unit to a section allowing a captain to command. Instead of Captain Henderson, E. David Mattioli was chosen to fill the position on October 19, 1987.

As would have happened in many professions, the highly competitive Henderson and Mattioli became rivals. Caught up in a vortex of circumstances, Ivan unwittingly became the victim of the personal animus between the captains. Ivan probably was Henderson's most prolific writer of affidavits, search warrants, and other sundry assignments relating to and securing wiretaps of the "muffs," as they were referred to by Henderson. Ivan was the senior trooper and the most experienced after many years of bookie cases, and as a result, he had established a retinue of confidential informants. He was also a Henderson loyalist.

Soon after the transition, an intelligence component was added to the section requiring additional troopers. The newly appointed Mattioli recruited personnel from his former position with the Worcester DA's office. Next to arrive on the scene of the enveloping vortex was C-3 Supervisor Special Agent James Ring, the former resident FBI agent for the Worcester area. He and Mattioli were allies.

After taking command, absent any viable state police policy about the use of informants, Mattioli pressed his troops to informally identify their "snitches," as they were affectionately called. Ivan pushed back because he didn't trust his new supervisor, and as he argued, there wasn't any official policy supporting Mattioli's demand. I had been recently promoted to staff sergeant as a patrol supervisor and transferred from the SSU with an office one floor below Ivan's in the Framingham barracks. One day, Ivan paid me a visit explaining to me his dilemma and seeking advice. I told him to peruse the *Boston Globe* obituary pages, pick a name or two, submit them to the brass, and let them prove otherwise. Ivan never revealed his informants to the captain. Upon reflection, I firmly believe that Mattioli already had a line on Ivan's informants.

Ring was FBI, but he was slowly interjecting himself in the formation of the newly crafted state police intelligence unit, wherein he strategically placed himself in a position to probe decades of confidential files through Mattioli. In retrospect, it was apparent that those files could have possibly flowed from Ring into the hands of fellow C-3 subordinate Special Agent John J. Connolly Jr., handler of informants Bulger and Flemmi. I am sure Ring did not consult with Mattioli about my assertion.

The Boston division of the FBI C-3 squad and the Massachusetts State Police, under the direction of Chief of Detectives Lieutenant Colonel John O'Donovan, forged a viable working relationship beginning in the 1960s that proved to be productive and beneficial to all parties, including the tax-paying citizens of the Commonwealth.

Colonel O'D, as he was commonly referred to, was a formidable figure both in fortitude and contrariness. In 1977, he attended the 111th FBI session of the very prestigious local and state police six-month training program at the FBI Academy in Quantico, Virginia, where he had the stones to announce to all in attendance that he believed Whitey Bulger was an FBI informant. The normal FBI lobotomy on the students did not faze the prophetic O'D, who faced down the doubters.

During the colonel's tenure, extremely successful joint FBI/MSP investigations flourished. Most noteworthy were the illegal gambling wire known as Operation Grandslam (circa 1975); the hijacking case of 1979, known as Lobster; the loan shark wiretap targeting Revere Mafia soldier hitman Frank Oreto Sr., in 1984; the Heller's Café money-laundering investigation in Chelsea; and the investigation of the extortionist acts conducted inside a sandwich shop involving Vincent Ferrara in 1986.

Ivan also was the trooper who provided informant information for the 1981 Lancaster Street affidavit application to bug the garage where Bulger, Flemmi, and the Angiulo brothers were targeted by the state police—only to possibly be thwarted by FBI C-3 squad members who were preparing a Title III wire on the North End meeting place of the Angiulos.

Scores of other troopers, including Ivan, had participated in one form or another, in several of these operations. However, at the time, Ivan would have had minimal knowledge of an FBI bug planted in a storage room adjacent to the Vanessa's sandwich shop at the Prudential Center on Boylston Street, Boston. This was where Ferrara and friends were overheard by FBI agents and state police troopers shaking down a couple of elderly Jewish bookmakers for a half million dollars.

On January 14, 1987, the sandwich shop storeroom bug picked up Harold "Doc" Sagansky and longtime partner Moe Weinstein being coerced into contributing to the future defense fund of Ferrara and his friends. The extortionists sold themselves short, however, because early in the '50s Sagansky became a multimillionaire operating an illegal numbers racket for the Angiulo crime family; Sagansky had paid tribute to them for years.

But oddly enough, on the same day that Doc and Moe were being extorted, subsequent incriminating conversations between the extortionist Ferrara and company came to an end as a result of unsubstantiated leaks. At the time, no legitimate attribution by either the bureau or state police had determined the source of the purported tip-off to the Mafiosa extortionist.

On April 4, 1987, James Tournas, a counter-electronic-surveillance expert, conducted an unsuccessful sweep of the shakedown storage room accompanied by Mafia capo "Sonny" Mercurio. Within days of the counter-surveillance, the bug intercept was discontinued by the FBI after operating for six months. There is nothing unusual about gangsters attempting to debug meeting places. In fact, the North End Mafia Lancaster Street debugging did not locate the state police–installed bug. Years later, Bulger found a bug in his motor vehicle, which was immediately retrieved by the DEA installers. Nonetheless, the following month, Ivan and Trooper Steve Lowell—with Norfolk County Assistant District Attorney Matt Connolly—began a wiretap operation targeting major bookies that took up most of the year.

Meanwhile, in June 1987, federal search warrants were executed for the premises of Vanessa's storage room and Vincent Ferrara's car. Little evidence was found in the room except loose dollar bills in a safe. Ferrara's car was another matter.

Found in Ferrara's car was a three-by-four-inch, seventy-page address book listing over 250 names, addresses, and phone numbers. In fact, the book contained the names of over a dozen Boston-area Mafia leaders and soldiers, including Sonny Mercurio, Dominic Isabella, and Carmen Tortora, to name a few. Money launderer Mike London was prominently listed along with Doc Sagansky and at least a dozen prominent Boston bookies, such as James Katz, Chico Krantz, Frank Russo, Richie Gambale, and Joey Yerardi. The name of Chelsea bookmaker Sammy Berkowitz, who received a presidential pardon by Ronald Reagan in 1984, was also included.

FBI agents leafed through the worn pages of the book like it was the latest issue of *Playboy*. One name was so intriguing that an FBI agent assigned to C-3 was tasked in the fall of 1987 to pursue this individual. What intrigued the agents was a local phone number printed next to the pseudonym Fran Mac. Normal investigative procedure by the FBI revealed that five years earlier, Francis J. McIntyre Jr., was arrested for illegal gambling when troopers from the SSU, led by Trooper Naimovich, raided the same address the phone number was listed for in Canton, Massachusetts. The FBI then set out "to develop probable cause setting forth McIntyre's activities as a bookmaker."

According to an FBI affidavit, "Subsequently, probable cause was developed on other bookmakers in the Boston area and the investigation into McIntyre's specific activities regarding illegal gambling was discontinued in September, 1987." The affidavit does not mention probable cause or what legal action was taken with those bookmakers, nor does the affidavit provide any names. Under normal circumstances, troopers assigned to the SSU should have independently pursued the bookie (if the FBI shared the phone book information), but as a matter of interest, the troopers did not pursue any major bookies listed in the Ferrara phone book. However, these were not normal circumstances because of a clandestine state police internal investigation targeting one of their own.

Even though the McIntyre investigation was discontinued by the FBI, under Mattioli, the state police, who were partners in the Vanessa bug operation, for some anonymous reason, subpoenaed telephone toll records for a phone number subscribed to Ivan at his New Hampshire summer home. (As a state police administrative matter, troopers have to provide all personal contact information, including phone numbers.) Ivan's New Hampshire toll records represented the months May through September 1987.

An analysis of the toll records included calls between Ivan and Fran Mac (who was listed in Ferrara's phone book), which may have retroactively spawned suspicion that Ivan was leaking to Mac about Vanessa's six-month bug in the aftermath of Vanessa's storeroom being debugged. But why did Ivan even come under suspicion in the first place, prompting Mattioli to request his phone toll information?

In October 1987, four months after Ferrara's phone book was seized, Mattioli requested Ivan's New Hampshire home phone toll records. That same month, an FBI document reveals an FBI confidential informant related an uncorroborated tale about another unnamed person who was a source of law enforcement investigative information being given to bookmaker Mac. The confidential informant further stated that Fran Mac (Francis McIntyre) paid money or rent to La Cosa Nostra to stay in business. That tidbit was already known to the FBI when Ferrara and Sonny Mercurio were recorded on December 22, 1986, on the Vanessa's bug discussing Fran Mac's rent payment.

Daniel Forte, also known as Tony Cee, was the informant who was alleging that confidential law enforcement information was being leaked to Fran Mac. Forte had been arrested in the Frank Oreto Sr., loan-sharking case in 1984, and his subsequent two-month stint as a snitch for Trooper Tom Foley and FBI Agent Nick Gianturco was unremarkable, as was his information.

The FBI C-3 Organized Crime Squad Supervisory Special Agent James Ring needed an insurance policy against what was coming, and the documented Forte / Tony Cee information would serve the purpose for his and the FBI's plausible deniability. On October 19, 1987, Captain Eugene David Mattioli officially assumed command of the Special Service Section, or SSS. At the time, Ivan and his mentor, internal affairs investigator Captain Henderson, had no idea that Mattioli was analyzing Ivan's and Mac's telephone toll records.

Paralleling Mattioli's cursory investigation of Ivan, an FD-302 report by Special Agent Nick Gianturco stated, "TONY CEE advised that he met 'LEMON LOU' FOTI at the NORTH REVERE CIVIC CLUB at approximately 12:40 p.m. and went with FOTI on his numbers pickup." Tony Cee was a pseudonym for FBI informant Daniel Forte, who had been tape-recording factions of the Vinny Ferrara crew on November 9, 1987. Tony Cee traveled by car with "Lemon Lou," picking up number slips at a half dozen locations throughout the North Shore of Boston before finally depositing them in an apartment mailbox on Salem Street in the North End in an attempt to get close to Ferrara for the purposes of informing. Tony Cee was also looking to borrow two thousand dollars from Ferrara using Foti as an intermediary. Presumably, Tony Cee needed the money for his lawyer, who was defending him in an earlier assault case at one of Ferrara's hangouts, Fasad's, in Revere.

Thanksgiving of 1987 was fast approaching when on November 25, FBI Special Agent Brian Rossi phoned Mac for the first time at his home to set up a meeting. As a result of Ivan's toll analysis, Rossi had just been informed that Ivan and Mac had been communicating. A review of Mac's toll calls revealed he made a one-minute call on the same day the agent visited him and a seven-minute call on Thanksgiving Day from his Canton home to Ivan, who was celebrating the holiday with his family in New Hampshire. Rossi's call was a pretext to see who Mac might call after Rossi hung up. Previous to the call, Mattioli had Mac's phone records in his possession containing Ivan's toll calls.

FBI Special Agent Vincent de la Montaigne was advised sometime in November by Mattioli that Ivan had been assigned to a "special electronic surveillance project" since November 1. In reality, Ivan had been working hand in hand with Norfolk County Assistant District Attorney Matt Connolly since May on a steadily progressive wiretap targeting some of the same prominent organized crime bookies, such as Abe Sarkis and Mel Berger, as the bureau. De la Montaigne was then slated as the case agent targeting Mac.

Former Norfolk County Assistant District Attorney Matt Connolly explains in his 2013 blog what happened next.

> On October 24 (1987) we went up on the Milton home of Abe Sarkas (sic). Abe has been mentioned in the Whitey trial [Matt wrote the blog during the trial] as the guy who ran all the booking for the Boston Mafia's Larry Zannino. We'd stay

up on that phone until December 14; we went up Mel Berger's phone in Newton. Mel was the man at the top of the Jewish bookmaking empire who was also mentioned during the [Bulger] trial and stayed up between November 1 through December 14; and we put a bug in Abe Sarkas's (sic) office between November 24 and December 9. We are knocking at the door of the leaders of organized crime including Whitey and Stevie (Flemmi).

Matt Connolly and especially Ivan were now in direct competition for the attention of Bulger and Flemmi. They were targeting the same bookies as those who were indicted in Grandslam, the 1975 FBI/MSP joint operation. Ivan had previously provided informant information for the 1981 Lancaster Street affidavit application to bug the garage where Bulger, Flemmi, and the Angiulo brothers were targeted by the state police, only to be thwarted by C-3 squad members who were preparing a Title III wire on the North End headquarters of the Angiulos.

The FBI still wanted to know why Mac's number was in the Ferrara phone book, so Agent Rossi again phoned Mac on November 30, and they agreed to meet at his home in Canton between 11:00 a.m. and 1:30 p.m. Mac told Rossi "that he had met Vinnie Ferrara approximately six (6) times about a year and a half ago." He further stated that sometime later he saw Ferrara's picture in the newspaper as being part of the "new faction" of the Boston La Cosa Nostra.

A portion of the interview with Mac was transformed into a de la Montaigne affidavit in support of an application to tap Mac's home phones. Within one month of rookie informant Dan Forte, also known as Tony Cee, wearing a wire targeting Ferrara, de la Montaigne wrote, "McIntyre further advised tha (sic) he knew of 'one guy' who was one of the biggest bookmakers in the Boston area and that this individual was 'Chico.'" Chico's true identity was Burton L. Krantz. McIntyre also identified Harold "Doc" Sagansky as being "big in numbers," but McIntyre provided no additional information regarding Sagansky. Another large-scale bookmaker identified by McIntyre was Melvin E. Berger. A review of the FBI's organized crime information system would reveal numerous references to Krantz, Sagansky, and Berger for "illegal gambling."

Chico Krantz was "One of the biggest bookmakers in the Boston area," according to McIntyre. Krantz became a bit of a celebrity, appearing on Boston's Channel 5 TV news program, pontificating about his wagering prowess. That was the year the New England Patriots football team began the 1985 season with a two and four record, finishing eleven and five. They beat the spread on points scored in twelve of fourteen games. The bookies were getting creamed that record-breaking year. Krantz presented himself on the program as an authority on sports betting, particularly the spread, or what is commonly referred to as "the line." His expertise was in structuring the lines, defined like this: the gambler usually wagers that the difference between the scores of two teams will be less than or greater than the value specified by the bookmaker. Spread betting was first introduced by Charles E. McNeil, a math teacher from Connecticut who became a bookmaker in Chicago in the 1940s. (Krantz was a key player in the Mike London 1986 money-laundering wiretap but was not indicted.) After a ten-year battle with cancer, he died in 1998 while in the federal Witness Security Program.

But I digress.

Mac was being extorted by Vinnie Ferrara, and the bureau knew it, yet Supervisory Special Agent Ring missed the opportunity to flip Mac into a potential confidential informant or cooperating witness. Instead, he decided it was more appropriate to tap the phones of the extortion victim to get another more important target: the law enforcement official who was allegedly leaking information. And that target would be Ivan.

De la Montaigne was looking to bolster intelligence and probable cause for his forthcoming affidavit, so, he installed pen registers on Mac's two phones on December 4, 1987. (There is no statute providing for a pen register in Massachusetts state wiretap law; only the Feds have such a law.)

This precursor for establishing probable cause would enable de la Montaigne to identify the phone number for outgoing calls and then subpoena the phone company for the name of the subscriber. For some unexplained reason, the pen registers did not function correctly and were abandoned a week later. Several weeks after the pen registers failed, de la Montaigne applied for the Title III without the benefit of "particularized evidence," which is a presumptive legal standard for probable cause. Days before Christmas, a federal judge signed the application for the tap on Mac's phones. Six weeks later, both wiretaps were terminated, and two days after that, a true bill, or indictment, was returned by a federal grand jury sitting in Boston immediately after the Feds and state police executed over a dozen search warrants for bookie offices, including Mac's home in Canton, on the night of January 29.

On the same evening, Mattioli and de la Montaigne proceeded to Mac's house and availed themselves of an opportunity to *interview* him for nearly four hours without the prerequisite Miranda warnings. Ivan's name never came up and was not the subject of conversation.

And yet, for the Feds, things were moving exceptionally fast because shortly thereafter a superseding indictment charged that John Naimovich and Francis McIntyre were engaged in criminal activity amounting to five counts of obstruction of justice and conducting an illegal gambling business, including federal violations amounting to thirty-three acts of racketeering.

Page 3 of the *Boston Herald* dated February 4, 1988, had a sensational headline—"Trooper 'Loses Gamble.'" Beneath the headline, a photo showed an unshaven Ivan wearing a scally cap leaving the Boston federal courthouse after his arraignment. According to the paper, he was charged with sharing sensitive information about organized crime investigations with a criminal ring of sports gamblers.

The related news article reported how Ivan had been arrested the day before in his Framingham office by State Police Colonel Thomas Fitzgerald and Commander Captain David Mattioli. What the article didn't mention, according to troopers who were present, is that Mattioli called an 8:30 a.m. meeting, and, in front of his fellow troopers, threw Ivan against a filing cabinet, had him spread-eagle his legs, handcuffed him behind his back, and frog-walked him downstairs to a barracks cell, in the process completely humiliating him for life.

The harsh treatment Ivan received at the hands of Mattioli was in sharp contrast to a 1974 *Boston Herald* photo depicting Steve Flemmi walking into Boston Police Headquarters, *uncuffed*, and being escorted by two Boston police detectives. He had just surrendered himself on a warrant issued by the Suffolk Superior Court in 1969 for the murder of William Bennett.

State Police Commissioner William McCabe was quoted in the *Boston Herald* as saying Ivan was a twenty-three-year veteran of the force who had betrayed his oath to uphold the law as well as his fellow officers. "It is therefore fitting that these same troopers whom he is charged with betraying were able to conduct this joint investigation," said McCabe.

But allowing troopers of the same rank and fellow union members to investigate a brother was a complete breach of investigative standards and ethics by McCabe; in retrospect, experienced internal affairs investigators should have been utilized to work with the FBI.

One problem, Captain Henderson, Ivan's former supervisor, was assigned to the unit by McCabe. The commissioner mistakenly displayed a bias and a lack of trust against internal affairs and the commissioned officers' mission of investigating troopers up to the rank of captain in favor of troopers assigned to the Special Services Section. A precedent had previously been set back in the early 1980s when the state attorney general was investigating a trooper, and McCabe's predecessor smartly assigned internal affairs officers to assist in the probe.

Not only had the *Boston Herald* convicted Ivan, but Commissioner McCabe sounded the clarion of gratification when quoted in the *Boston Globe*, stating, "It's a sad day, but there is a certain amount of pride knowing we did it ourselves." High-ranking federal and state law enforcement officials in Massachusetts, from US Attorney Frank McNamara, head of the justice department organized crime strike force, to Jeremiah O'Sullivan; Special Agent in Charge of the Boston FBI office James Ahern; Commissioner McCabe; and Colonel Fitzgerald, were all quoted in the Boston papers deriding the yet untried trooper.

This bunch could have formed their own Boston chapter of the iconic Irish Clover Club (no women allowed): the Hibernians' answer to the crusted Brahmin-established Algonquin Club.

Conspicuously absent from the public relations circus was the C-3 supervisor since 1983 who did not publicly comment. Agent Ring had supervised the affiant and case agent de la Montaigne in Ivan's case. Shortly after Ivan's arrest, Ring passed me in the state police Framingham barracks parking lot. He stopped his vehicle, leaned out the window, and said—I paraphrase—"I'm sorry about John's arrest." I was in no position to be placated, one way or another, because I had no idea or inkling at the time about Ivan's guilt or innocence.

A twenty-eight-page superseding indictment charging Ivan and Fran Mac was presented covering the period "from on or about 5-1-85, and continuing to on or about 2-2-88." The justice department charged the defendants with everything short of corrupting the youth of America.

Mac signed a memorandum of agreement authored by cosignatory Jeremiah O'Sullivan on March 1, 1988, stipulating that as a cooperating witness, he had to agree to "cooperation in the investigation and prosecution of Vincent Ferrara, John Naimovich and others." The memo was structured in such a way if he entered a guilty plea and was not truthful about everything he knew about Ferrara and Ivan, he would face prosecution for perjury.

I'm sure Mrs. Mac could not have been very pleased when state troopers in street clothes came busting through her residence in 1982 looking for evidence of illegal bookmaking apparatus. The search of the four-bedroom center-entrance colonial situated in a rather tony neighborhood produced enough evidence to arrest Mac for registering bets and using the telephone for illegal gambling. Before the year was over, he would plead guilty in Stoughton District Court, paying a two-thousand-dollar fine for both charges. For the next five years, Mac had gotten the proverbial "pass"—a term which became prominent at the upcoming trial of both defendants. The Latin translation for *pass* in civilian life is "quid pro quo." As long as Mac was the gift that kept on giving, he was allowed to stay in the bookmaking business.

Ivan hired two highly respected former assistant district attorneys, Tom Drechsler and Alex Nappan, for his defense. The full resources of the federal justice system and the wrath produced would be enormous. Troopers who did not care for the usually bellicose defendant did not wish him well, surmising he was guilty as hell. The normal professional rivalry between the bureau and state police was acute but not as problematic as within Ivan's brotherhood. Rumors had been around for years that Mattioli and Henderson did not care for each other, as their careers were paralleling. Ivan was a tremendous asset for the SSU and Henderson. His talents made the lieutenant look good, and Henderson appreciated it. But Mattioli was cautious and skeptical of Ivan and didn't trust him, probably because of his relationship with Henderson.

CHAPTER 26

My Informant, Your Informant

Nearly a year after Ivan's arrest, the legal machinations began when Mattioli had to respond to a letter sent by Ivan's defense attorney, Alex Nappan, in response to his January 1989 inquiry questioning state police written policy regarding identifying informants. Mattioli stated, "Prior to my assuming command of the Special Service Section there was no written policy concerning the identification of informants. It is my understanding that the section commanding officer [Henderson] knew the identity of each Trooper's informant(s)."

"Since I assumed command of the Special Service Section, on October 19, 1987, I required that each informant's identity be documented in writing and this documentation be maintained under my control."

The remaining scripture as written by Mattioli related to exculpatory information pertaining to the upcoming trial of Ivan.

Mattioli concluded, "I understand that it is essential for a defendant to have the necessary information available to him to prepare for trial. I would suggest the best avenue for information you are requesting is through the formal filing of motions in the federal court."

Without knowing Mattioli's thought process in analyzing his logic (or that of whoever penned the letter), he pivots by attempting to focus blame on the lack of a state police informant policy, but he understands his predecessor, Captain Henderson, "knew the identity of each Trooper's informant(s)."

If there was no policy and the previous commander knew the identity of the trooper's informants, why didn't Mattioli simply ask Henderson, the senior officer in charge of internal affairs? Upon receipt of Nappan's letter to Mattioli, the defense motions were coming in all directions toward the prosecution. Mattioli had gotten his wish.

In response to defense attorney discovery motions, Mattioli then had to compose an affidavit. He defended his lack of awareness that Mac was Ivan's informant before the de la Montaigne affidavit was submitted, and neither then Major Henderson nor Corporal Haley (Ivan's immediate supervisor) told him "the identities of any of Naimovich's informants." He then denied withholding any information from de la Montaigne about Ivan's activities and affirmed he did not lie about contributing information to the affidavit nor was that information "intentionally or recklessly misrepresented." He signed the affidavit under pains and penalties of perjury on March 10, 1989, notarized by former Democrat Massachusetts attorney general Martha Coakley.

In addition to his initial twenty-eight-page affidavit, Agent de la Montaigne coincidentally filed a ten-page affidavit on the same date as Mattioli, which I interpret as de la Montaigne's *mea culpa, mea culpa, mea maxima culpa*. I suspect de la Montaigne realized Ivan was being railroaded.

After agreeing with prosecution to throw Ivan under the bus, Mac had a new ride. During his debriefing by the FBI and state police, they first learned that Mac had lied about Ivan leaking information to him, which was contained in de la Montaigne's original affidavit.

Mac recanted his statement that Ivan told him about a barbooth game in the North Shore of Boston, but the agent still thought it possible Ivan could have "tipped the operators…through another means other than McIntyre."

Paragraph 7 of the de la Montaigne affidavit reads as follows:

> McIntyre also revealed that while Naimovich had told McIntyre in advance that the Prudential Center would be searched, Naimovich had not informed him that the electronic surveillance was being conducted at that location until sometime in June 1987.

(If true, it was two months after the bug was terminated at Vanessa's.) De la Montaigne continues,

> Accordingly, McIntyre did not tell Ferrara earlier, as had been believed, that the location at Vanessa's was bugged, resulting in criminal conversations diminishing and an electronic sweep being conducted to locate listening devices in April of 1987. However, because of another piece of information leaked by Naimovich and provided to Ferrara, it is believed that existence of electronic surveillance was incidentally revealed by McIntyre.

This last sentence is confusing because Naimovich allegedly provided information to Ferrara, and McIntyre revealed the wiretap, but the agent did not provide any corroboration or evidence of either accusation.

Paragraph 10 may be bordering on the willful giving of a false statement, wherein the agent cites,

> At the time of the execution of the electronic surveillance affidavit, I was completely unaware that McIntyre had an informant relationship with Naimovich. My primary contact

at the State Police for the investigation was Captain E. David Mattioli.

Mattioli joined Ivan under the bus.

Preceding the de la Montaigne involvement in the investigation, he was undercover in a five-year East Boston Mafia assignment. He may not have been tuned in to the state police players and was thrown into a conundrum not of his making by his supervisor, Agent Ring.

The remaining twelve paragraphs pertain to de la Montaigne maintaining McIntyre was given a pass because he was an informant for Ivan and that Corporal Haley was not interviewed "due to the extremely sensitive nature of the investigation until after the electronic surveillance had terminated and the original nature of the indictment had been returned." On two different occasions in August 1987, the agent inquired of unidentified troopers as to their knowledge of Mac. He further stated, "my inquiries were met with negative results. At no time was I told that McIntyre enjoyed an informant relationship with Naimovich, nor did I have any reason to suspect that he did." Imagine a state trooper investigating Whitey Bulger and inquiring if Agent John Connolly was sharing confidential law enforcement secrets with Bulger. Agent Ring would likely have had the trooper indicted for treason.

March 1989 proved to be a fortuitous month for filing motions by the opposing counsels. The justice department made an innocuous attempt to deflect Ivan's defense motion to suppress the electronic surveillance, arguing their position in the following excerpts garnered from footnote 3. "It [informant] believed in good faith that all the information contained in the (de la Montaigne) affidavit was true and correctly reflected the relationship between McIntyre and Naimovich," ending with "but also because the errors go only to the inferences drawn by the facts and not the facts themselves." In other words, the facts are okay. It is how one infers the manner they are implied. So, if you look out the window and it is snowing, that is a fact, but how one infers the weather conditions could be in dispute according to the prosecutor's theory.

By virtue of discovery motions, Ivan's lawyers were desperately trying to break down the government barrier pertaining to exculpatory evidence they had that could possibly clear their client. The Boston FBI office supervisor of C-3, James Ring, begrudgingly complied.

The Honorable Judge Joseph L. Tauro was the sitting federal justice hearing the pretrial motions submitted by the opposing parties. After holding an in camera (secret) review requested by the prosecution, in a stunning rebuke to the FBI, the judge wrote the following:

> Angela Blanco worked as a stenographer for the Federal Bureau of Investigation. From late 1987, *through the period covered by the indictment* [my emphasis], Ms. Blanco's brother, Anthony Corrado, is known to have a relationship with Vincent Ferrara. Because of Ms. Blanco's employment, she had access to the information contained in the attached F.B.I. Form-302. At this time no confidential information is known to have passed from Ms. Blanco to Mr. Ferrara. However, an investigation of Ms. Blanco and Mr. Corrado is currently being conducted by the Federal Bureau of Investigation.

Before the judge signed off on the order on March 13, 1989, three days after Mattioli and de la Montaigne submitted their affidavits to the same judge who would hear Ivan's trial, Tauro declared the "circumstances under which the government became aware of the information set forth in paragraph 1 is not exculpatory and therefore is not subject to discovery by the defendants."

My contrarian view is the *circumstances* were such that Agent Ring had set up Daniel Forte as a proxy informant in late 1987. He was interjected into the conversation to falsely direct suspicion of leaks away from Boston FBI agents or civilian pool stenographers and toward Ivan because I believe Ring knew he had an unidentified leaker in his bureau office as early as the spring of 1987. FBI Agent Connolly then hypothesized in an interview with the *Boston Globe* in 1988 that Ivan "wanted to do Vanessa's," but the bureau beat him to the punch. Connolly apparently assumed that Ivan told his informant Mac about the Vanessa's bug, and he in turn advised Ferrara. The common denominator in this fiasco was Ferrara, whom Blanco was passing confidential information for years through her low-level bookie brother, Anthony. Although Ring had to admit to ongoing internal leaks in early 1988, in close proximity to Ivan's arrest and thirteen months before Tauro's order, he simultaneously was trying to build a case against Ivan for leaks perpetuated by the compromised Ms. Blanco. She was the supervisor of the steno pool with a top-secret clearance allowing her access to confidential documents during her ten years with the bureau.

FBI Director William Sessions signed Blanco's resignation on February 2, 1988, the day before Ivan was arrested. Neither she nor her brother were criminally investigated or charged, but in order for the FBI to save face, Ms. Blanco was allowed to resign rather than being arrested followed by an ugly trial, which would have exposed the Boston office of the FBI as less than austere in internal matters of confidentiality, to put it mildly. Ivan was indicted for less.

Blanco's demeanor during our February 2016 meeting was blasé. Her gratitude toward the FBI for giving her a pass (a word you will read more about) was less than enthusiastic when she directed the following comment at yours truly, "you people [FBI] are more corrupt than the people out on the street." She also disparaged a retired agent in the process. (I had already introduced myself as a state police retiree doing independent research.) Ms. Blanco was an FBI employee during the John Connolly and John Morris FBI era of corruption. I cannot explain her motivation for disavowing her oath of office, but in her case, blood was thicker than water.

The Cleveland, Ohio, office of the FBI had a similar internal problem back in the '70s involving a female clerk who was bribed by the local Mafia into updating them on organized crime and government informant information. An elderly Cleveland mobster "Blackie" Licavoli later told one of the FBI's top informants, Jimmy "Weasel" Fratianno, "Jimmy, sometimes, you know, I think this (expletive) outfit of ours is like the old Communist party in this country. It is getting so that there's more (expletive) spies in it than members." It was Licavoli who compromised the FBI clerk.

Agent Ring wasn't acting out of any largesse for Ivan when he stunned the defense with the Blanco disclosure. Retired State Police Superintendent Tom Foley would write a book in 2012, *Most Wanted*, with John Sedgwick. Foley, Major Tom Duffy, Detective Lieutenant Steve Johnson, and DEA Agent Dan Doherty, among others, were all enormously instrumental in dismantling the Winter Hill mobsters Bulger, Flemmi, and Martorano.

Foley wrote in October 1986 he was called into a meeting at the Boston FBI office with Agents Ring and Nick Gianturco. Mattioli and State Police Sergeant Ed Sullivan were also in attendance to discuss Daniel Forte, who was cultivated as an informant by Foley and Gianturco, resulting from his loan shark arrest in 1984. Ring led the get-together, asking Foley, "Based on what some of our sources deep in LCN (La Cosa Nostra) are telling us Vinny Ferrara has obtained information about Forte's activities that matches your report word for word…Can you explain that?" Ring probed further, "Did you divulge this information to anyone else?"

Ring's "sources deep in LCN" was FBI Agent John Connolly's informant and coconspirator extortionist of elderly bookies, Angelo "Sonny" Mercurio. Ferrara called a meeting expressing concern to Mercurio that someone was walking around wearing a wire targeting Ferrara. He learned this information from Anthony Corrado, brother of FBI steno Ms. Blanco. Mercurio passed the information to Connolly, who in turn advised Ring. It is unclear at what point in time Ring learned that Corrado was Ms. Blanco's brother.

Foley shared the information, stating, "Yes, one other person. On Dave's instructions." I turned to Mattioli. "I told him Trooper John Naimovich of the State Police."

"We'd better get Forte out of there. I'll get started putting him and his woman friend into the Program." (Presumably the Witness Security Program run by the US Marshals Service.)

Ring responded, "Do that."

The preceding FD-302 authored by Agent Gianturco in November 1987 classified the bearer of the wire against Ferrara as Dan Forte, also known as "Tony Cee." He eventually was accepted into the Witness Security Program with his girlfriend, Darlene, after being denied many family members.

Naimovich once again was vindicated.

Foley then asserts in his book that Ring was of the opinion Mac was acting as a middleman, passing confidential police business directly to Ferrara. Unless Foley is giving the reader a head fake, the October 1986 meeting more likely occurred in October or November 1987. Ivan and Mac were indistinguishable blips on the radar of any police agency, given the fact Mac's name did not surface until December 22, 1986, when Ferrara threw out his name in a recorded conversation at Vanessa's, not to mention Mac's name was listed in the alleged Ferrara phone book but wasn't discovered until April 1987.

The pressure was off Foley and immediately transferred to Ivan because he reviewed a Foley report at Mattioli's direction. Foley then implicates Mattioli, writing, "Mattioli checked later, and Naimovich was using Frannie Mac." It is unknown when Mattioli "checked," but in his March 1989 affidavit, he denies knowledge of Naimovich "using" Frannie Mac. Presuming Mattioli and Foley were familiar with the informant relationship before, during, and after wiretapping Ivan and Frannie Mac, neither trooper officially advised de la Montaigne in his effort to acquire just that type of information in approximation to the possible fall 1987 Foley meeting with Ring.

After several months of physical and electronic surveillance targeting Ivan, Foley writes, "Precious little of it supported the core charge from Ring and the FBI that Naimovich was supplying information about Forte's movements to Ferrara."

Lacking evidence to the contrary, Foley met in Ring's office, and as he was departing, he overheard Ring tell Agent Nick Gianturco, "Now we have to take care of our problem."

At a later undated conversation with Mattioli, Foley told him he was perturbed to the point that he let his superior know about the lack of evidence against Ivan. Another meeting with Ring was arranged by Mattioli. Nearly choking, Ring coughed it up that "our problem" was a typist in the steno pool (Angela Blanco), who was the source of information passed to Ferrara through her bookie brother, Anthony Corrado, and not Naimovich.

Ring proclaimed Naimovich "is a bad cop and he will be convicted, believe me."

"Not if the jury hears the truth about your steno he won't," the usually calm Foley retorted.*

In a preemptive move, three days before Tauro's order identifying Blanco was disclosed, Mattioli and de la Montaigne filed separate motions. Mattioli wrote, "At the time the electronic surveillance was submitted I was not aware Francis J. McIntyre Jr. was an informant for Naimovich."

---

* Foley testified in the 2013 RICO trial of Bulger stating he felt the FBI was focusing on him as a leak when in fact Defense Attorney Brennan got him to admit it was "a stenographer in the Department of Justice, correct…And that stenographer had contacts with organized crime." Brennan questioned Foley if her last name was Blanco, but he could not remember her last name.

CHAPTER 27

Mac and Ivan Go on Trial

State Police Sergeant James Murray was the first member of the former Special Service Unit to testify for the prosecution on May 25, 1989. He was preceded by FBI Agent de la Montaigne, defendant Francis McIntyre, New Jersey State Police Detective Charles Brennan, and FBI Agent John Massey. Murray was assigned to the unit from 1980 to late 1984 and then transitioned to the intelligence unit where he remained until 1987. At the time of his testimony, he was in charge of the Organized Crime and Vice Control Unit.

Trial defense attorney Alex Nappan cross-examined Murray as a result of the witness silently reading an FBI report stating FBI Agent Don Palmer said he, the agent, "was aware that Francis McIntyre…was an informant for the Massachusetts State Police?" Murray responded, "Yes, sir." Agent Palmer coordinated with the New Jersey State Police in tracking down Frank Russo, an elusive Cape Cod bookie in a multistate gambling investigation on which Ivan wrote a report subsequent to being contacted by New Jersey in 1985 outlining what intelligence he had garnered about Russo. The FBI agent became aware in February or March 1988 that McIntyre was an informant well over a year before Ivan's trail. Whether the agent knew McIntyre (also known as Frannie Mac) was Ivan's informant is speculative. Nappan continued questioning Murray, "So there's no question that the FBI, specifically the agent that wrote this report, was aware at the time that Francis McIntyre was a source of information, an informant for the Massachusetts State Police; isn't that correct?" The prosecution immediately objected and just as quickly was overruled by the judge allowing the witness to answer, "Yes, sir."

For months beginning in 1980, SSU troopers and the Worcester DA's office tapped the phones of area organized crime figure Carlo Mastrolotaro and two of his Worcester storefront distributors of pornographic material, James Roche and Maurice "Moe" Hagerty. In what became Operation Big League, Nappan asked Murray, "Who was the affiant in that?"

"John Naimovich," replied Murray.

Nappan pursued his line of questioning about an informant used in the first affidavit to get a court order to electronically surveil the phones of Mastrolotaro, who at the time was on an equal footing with Jerry Angiulo in the hierarchy of mob bosses in New England. Murray confirmed SSU Trooper Rod Beaton had passed off his informant to Murray, who in turn supplied information for Operation Big League. Nappan asked, "During Operation Big League, were you in contact with a special agent for the FBI by the name of Ring?"

Murray, "Of course, yes, sir."

The cross-examination moved forward when Murray, who was the point man in the wiretap, factually stated the FBI became involved in the spring of 1980 because the investigation crossed state lines into Vermont. Murray then had to agree with Nappan that Ring was intercepted on the wiretap conversing with an informant (without specifying exactly when). It is alleged that on a Saturday afternoon interception, while in midconversation, Ring's informant had to answer the doorbell, prompting Ring to start singing to himself "Hello, Charlie" to the tune of "Hello, Dolly." His childish skit may have been in reference to Staff Sergeant Charles Henderson, who at the time was commanding SSU and the leader of the investigation. Nappan wanted to know from the prosecution witness if Ring was investigated for his contact with the informant when Prosecutor Sullivan jumped to his feet yelling, "Objection, Judge."

Murray was allowed to answer, "I was not made aware of any investigation in regards to Mr. Ring and the informant."

In closing, Nappan presented a narrative for the jury, theorizing a double standard of prosecuting Ivan for the same offense Ring may have committed. He asked Murray, "But there's no question in your mind, is there, sir, that Agent Ring was intercepted speaking to a target of the investigation?"

Murray could only answer, "Yes, sir, he was."

"Lieutenant Saccardo, directing your attention to January 24, 1988, did you receive a phone call from the defendant that evening?"

"Yes, I did," I said in response to the prosecution. Ivan returned a call from me because I had asked him to check out a subject for me. "And after we discussed the subject, the defendant started to query me with regards to who may be going into the grand jury in the Hellers investigation, and where we were at." (Approximately halfway through the trial, I was called to testify on May 30, 1989.)

Prosecutor Sullivan wanted to know what the specifics were when Ivan asked me about the progress of the Heller's investigation. "And did that conversation or those inquiries from the defendant concern you?"

"Yes" was the answer, and "Why?" was Sullivan's next question. Nappan objected and was sustained. I then had to explain to the jury and an assistant US attorney, without getting into detail, "that there may be a possible leak surrounding the grand jury investigations from Heller's?" Nappan again objected, winning a sustained from the judge along with striking my answer. I then testified I had called the assistant US attorney Mitch Dembin, conveyed my conversation with Ivan, and told Mattioli at a later date. This turn of events became a point of contention by incorrectly implying that Ivan was leaking about the Heller's grand jury investigation. The prosecution then rested.

Nappan came out firing, asking, "The investigation was successful, wasn't it?"

I answered, "It's still ongoing."

Further into my testimony, he brought up something about a pass. My first inclination was to think this must have something to do with giving somebody a break or "judicial adjustment" until he stated that Henderson condoned giving passes to bookmakers who were also informants: a situation I had not experienced. After Sullivan's objection was overruled, Nappan explained in better detail what a pass was. Never having heard that particular jargon in those terms, I responded, "I see, okay."

Nappan later came back to the issue of a pass asking, "Is it fair to say that you understand the concept of a pass, do you not, sir?"

I answered, "Now I do, yes. It's the first time I've heard that."

Then he asked, "The concept of a pass facilitates a gaming operation?"

"Possibly."

Sullivan objected. Overruled. He moved to strike, and the judge denied the move. Then Nappan hit me with, "Is it fair to say, Lieutenant, that…you said 'possibly.' Is that true? That was your answer, 'possibly.'"

"Yes."

Nappan then ranted on about a hypothetical, which I was interpreting as an assumption, and I told him I did not understand. He then shocked me with the following: "Is it fair to say, Lieutenant, that your failure to understand the question reflects a concern on your part that you might be indicted for facilitating—"

Before he could finish his question, I angrily retorted, "Absolutely not."

The trial was nearing an end when Captain E. David Mattioli took the stand on June 1, 1989. Mattioli was asked under direct examination by Assistant US Attorney Sullivan about the inception of the intelligence unit he took command of in May 1984 and how it was created. Mattioli said, "That unit was created by agreement with then Commissioner Frank Trabucco, and the Boston office of the FBI, for the purpose of working joint cases on organized crime figures in the state."

Ring had just taken over supervision of the FBI organized crime squad known as C-3 in 1983. Bulger, Flemmi, and John Martorano continued to create chaos, having just been directly involved in the murders of World Jai Alai owner Roger Wheeler; FBI informant Brian Halloran; John Martorano's *friend* and former World Jai Alai employee John Callahan; bank robber Arthur "Bucky" Barrett; and IRA sympathizer, gunrunner, and drug smuggler John McIntyre. Also, Ivan was the affiant in the successful Worcester organized crime prosecution of Ring's informant and major porno supplier. Either Ring's FBI C-3 squad needed assistance in ferreting out intelligence other than what the bureau's Top Echelon informants Bulger and Flemmi were feeding, or there was another more sinister reason: Ring wanted to infiltrate the newly formed unit to his and the bureau's advantage in securing the unit's sources of information and targets of investigation, keeping in mind how close the 1981 State Police Lancaster Street investigation was to snagging Bulger and Flemmi.

Well into Mattioli's testimony, the prosecution probed when and how he became involved in the investigation of Ivan. The judge sustained the objection of the defense. The prosecution tried a different line of questioning, asking Mattioli if he received a phone call from the FBI on November 19 (1987). Again, the judge sustained Nappan's objection, resulting in Sullivan requesting to approach the judge. In the sidebar conference, Sullivan tried to establish while Mattioli was in internal affairs.

> Mattioli explained that there was a breach of security involved with the defendant that was brought to the attention of the FBI. He had conversations with Commissioner McCabe as to how the investigation was to be handled. That would have included the fact that at that time police internal affairs would not be involved in the investigation.

Before Sullivan could finish his thought, the judge sustained the objection for the second time. By his own verbal introductory résumé, Mattioli did not mention being assigned to internal affairs, nor was the "breach of security," as alleged by the FBI, ever fully explored. The only nonpublic breach of security was the FBI steno pool supervisor, Ms. Blanco.

Mattioli went on to testify that Ivan came into the investigation of Frannie Mac approximately November 19, 1987, but he was not a target even though his name had surfaced. Subsequent to the phone call made by an unknown FBI agent to Mattioli, the bureau proceeded to accumulate telephone toll records of Ivan and Frannie Mac, institute a malfunctioning pen register, rely on a less-than-reliable informant, perform minimal physical surveillance of the targets, and completely disregard an internal affairs investigation by seasoned state police commissioned officers in preparation for an affidavit prepared and submitted by FBI Agent de la Montaigne for an application to conduct electronic surveillance on Frannie Mac's phones, which was signed by a federal judge one month later on December 21, 1987.

On December 23, 1987, troopers from the organized crime unit and Ashland police raided a bookie's office. Several days later, Mattioli sent himself an anonymous letter containing a new telephone number for the raided bookie's office. A sidebar conversation between the judge and opposing lawyers caused more confusion about the letter. Without any discernible reason, Mattioli was attempting a sting operation in order to entrap Ivan into notifying the bookie to relocate his office. On cross-examination, Nappan got the witness to agree that both Henderson and Haley knew the identity of Frannie Mac as being Ivan's informant.

Mattioli also admitted Frannie Mac's phone number was the only number found in Ferrara's phone book that warranted an investigation by the FBI and state police, ostensibly resulting from the informant's name being overheard on the Vanessa's bug as paying rent to Ferrara. What attracted the attention of the FBI and state police to target one low-level bookie's name in a sea of high-level Boston and Providence Mafiosi, numbering over a dozen hoods, including the biggest bookies in the area, many of whom were paying rent to the same hoods? But none of the few, the proud, and the unindicted were Ivan's undocumented informant.

Nappan and Mattioli parried about whether or not Ivan and Frannie Mac had a legitimate relationship. Mattioli had already penned a March 10 affidavit swearing that he "had not received information from either Major Henderson or Corporal Haley concerning the identities of any of Naimovich's informants," because he never asked what he didn't want to hear or already knew. Nappan asked, "When did you believe there was an informant relationship?"

"After the call on December 23."

December 23 was the second day of the wiretap on Frannie Mac's phone and the very first call between the defendants, which convinced Mattioli of the informant relationship.

Frannie Mac signed a memorandum of agreement with the US attorney's office representative, Jeremiah T. O'Sullivan, in March 1988, a month after the state police raided his house and the arrest of Ivan. If he cooperated in the investigation of Ivan and Vinnie Ferrara and after he pleaded guilty to any impending indictments, the federal government would bring such acquiescence to the attention of the sentencing judge. During his subsequent debriefing, Frannie Mac put on a masterful performance of composing and singing for a rapt audience of O'Sullivan and the jurors. Mattioli was so confident of Ivan's guilt he told a *Boston Globe* reporter in a confidential interview following Ivan's arrest that he compromised the Vanessa's surveillance and was further quoted saying, "I can't wait until it's all out. We've taken it on the chin because we can't say anything."

As difficult as it was, the defense demonstrated to the jury that Mattioli never even made a threshold inquiry into whether or not Frannie Mac was Ivan's informant. By his own admission, Mattioli realized after the second intercepted phone call between Ivan and Frannie Mac that they had a legitimate relationship. In spite of that fact, he neglected to confidentially consult with Henderson or Haley to confirm the truth of the matter.

After establishing the former, Nappan didn't hesitate in his continued cross-examination of Mattioli. He concentrated on impeaching Frannie Mac's previous testimony directed at his preconfessional deferential position toward Ivan as opposed to his postabsolution accusations toward the defendant in agreeing to "complete cooperation" with O'Sullivan.

In a series of rapid-fire questions that were structured to elicit yes or no answers, Nappan stripped away the veneer of the government star witness Frannie Mac's truthfulness while exposing the logical conclusion that the justice department attempted to frame Ivan.

Some of the most glaring rebuttals by Mattioli in relation to Frannie Mac's first interview, which morphed into his plea agreement accusations against Ivan and resultant contradictions, were that Ivan did not leak the raids at Vanessa's, Ivan did not tell Frannie Mac somebody was wearing a body wire against Ferrara, and Ivan did not accept money or liquor from Frannie Mac.

Nappan then read aloud a letter to Mattioli and the jury, which was sent to Frannie Mac's attorney, promising his client if he submitted to an interview by the FBI and Massachusetts State Police, "that whatever admissions that your client makes during this interview will not be used against him in any way." Nappan followed with "the decision on whether or not Mr. McIntyre's story would trigger the prosecution against him was Mr. O'Sullivan?"

The prosecutor unsuccessfully objected before Mattioli answered, "Yes."

In conclusion, Nappan reiterated a conversation Mattioli, de la Montaigne, and O'Sullivan had had with Frannie Mac the day after raiding his house on January 29, asking Mattioli, "Do you remember any promises being made to Mr. McIntyre to induce his cooperation in this matter?"

Mattioli responded, "Yes."

It was revealed for the second time in open court that O'Sullivan promised to protect Frannie Mac's family; there would be no asset forfeitures and a negligible sentence if he cooperated.

FBI Special Agent Vincent de la Montaigne had earlier testified on May 17 but was recalled for further examination on June 5 by the defense. The prosecution honed in on an intercepted phone call Ivan made to Mac to set up a meeting with him to discuss Alan Dvorkis, who was the subject of an illegal sports investigation. In early January 1988, Mattioli's intelligence unit was simultaneously surveilling Ivan while deceptively inducing him into a joint operation with the Watertown Police Department. After being briefed, Ivan made a call on January 5 to Frannie Mac, allegedly reciting details of the investigation to him. (No intercepted phone calls between Ivan and Frannie Mac we're allowed to be heard during the trial.) The two defendants met later that day at a grocery store parking lot where Frannie Mac accused Ivan of telling him to get "the word out and warn Dvorkis," according to de la Montaigne's testimony as related to him by Frannie Mac's initial debriefing on January 29. It was later discovered in cross-examination of the witness de la Montaigne by the defense that there was a leak in the Watertown Police Department who gave up information about the potential joint investigative wiretap to a large-scale bookie, Frank Russo, who was a cohort of Dvorkis's and subject of the New Jersey State Police gambling investigation.

The defense finally got to call a witness who was not being investigated by Ring or Mattioli. For more than a year that Ivan was under electronic and physical surveillance, he was tied up for most of 1987 doing the exact same thing with Trooper Steve Lowell in Norfolk County investigating top-level bookies. Lowell gave a truly honest appraisal of his thoughts about informants and a heroic assessment of Ivan's talents. While questioning Lowell, one of the more serious cross-examinations by the prosecution was when Sullivan tried to make a big deal out of Ivan calling into his office when he was supposedly at his summer home in New Hampshire. The defense objected, and Judge Tauro replied, "I'm going to sustain the objection. This is nonsense."

Next to take the witness stand in defense of Ivan was First Assistant District Attorney Mathew Connolly of Norfolk County. The county is just south of Boston and had been a safe haven for bookies for years until Connolly made a difference by utilizing the services of Ivan and the state police organized crime unit. Connolly had been doing wiretaps for years and had been on the verge in 1987 of cracking into a major bookie operation that was paying rent to Ferrara, Bulger, and Flemmi. Out of respect for a legal approach as specified by the very stringent Massachusetts wiretap law, Connolly contacted O'Sullivan asking for information about the subjects who were under scrutiny. O'Sullivan stated he would have an FBI agent contact Connolly, but no one from the bureau ever called.

The most illuminating and educational moments of Matt Connolly's testimony were a ten-minute tutorial on why he did not implement an informant policy for police officers working with him in Norfolk County.

On June 9, 1989, Ivan was found not guilty on four counts, and there was a mistrial on the fifth. Nearly every statement of fact that was alleged by the prosecution was proven at trial to be misconstrued, unproven, or a false statement given by the government's cooperating star witness, Francis J. McIntyre, who had been identified by Vinnie Ferrara as Frannie Mac and Sammy by Ivan.

Ivan's favorite affidavit phrase was "the aforementioned," so in his memory, *the aforementioned* Ferrara phone book should be considered a candidate to be enshrined in the FBI Museum of Blunders. *Ivan had been framed.*

Long before SSU transitioned from a unit to a section, commanded by Ring's comrade in arms Mattioli, Ring positioned himself and the bureau in such a way as to effectively infiltrate the best organized crime investigative body in the state while being privy to a constant flow of intelligence and informant knowledge in order to provide cover for the bureau's Top Echelon informants Bulger and Flemmi.

Ring's seven-year reign as supervisor of the bureau's organized crime squad and overlord of the Top Echelon Informant Program coincided with the deaths of Arthur Barrett, John McIntyre, and Debbie Hussey; an infestation of illegal drugs into South Boston neighborhoods; and an assortment of heavy-handed extortions amounting to millions of dollars all committed at the hands of Bulger and Flemmi.

In spite of the fact Ivan's lawyers were receiving favorable exculpatory evidence for their client, the Feds pressed forward in their pursuit of justice, but justice took a holiday. FBI Supervisory Special Agent James Ring married his second wife, twelve years his junior, Marita Hopkins, at the Old North Church in the Italian North End on June 3, 1989, days before Ivan was found not guilty on four counts. Ivan's chief protagonist, Assistant US Attorney Jeremiah O'Sullivan, joined the newlyweds on their honeymoon in Italy, leaving the trial to another Sullivan named Gregg (sans the O). I propose the groom and his fellow traveler properly assumed they had a losing cause and did not want to be confronted by the media and other inquiring minds. Neither man was ever taken to account for ruining the reputation of an innocent state trooper, preferring to genuflect before the destructive altar of the other dynamic duo: Bulger and Flemmi.

The wounded heart and soul of Trooper John Zannon Naimovich began to deteriorate the day he was arrested and slammed into the office filing cabinets by Mattioli. Ivan suffered debilitating anguish and anger at the hands of the US attorney for the District of Massachusetts, the Boston office of the FBI, and, most regrettably, the Massachusetts State Police.

Ivan was forced to retire because of a plea bargain deal, and in return, the mistrial count was dismissed. He never applied for his state pension.

He died of a heart attack at the age of forty-nine in 1991, two and a half years after he was found not guilty of being Ivan.

Colonel Charles Henderson retired in 1996.

Retired Captain Dave Mattioli has been collecting his pension since the early '90s.

Agent James Ring went into the private sector in 1990 and continues to receive his pension until death.

Agent Vince de la Montaigne retired in 2000 and went to work security for the National Football League.

Steve Lowell retired a lieutenant and became a successful lawyer.

Former ADA Matt Connolly is a prominent blogger and author of *Don't Embarrass the Family*.

Jeremiah O'Sullivan died of cancer and heart disease at the age of sixty-five.

Defense attorney Tom Drechsler was appointed an associate justice in the Massachusetts Superior Court.

Defense attorney Alex Nappan retired in western Massachusetts after practicing law for many years.

Francis McIntyre, also known as Frannie Mac, and Sammy received an imposition of a sentence, which was suspended, and he was placed on probation for twenty-four months at the government's request. He pled guilty to racketeering conspiracy, and the remaining four counts were dismissed with a special assessment of fifty dollars.

Shortly after completing the Ivan chapters in June 2019, I had a doctor's appointment at a Boston hospital. In order to while away the office wait time, I bought a Boston newspaper for the first time in several years. For some reason, I checked the lottery numbers for the previous day. Sitting side by side, in no particular order, the winning numbers turned out to be Ivan's state police identification, 754, and mine, 821. Ivan had played his number, winning many times, but on this occasion, my numbers paid out more than his. My personal interpretation: I would like to think this was not a coincidence.

CHAPTER 28

De Facto Immunity

When John Martorano discovered Flemmi had been an FBI informant for nearly four decades in 1998, he began the process of unloading his serial-killing career in the name of justice and revenge to anyone who would listen in the Boston US attorney's office.

Ultimately, it was justice for himself and not the many family and friends of his twenty confessed victims, not to mention retaliation against Flemmi for not being a true criminal friend and finally realizing his ignorance to not recognize the difference.

John Vincent Martorano had previously admitted to killing twenty men and women in a plea bargain agreed to in 1998. Part of his immunity deal involved testifying for the federal government against Connolly, whom he alleged alerted Bulger and Flemmi they should leave town because of impending grand jury arrest warrants.

The so-called gangland war of the '60s produced a landmark year in

1965, which resulted in over twenty-five shootings, a majority of which were homicides, and missing persons believed dead. Ironic that the Vietnam conflict was escalating parallel to the Boston killing fields. From 1960 through 1978, the year Martorano fled his indictment for RICO violations, there were approximately seventy-five gangland-related homicides in Boston and environs of which Martorano accounted for at least eighteen or an estimated 20 percent. His fugitive status in Florida did not impair his ability to perform out-of-state hits in 1981 and 1982 in Oklahoma and Florida, respectively.

Former FBI Special Agent John Connolly was charged in 2002 with various racketeering (RICO) violations and was found guilty in all instances at the central Massachusetts federal courthouse in Worcester. John Vincent Martorano had previously admitted to killing twenty men and women in a plea bargain agreed to in 1998 as a result of good lawyering. Part of his immunity deal involved testifying for the federal government against Connolly, whom he alleged alerted Bulger and Flemmi they should leave town because of impending grand jury arrest warrants.

In *USA v. John J. Connolly Jr.*, Martorano's testimony for the prosecution covered over two hundred pages. Direct examination in May 2002 by federal prosecutor John Durham chronologically walked his handheld-star witness through the psycho's decades of serial murders starting with the historical perspective of Martorano's beginnings with Bulger, Howie Winter, James Sims (missing), Joseph McDonald (deceased), and other members of the Somerville-based Winter Hill gang. At the time of his testimony, Martorano had been incarcerated for four years in a secret federal location as a cooperating witness, much like Steve Flemmi has been since the late '90s. Martorano's first (November 15, 1965) and third (September 28, 1966) admitted murders were to protect the Flemmi brothers, although he testifies (and may have perjured himself) he killed the witnesses to the Sylvester murder (November 10, 1964) to protect his brother, James.

Durham did not question Martorano in the murder of Tony Veranis (April 26, 1966), who was shot to death at the Flemmi after-hours bar in front of numerous witnesses. He also initially failed to mention three black victims

(January 6, 1968), two of whom were innocent teenagers. Nor did he reference another black victim, Ronald Hicks (March 19, 1969), an innocent witness to a triple murder committed by the Campbell brothers, who were notorious criminal associates of the Martorano brothers in the black community.

In what must have been a psychopathic fit of rage, Martorano testified he stabbed a pimp named John "Touch" Banno (September 25, 1969) twenty times in the heart, out of revenge reminiscent of the Sylvester slaughter. Approaching the end of the volatile '60s, Johnny "B'wana" had killed five blacks (two of whom were witnesses), a tough guy he knew he couldn't beat in a fistfight, and a pimp. The '70s were no less disturbing.

Martorano went on a killing spree in March 1973. He admitted killing three men and wounding five people, including three innocent males and a female. At the Connolly trial, for the first time, he implicated Howie Winter in all three murders, along with Winter Hill associates James Sims, Bulger, and other unnamed victims in the murder of an innocent bartender, Michael Milano (March 8, 1973). The next month, he and another Winter Hill associate, Joseph MacDonald (and unnamed others), whack out the first of the Notarangeli brothers (April 18, 1973). In December, Martorano, Winter, MacDonald, Bulger, and the ever "anonymous others" killed James J. "Spike" O'Toole (December 1, 1973).

The next year, Martorano caught up with "Indian Al" Notarangeli (February 22, 1974), the brother of Joe, assisted by Winter, Bulger, and unnamed individuals. In May, Steve Flemmi returned from the lam and joined gang members Martorano and Winter in killing James A. Sousa (October 6, 1974).

Once again, Durham neglected to query Martorano in another admitted homicide involving Eddie Connors (June 12, 1975) when he, Bulger, and Flemmi fatally shot Connors in a Dorchester phone booth. Durham did get Martorano to answer to the missing body of Thomas King (November 5, 1975), which was uncovered from a grave in 2000 alongside the Neponset River in Quincy. Martorano then incriminated Winter and Bulger in the shooting death of King.

FBI informant Richard Castucci's body was found December 30, 1976, in his Cadillac at a Revere mall. Martorano, Winter, Bulger, Flemmi, and several others participated in his death, which occurred in a Winter Hill hangout in Somerville.

Howie Winter, the one-time leader of the Boston Irish and Italian Winter Hill gang was a willing assassin, coconspirator, and accessory either before or after the fact of eight homicides committed with John Martorano, who had admitted twenty murders under the penalties of perjury in the Connolly trial. Also, unnamed individuals criminally participated in four of the twenty. As part of Martorano's plea agreement, federal prosecutors agreed to indirectly immunize Winter and unnamed others and got nothing in return from coconspirators. A prerequisite to his August 1999 plea agreement, John Martorano was debriefed by the DEA and the state police for over a year before signing off to the twenty murders, of which approximately eleven were committed with a person commonly known as "unknown individual." Coconspirators in the murders were Bulger, Flemmi, James McDonald, James Sims, and other named Winter Hill gang members; however, Howie Winter was suspiciously missing from being named in the debriefing. As part of Martorano's plea, federal prosecutors agreed to indirectly immunize Winter and unnamed others in what I describe as de facto immunity. The Feds got nothing in return from the coconspirators namely because Bulger was a fugitive, Flemmi was gearing up to be immunized, and McDonald and Sims were either missing or dead.

Martorano committed two murders in Middlesex County, but no record of plea agreements with then District Attorney Martha Coakley could be located. According to Assistant US Attorney Fred Wyshak, DA Coakley decided not to enter into a formal plea agreement with the justice department, citing double jeopardy as relates to Martorano being charged in both state and federal court.

Wyshak further stated there is a confidential document between the two parties not available to the public. Undocumented reports indicate Winter had been an FBI informant for years.

Martorano was briefly questioned about the triple murder of Herbert "Smitty" Smith, Elizabeth Dixon, and Douglas Barrett (January 6, 1968). Of the three black victims, the teenagers Dixon and Barrett were collateral damage in Martorano's thirst to kill Smith as a favor to Steve Flemmi because according to Martorano, while two wise guys beat Flemmi, Smith held his arms.

Tracy Miner, Connolly's defense counsel, followed Durham's questioning when she cross-examined Martorano about the unsolved 1966 murder of Kathryn Murphy.

> Q. How about Kathleen (sic) Murphy; do you recall her?
> A. Don't know her.
> Q. Do you recall a girlfriend of Billy Kearns?
> A. Billy who?
> Q. Kearns.
> A. Billy Kearns, yeah.

Martorano knew Kearns's first name was Jimmy not Billy, but of course he did not take the opportunity to correct Miner. He realized if he made a connection between Kearns and Murphy, in theory, he could deflect any suspicion off himself or Kearns in the 1966 murder of Kathryn Murphy. Kearns was the original single suspect in her death and immediately lawyered-up. He died a natural death at a federal prison in 2005 while serving a term for the attempted murder of an assistant US attorney. Murphy was a nineteen-year-old recent high school graduate who frequented a Boston after-hours bar run by Steve Flemmi and the Bennett brothers. She was discovered shot to death near her Boston home on an early Sunday morning in June 1966. The evening before, she was last seen at the same bar where, two months earlier, Tony Veranis was murdered by John Martorano in front of a dozen witnesses. As reflected in Martorano's own testimony, he had a penchant for killing witnesses.

Florida v. John J. Connolly Jr.

For two days in September 2008, John Martorano was a prosecution witness for the Florida state attorney's office in the John Connolly murder trial. Martorano was a free man, resolving to go straight after being sentenced by federal judge Mark Wolf and serving twelve years for twenty murders, or approximately seven months per murder, two of which were committed in capital punishment states. If Martorano hadn't admitted to the murders, he was facing a four- or five-year state sentence for the race-fixing scheme. When questioned by Florida State Attorney Von Zamft about his motivation for ratting out Bulger and Flemmi, he responded, "Because I wanted to put a stop to what was going on." This altruistic statement came from a man who may have killed more people than Bulger and Flemmi combined.

Martorano accused Connolly, a person he admitted never meeting, of tipping Bulger that John Callahan could be a material witness to the murder of his former boss and the owner of the Miami World Jai Alai, Roger Wheeler. Connolly was on trial for the second-degree murder of Callahan. It was determined by Bulger and Flemmi that Martorano would kill Callahan. The fugitive Martorano probably figured if he didn't kill his best friend, his partners probably would have outed his location to Agent Connolly. Martorano left Callahan's body in the trunk of his own car at the Miami-Dade International Airport, and it was discovered on August 1, 1982. Martorano, the prosecution's star witness, had previously pleaded to seventy-nine felony counts in federal court.

Florida State Attorney Von Zamft questioned Martorano on direct examination about whom he would testify against. Howie Winter and South Boston hood Pat Nee were not on the list.

Cross-examination by defense attorney Manuel Casabielle prompted Martorano to respond to a question about being an informant. "You can't rat on a rat," stated Martorano. He told Casabielle that he had a plea agreement not to testify against Winter and Nee but admitted Nee was a "possible" in some of Martorano's murders. He stated he killed his first victim (Palladino) "in self-defense and that he was doing the right thing for Steve Flemmi." He killed his third victim (Jackson), because he was told "he was going to be a witness against my brother (James) wrongfully in a murder case." In both instances, that would be the Margaret Sylvester homicide. Concerning the 1973 James O'Toole murder, Martorano said O'Toole was "talking about killing a friend of mine, Howie Winter." Martorano killed Al Notarangeli for Jerry Angiulo in 1974 for the handsome sum of fifty thousand dollars. Nine months previous to the Connolly trial, on January 6, 2008, Martorano was quoted during an interview with Steve Kroft on the nationally acclaimed Sunday night television program *60 Minutes*, stating, "You could never pay me to kill anybody." He told the truth under the penalty of perjury in the Connolly trial but lied to millions of television viewers.

It was no secret that for decades starting in the 1960s the so-called Winter Hill gang was a wholly owned subsidiary of the Angiulo organized crime family under the tutelage of consigliere Ilario Zannino, also known as Larry Baione. (Zannino died in the Springfield, Missouri, federal prison at the age of seventy-six.) Two prime examples are the 1974 murder for hire of Al Notarangeli and the 1980 state police audio and video investigation of Danny Angiulo meeting with Bulger and Flemmi in a Lancaster Street garage only minutes form the Boston Mafiosa seat of power in the North End.

Martorano's last victim in 1974 was James Sousa in order "to prevent an indictment or a case going forward," according to his testimony. Sousa's body has never been found.

The jury deliberated for thirteen hours before convicting Connolly of second-degree murder nearly three decades after the death of John Callahan. After hearing testimony from a heavily immunized trio of two admitted hitmen (Flemmi and John Martorano), a gangster who assisted in five homicides with Bulger and Flemmi (Kevin Weeks), and corrupt FBI agent Paul Rico, former FBI agent John Connolly, who at one time had the key to the safe deposit box of the FBI's most valuable informants, would be facing thirty years in a Florida state prison for being armed with his issued service weapon during a murder in Miami while the agent was living 1,500 miles away in Massachusetts.

My parochial school education informs me that venial sins are less severe than mortal sins. Agent Connolly may have committed venial sins during his career but not the type of mortal sins, such as murder, like those gangsters, who themselves were complicit in over forty murders, did. Unless released on appeals, the then sixty-eight-year-old Connolly faces the reality of not outliving his thirty-year prison sentence.

In February 2021, John Connolly was released from a Florida prison for humanitarian reasons due to terminal cancer after serving eight years for a murder he never committed. He will be allowed to return to Boston, but he has initially decided to reside in southeast Florida with either his brother Jim, who is a retired DEA agent, or the former honcho of the Massachusetts Convention Center, Franny Joyce. Connolly is but a stone's throw from Lauderdale-by-the-Sea, which serves as Southie's City Point south for the patrons of the Village Pump bar.

CHAPTER 29

Happy St. Whitey's Day Lasted Sixteen Years

The *Boston Sunday Globe* ran a front-page special report, consisting of five full pages, titled "Whitey in Exile" on October 9, 2011. The newspaper chronicled Bulger's sixteen-year odyssey ending with his and Catherine Greig's arrest by the FBI on June 22, 2011. A former Hollywood actress and model paid enough attention to the FBI public relations media blitz featuring Greig, and the fact they shared a common interest in cats brought her to make a two-million-dollar reward phone call from her home in Reykjavik, Iceland, to the FBI in Los Angeles. Anna Bjornsdottir recognized Bulger and Greig as her former Santa Monica neighbors, Charles and Carol Gasko, who had taken up residence at the Princess Eugenia Apartments, 1012 Third Street, #302, only blocks from the famous Santa Monica Pier. Ironically, Bulger's attempt at concealment as a free man during the 1980 funeral service for his mother at St. Monica's in South Boston was contrary to his hiding in the open in Santa Monica, while law enforcement worldwide sought him out.

St. Monica is revered by the Catholic Church as the patron saint of wives and abuse victims.

In *USA v. James J. Bulger Jr.*, retired State Police Colonel Thomas Foley was the first to take the stand and testify against a man whom he had never met but who had caused the colonel nearly twenty-five years of consternation.

Further into his testimony, Defense Attorney Brennan asked Foley if the debriefing information John Martorano gave him concerning his involvement committing murders with Winter Hill leader Howie Winter and Bulger associate Pat Nee led to developing a case against the two men. Brennan went on to impeach the witness, reading from the 2006 Florida murder trial of former FBI Agent John Connolly, stating, "Did you make any efforts to develop a case against Mr. Winter and Mr. Nee?" Brennan pushed Foley asking, "What was your answer back in 2006?"

Foley retorted, "I said, 'No, sir, I didn't.'"

Federal prosecutor Fred Wyshak cross-examined Foley on the matter of a racketeering statute of limitation when the federal government may prosecute a common-law murder. Foley answered the statute of limitation was five years.

In general, 18 US Code 3282 states, "Except as otherwise expressly provided by law, no person shall be prosecuted, tried, or punished for any offense, not capital, unless the indictment is found or the information is instituted within five years next after such offense shall have been committed."

Under state law, there is no statute of limitations for murder. The federal RICO law should be repealed, allowing for the same provisions as the state law for capital punishment involving murder.

Wyshak further drilled in on the fact that John Martorano began to cooperate with the federal government in 1998, and in the process, he tried to clarify that neither Winter nor Nee were part of the RICO enterprise because both had been in prison since 1993, thereby negating the five-year look back under the statute, allowing no federal prosecution of the two hoods.

Brennan then cross-examined Foley, outlining in his 2002 book the difficulty he had "pursuing organized crime based on the conduct of the FBI and the Department of Justice, that was true?"

"Yes."

Tom Foley admitted to Brennan that he authored the debriefing of John Martorano in 1998 and forwarded the report to the US attorney's Boston office.

On May 1, the same year Foley's book was published, a twenty-two-page, single-spaced confidential debriefing of John Martorano containing unredacted classified information about Bulger, Flemmi, and other organized crime figures was faxed from the Massachusetts State Police General Headquarters in Framingham to at least one recipient who was a Boston media personality and author of several books about the Boston Mafia.

Either just before or just after the debriefing was released, John Martorano's sixteen-page plea agreement, dated August 24, 1999, was sent by fax dated January 24, 2000, from an unknown "US ATTORNEY OFFICE—PO&COURT HOUSE." (PO is the old Post Office Square Courthouse in Boston where the US attorney was located.) The cosignees were Assistant US Attorney Chief of the Boston Criminal Division James B. Farmer, Suffolk County Assistant District Attorney Chief of the Homicide Bureau David E. Meier, Tulsa County District Attorney (Oklahoma) Tim Harris, and Florida Assistant State Attorney Deputy Chief for Special Prosecutions Mary Cagle. Martorano signed the document on August 23, 1999, and his defense attorney Francis DiMento, Esq., signed on September 7, 1999. The last page of the copy that I have in my possession was titled "Attachment A" and listed the names of eight homicide victims from 1965 through 1969 whom John Martorano confessed to killing.

David E. Meier and his boss, Suffolk County District Attorney Ralph Martin, absolved Martorano of sixteen homicides committed in Suffolk County, a majority of which occurred in Boston. Two unanswered voice mail messages were left with Meier at his private law practice. I then sent him a letter addressed to his Boston law firm, asking if he ever had the opportunity to read the Martorano debriefing. He avoided all my inquiries.

John Martorano was an early prosecution witness when he testified at the Bulger trial, allowing him a public platform to get another bite of the proverbial apple to defend himself as to why he murdered twenty innocent people without being tried at the expense of Bulger. He brushed off the offer made by the US Marshal Service, refusing to enter the Witness Security Program.

Federal prosecutor Fred Wyshak promptly got the niceties on the table the first day of Martorano's testimony in June 2013 at Bulger's racketeering trial. On direct examination, Wyshak is more concerned with the aftermath of the 1964 Margaret Sylvester murder witnesses, when Martorano explains why he killed Robert Palladino in self-defense with his brother, James, at the scene of the crime sitting in a car. (James was found guilty of accessory after the fact of the murder of Sylvester.) Wyshak then asked, "Did you find the other fellow, John Jackson, at some point?"

"He was sort of on the run. He was evading everybody. I guess he was in there testifying. So we knew he was coming home one night and waited for him," replied the serial killer. Brother James had already been indicted for accessory after the fact in the Sylvester murder when brother John had the stones to eliminate a grand jury witness to the murder.

Wyshak wanted to know, "Who is the we?"

Martorano then incriminated three dead hoods, including James Kearns, in the murder of John Jackson.

The inquisition continued with follow-up queries by Wyshak about the 1966 Tony Veranis murder. Martorano goes into depth explaining Veranis came over to him at Bennett's after-hours place and "started mouthing off about he just gave my brother a beating, some stuff like that, and 'F' him, 'F' you, and went to pull a gun, and I shot him." By this time, Martorano was probably wishing he had a sister instead of a brother who was a criminal just like him.

The next day, Bulger's cocounsel, Hank Brennan, started his cross-examination, asking Martorano how many times he stabbed John "Touch" Banno.

He answered, "Somebody told me twenty." (Sylvester was also stabbed multiple times.)

The year after Joe Notarangeli was murdered by Martorano, he killed his brother Al on February 2, 1974, with a crew of seven guys in different vehicles, per Martorano. Howie Winter was in the murder vehicle with Martorano when he shot Al to death. Other than Winter, he named Bulger as being in the vehicle behind him. (Bulger was proved not guilty.) Martorano decided to kill Al Notarangeli in order to impress upon Jerry Angiulo that Winter Hill had a *capable* crew (my emphasis). Translation: Winter Hill would kill for Angiulo. After serving twenty-four years in prison for RICO charges, two years following his release, Jerry Angiulo died at the age of ninety in 2009.

Brennan moved on, questioning the cooperating government witness about killing women, specifically, Elizabeth Dixon (1967), the innocent black female victim in the car with Smitty and a second male.

> Q. Do you have any hesitation admitting that you knew this was a young girl before you killed her?
> A. If that's what I knew before I killed her, I would have said that.

How could he not know? Martorano was sitting in the rear passenger seat behind the driver, Herbert Smith, forty-nine, in Smith's borrowed 1967 Mercury station wagon when he first shot Smith behind the right ear. Sitting in the front passenger seat was the nineteen-year-old recent high school graduate Elizabeth Dixon. She had no outer winter clothing on that could possibly conceal her gender when Martorano jumped into the back seat. Douglas Barrett was sitting adjacent to Martorano in the back seat when he was shot at close range above the left ear.

The Sylvester murder came up again, this time under cross-examination by defense attorney Hank Brennan. Martorano said Steve Flemmi and

Winter told him the witnesses "were going to say something against my brother."

Brennan continued the next day with the same line of questioning, asking Martorano,

> Q. Were you willing to talk to the federal government and offer evidence to prosecute your brother?
> A. Yes, I told them he was with me on a certain murder.
> Q. And you were willing to assist them in prosecuting your brother?
> A. If I was subpoenaed, I'd have to go.

Needless to say, Brennan refutes that claim and continues to cross-examine.

> Q. And you were not willing to testify against your brother, right?
> A. I was not willing to testify against everybody and anybody. That's what they said.
> Q. Well, everybody and anybody, that includes your brother, doesn't it?
> A. Included him.
> Q. And it included Howie Winter?
> A. Included anybody.
> Q. Well, did it include Howie Winter?
> A. Yes.
> Q. Did it include Pat Nee?
> A. Correct.

Of the twenty murders Martorano had confessed to spanning over two decades, it is unknown how many of those murders he was an actual suspect in with federal and state law enforcement. He certainly was a target of the state police enforcement of illegal gambling when he was arrested for sports betting in December 1976. Before the Christmas holiday season was over for that year, while out on a ten-thousand-dollar bail, he assassinated known bookmaker and FBI informant Richie Castucci. Three years later, he was indicted for various state and federal violations, fleeing the charges in 1979. From that year until his Florida arrest in 1995, he never took another pinch. After realizing Bulger and Flemmi were exposed as longtime FBI informants, resulting from the 1998 so-called Judge Wolf hearings, Martorano blithely skipped to the other side. Point being, how many of his twenty homicides were the DEA and state police able to corroborate before the Butcher of Basin Street gave it all up? And how many did he not confess?

The FBI suspected Martorano in the Castucci hit. When he started saving his ass from capital punishment in two states, the FBI was a nonentity as far as communicating with their suspect. The Boston police were on the periphery, although a large percentage of the murders were committed in their city. The DEA normally does not get involved in homicide investigations, but a special agent became a primary interrogator in the Martorano debriefings. That left the Massachusetts State Police Intelligence and Special Service Section to research, document, and corroborate the murderous résumé of the serial killer. Many of the troopers were from Worcester County, sixty miles west of Boston. By what criminal investigative vehicle did the strike force travel?

I suspect the group had inside knowledge. Bulger was on the run. Frank Salemme was in prison during the height of Martorano's killing spree. He was not particularly close to Martorano or the Winter Hill gang. That leaves Steve Flemmi. Martorano had beaten Flemmi to the immunization sweepstakes in 1998. Flemmi allegedly didn't come around until sometime later. Both men sacrificed Agent Connolly on the road to eventual freedom for Martorano and life in a prison for cooperating witness Flemmi. My money is on Flemmi cooperating with the strike force about John Martorano's homicidal tendency earlier than we have been led to believe.

One month after Martorano had testified at the Bulger trial, the first question asked by federal prosecutor Brian Kelly was "Please state your name, and spell it for the record, sir." "Joseph C. Saccardo, S-A-C-C-A-R-D-O," I answered, in response to having been called as a government witness in July 2013. Bulger certainly was more than familiar with Martorano, but in all probability, he said to himself, *Who the hell is this guy?* In the theater of the absurd, previously seated in the witness chair less than ten feet away from "Himself" was John Martorano and then me. Two individuals with completely disparate backgrounds gave testimony to the evils committed by Bulger—Martorano giving immunized testimony about murdering people with Bulger and I testifying about unsuccessfully trying to find Debbie Hussey, one of Bulger's and Flemmi's many victims.

Following a brief recital about my state police résumé, Kelly asked, "And, sir, do you know a woman named Marion Hussey?" After I answered in the affirmative, Kelly then walked me through my decades-long personal relationship with the mother of the deceased woman, Debbie Hussey. I was asked to identify a picture of Hussey for purposes of entering the photo into evidence. My cameo appearance ended with just a few inconsequential questions by Defense Attorney Jay Carney.

Bulger was charged with nineteen murders and found guilty of eleven, including Debbie Hussey's, in August of 2013. He was sentenced to enough years of incarceration guaranteeing that he would die in prison.

In *USA Appellee v. James Bulger*, dated August 14, 2014, Defense Attorney Hank Brennan argued in Bulger's appeal the following text:

> The government also convincingly presented witnesses and documents in an effort to support its theory that Mr. Bulger was an informant during the 1980s and 1990s. This informant claim was central to the government's argument that John Connolly was a rogue agent who masterminded Mr.

Bulger's success, rather than acknowledging the liability and complicity of the DOJ.[*]

John Martorano admitted to killing twenty people. Two of those murders involved the death penalty. (Tr. 2:74; Ex. 1157; Ex. 1159). His plea agreement called for a sentencing range of twelve-and-a-half to fifteen years and not being subject to the death penalty in two capital cases in exchange for his cooperation and future testimony. (Tr. 4:69). The Honorable Mark Wolf sentenced him to fourteen years in prison.[†] (Tr. 4:69).

He [Steve Flemmi] was never prosecuted with the Poulos murder [9/29/69] in Nevada despite his confession (Tr. 27:152), and his plea bargain in Florida allowed for a future Rule 35 motion (Tr. 29:26–32).

The government opposed numerous discovery requests including those related to tacit promises (D. 785; D. 854; D. 859; D. 860; D. 881; D. 900) and denied that they had promised Martorano that he would not have to testify against his

---

[*] Trooper Thomas Foley testified: "Q. So when you said in the book (*Most Wanted*—2012) that the federal government stymied your group's investigations, they got you investigated on bogus claims, tried to push you off the case of pursuing Winter Hill and Mr. Bulger, got you banished to a distant barracks, phonied up charges against other members of the State Police, lied to reporters, misled Congress, drew on the President of the United States to save themselves, and nearly got you and your investigators killed, that was the truth wasn't it? Yes, it was." (Tr. 2:125–36).

[†] In D. 768 at n. 10, the defense reproduced Judge Wolf's statement at John Martorano's sentencing hearing: "He [Martorano] did say he didn't want to testify against certain people, Pat Nee and Howie Winter, and I continue to have concerns that in cultivating this relationship, all of the relevant questions with regard to those individuals were not pursued, Mr. Nee being the last person, according to the evidence present to me in 1998, to have been with John McIntyre before he disappeared and we now know he died." Martorano Sentencing Hr'g. 109:12–19 (June 24, 2004).

brother, James Martorano, Pat Nee,* Howard Winter,† and others (Tr. 2:207-09; Tr. 6:103).

The defense independently learned that an active twenty-year veteran of the Massachusetts State Police had made a complaint alleging that John Martorano was involved in ongoing crime and that his handler, and key member of the prosecution team, Trooper Steve Johnson, was obstructing an investigation into the Martoranos criminal activity. (D.979). The prosecution refused to provide these materials to the defense and the court denied the defense attorney discovery requests without an evidentiary hearing. (D. 988; PT 6/11/13 (pm):4). The court also precluded the defense from calling the trooper who made the complaint and Martorano's associates listed in the reports as witnesses at trial (Tr. 29:160–61).

---

* John Martorano told Trooper Foley that Pat Nee was involved in murders with him. (Tr. 2:165-66).
† Martorano testified about Howie Winter's direct involvement in nine murders (1) Milano (Tr. 4:121); (2) Plummer: (Tr. 4–128); (3) O'Brien: (Tr. 4:129; Tr. 5–174); (4) Joseph Notarangeli (Tr. 4:133); (5) Al Notarangeli (Tr. 4:138:15); (6) O'Toole (Tr. 4:144); (7) Sousa (Tr. 4:148–49); (8) King (Tr. 5:27); (9) Castucci (Tr. 5:42).

• • • •

Four years after Bulger's appeal was filed, it was reported that his health was deteriorating, prompting a transfer from his Florida federal prison to an interim facility where he would await transfer to a prison that allegedly would address his health issues. Several days later, within hours of the transfer to one of the most violent federal prisons in the country, US Penitentiary Hazelton, Bulger was beaten to death in the early morning hours by two suspected inmates on October 30, 2018. A year later, Hank Brennan and David Schoen, attorneys for the Bulger family, filed a wrongful death lawsuit in the murder of Bulger in the West Virginia prison where eight inmates have been killed since 2014.

CONCLUSION

In 1998, former *Boston Globe* columnist Mike Barnicle wrote a poignant article titled "Introducing John Martorano." He severely criticized the US attorney and the FBI in Boston for giving Martorano trophy status "simply because he can't stop talking," while noting "the Justice Department is on the verge of forgiving the man for multiple homicides he is believed to have committed over three decades." Renowned Boston Police Detective Ed Walsh (then retired) added an exclamation point to the column when Barnicle quoted Walsh, "There was this girl in the rug at Luigi's. That was a place upstairs from the Intermission Lounge, an after-hours joint. He, John, killed this girl and wrapped her body up in a rug. I know he did that one. Long time ago, too."

By the time John Martorano started cooperating with Department of Justice lawyers in 1998, all but he; his brother, James; and their mother were deceased. Dead people don't talk. John Martorano won the immunity race, leaving Flemmi in the dust when he proclaimed he was beatified with immunity bestowed upon him by the FBI.

In the presence of his attorney, Francis DiMento John V. Martorano signed his plea agreement on August 23, 1999. Page 6, paragraph 2, states,

> If the Defendant breaches this Agreement by making any false, incomplete or misleading statement, or by providing any false, incomplete or misleading information to any law enforcement personnel, grand jury or court, the Government may terminate this Agreement as set forth below, and may also prosecute Defendant for any and all offenses that could be charged against him in the District of Massachusetts and elsewhere, including, but not limited to, false statements and perjury.

It is telling the first murder Martorano speaks to in his 1998 debriefing but does not confess is the brutal stabbing death of Margaret Sylvester. It was a family affair in as much as it was a crime of passion. John stated his father, Angie, was having an affair with the victim while his brother, James, was allegedly cavorting with the prosecution's star witness turned perjurer, Patricia Cowell. She was cowed into giving false testimony in the accessory-after-the-fact trial of James thereby absolving the entire Martorano family of the Sylvester murder. John fingers four people who were at the scene of the murder previous to Sylvester's demise, but he conveniently does not mention anyone in his family, leading one to believe that a family-run business had no one working the night of Sylvester's homicide. Yet he takes a huge risk in eliminating two of the witnesses at the request of Steve Flemmi, who it appears had nothing to do with the scheme. It just does not add up. The silence of John Martorano not being required to name Sylvester's killer(s) as part of his plea agreement is prosecutorial malfeasance amounting to John's complicity, which is conceivably verging on perjury and obstruction of justice. John Martorano's silence is deafening in not disclosing who killed Sylvester. It does not strain one's imagination that there is reasonable probability that a Martorano of the male species killed Sylvester.

From 2013 up until the publication of this book, Steve Flemmi and I have discreetly corresponded with each other via Christmas cards, personal letters, and phone calls. He has been imprisoned since early 2000 in a federal prison for cooperating witnesses in New York State.

I initiated the outreach when I sent a pretextual letter in July 2013 to Flemmi along with my business card, asking if he would respond to questions about unsolved homicides that I was independently researching.

Within a month, Flemmi called on my cell phone. At the time, I was more interested in picking his brain about the 1990 Gardner Museum art theft. He stated he and his criminal associate Whitey Bulger had unsuccessfully made an effort to find out which if any Boston hoods were involved in the multimillion-dollar heist. The intent was to get a piece of the action or extort the thieves. The robbery of irreplaceable art greatly intrigued my imagination and interest, which eventually morphed into a hobby in pursuit of trying to find the paintings.

In August and September of the same year, I followed up our conversation with two letters. He responded with a call at the end of September stating he would not be able to answer any more of my inquiries about the unsolved homicides unless cleared by the Boston US attorney's office.

Months passed without any direct contact with Flemmi until November 2014 when we had a monitored telephone conversation discussing the Gardner theft suspects.

After swapping birthday and Christmas cards with him for the next six years, I wrote a letter to Flemmi in June 2020 specifically requesting his version of who he thinks may have killed Margaret Sylvester. Several days passed when he called me, wherein I read to him verse for verse John Martorano's statement that he killed two witnesses to the Sylvester murder as a favor to the Flemmi brothers while subtly asserting that Steve's brother, James (Vinnie), had a hand in the execution. He became very agitated with that prospect, stating he had never read Martorano's debriefing, but he insisted he would need permission from Assistant US Attorney Fred Wyshak to talk to me about the matter. Wyshak essentially controls Flemmi's outside contacts. Two days later, I left a voice mail message with Wyshak.

The following day, Flemmi called again wondering if I had called

Wyshak, who had not returned my call. The same day, I sent Flemmi a copy of Martorano's debriefing relating to the Sylvester murder. On June 19, 2020, I made my last unanswered call to Wyshak.

I waited patiently for nearly a month before I sent Wyshak a letter. I wrote, "There are at least two living men who know who killed Margaret Sylvester: the Martorano brothers. And one person who can add or detract from John Martorano's debriefing on the subject: Steve Flemmi."

I implored Wyshak to "Please allow me to have further conversation with Steve Flemmi to try and clarify my apprehension of who actually committed this heinous crime."

Within weeks, Wyshak called. He explained because I was writing a book, I was considered media; therefore, if he let me talk to Flemmi, then all other media would be looking for the same privilege. He added only law enforcement would be allowed to talk with Flemmi.

Since the Sylvester murder came under the jurisdiction of the Boston police, I set up a meeting with a couple of cold case detectives in December 2020. The proposition was after getting permission from their superiors, an interview with Wyshak would be requested. The good news was they were interested. The bad news was the Sylvester homicide case file was missing. Nothing ever materialized.

Several days after Christmas 2020, I received some interesting material from Flemmi. One item was a makeshift holiday card wishing me and my family a "Nice Christmas." What I found most compelling was a two-page illustration of emblems of military designations depicting Flemmi's US Army service with the rank of corporal as a paratrooper with the 187th Airborne Regimental Combat Team during the years 1952 and 1953. Listed on another page were seven military awards and medals, including a Korean Service Medal with two Bronze Stars. Additionally, parachute badges were listed, designating seven foreign parachute jumps in countries such as Russia, Israel, and China, which qualified Flemmi as a member of the International Association of Airborne Veterans. Putting aside his criminal life, I was impressed.

I was not surprised in February 2021 when Wyshak retired because in an earlier conversation with him, I learned he had been thinking about the decision. Unfortunately, before he left, I was not granted access to Flemmi.

Margaret Sylvester died a horrible death, but I am going to memorialize her murder and others for as long as I am alive and hopefully beyond.

Addendum

Under the Freedom of Information Act, I requested the names of all murder victims for the years 1958 through 1980 from the Boston Police Legal Department. Specifically, I wanted to know if the homicide was open or closed and the victims' date of death. A cursory review of the state vital records of the requested categories revealed an inordinate number of female victims, particularly women of color, as noted in the certificates of birth and death. My interest piqued as I theorized the percentage of females of color seemed to be high in proportion compared to white female victims, who in the '60s represented a majority of the population for Boston residents. Nonwhite females accounted for approximately 10 percent of the total Boston female population as reported in the 1960 Census Tracts.

ACKNOWLEDGMENTS

No writer authors a book alone, least of all me. Not to get all religious, but a bit of divine intervention helped me along the way, including the following individuals whom I will be forever grateful.

I spent an enormous amount of time and sweat equity at Boston Police Headquarters researching organized crime files and unsolved homicides. Superintendent-in-Chief and Acting Commissioner Greg Long was instrumental in making that happen. He allowed me to work with Det. Sgt. Bill Doogan (ret.) of the Cold Case Squad and Det. Fred Waggett (ret.) of the Special Investigations Unit. Also, Det. Sgt Joe Fiandaca (ret.) formerly of District 7, East Boston, and Det. Jim Carr, formerly of Suffolk County DA's Office, brought a new insight for me into the criminal investigations of working cops. Semper Fi, Marines. Thank you all.

During the process of researching the book, I made new friends and renewed old ones from the Massachusetts State Police retirees. Det. Lt. Jack Walsh, Sgt. Bill "Beeper" McGrail, and Tpr. Ed Whelan were gracious enough to put up with my many calls and questions. Each of these troopers could write their own book. Semper Fi, Jack.

My two partners in the 1986 Mike London money laundering investigation at Heller's Cafe in downtown Chelsea, Massachusetts, FBI Special Agent Matt

Cronin (ret.) and IRS-CID Special Agent Bob Rooks (ret.) have never fully received the recognition they deserve for the part they played in that case. Thanks for your friendship and material I couldn't use in the book.

Another Boston-based FBI Special Agent, Nick Gianturco, made describing his undercover role in Operation Lobster easy for me to explain.

Renowned photojournalist and lifelong friend Bill Brett was an early supporter of this book. Bill, I really appreciate your support and interest along the way.

Author Steve Kurkjian was appointed by me as my pro bono lawyer and consultant. He was helpful in so many ways, and it only cost me a breakfast or two and a few beers.

My first editor, Stephanie Scholow, is owed my gratitude for putting the chapters together in a manner that pulled it all together.

My fortunate collaboration in research with Jason Bowns provided important content that greatly enhanced important chapters in the book.

My thanks to John, Will, and Hanna at the Massachusetts Vital Records in Dorchester.

Lastly, the Mascot Books staff of Julia Steffy and Kristin Perry are to be congratulated for putting up with a rookie writer the likes of me.

ABOUT THE AUTHOR

Rather than record the requisite resume, I am going to forgo that privilege and let the book speak for itself. For more insight on the subject, join me in listening to my two-year-old podcast, also called *Capable*, on most pod platforms.